Forging
Capitalism

Forging Capitalism

Rogues, Swindlers, Frauds, and the

Rise of Modern Finance

IAN KLAUS

Yale

UNIVERSITY PRESS

New Haven and London

Published with assistance from the
Mary Cady Tew Memorial Fund.

Yale University Press books may be purchased in quantity for
educational, business, or promotional use. For information,
please e-mail sales.press@yale.edu (U.S. office) or
sales@yaleup.co.uk (U.K. office).

Set in Minion type by Westchester Publishing Services.
Printed in the United States of America.

Library of Congress Control Number: 2014943071
ISBN: 978-0-300-18194-4 (hardcover: alk.paper)

A catalogue record for this book is available from the British
Library.

This paper meets the requirements of ANSI/NISO Z39.48-1992
(Permanence of Paper).

10 9 8 7 6 5 4 3 2 1

For Laurie

Drink a health to the wonders of the western world, the pirates, preachers, poteen-makers, with the jobbing jockies; parching peelers, and the juries fill their stomachs selling judgments of the English law.
—J. M. Synge, *The Playboy of the Western World*

Contents

A Definition; An Argument

T rust, to be simple with our definition, is an expectation of behavior built upon norms and cultural habits. It is often dependent upon a shared set of ethics or values.[1] It is also a process
orchestrated through communities and institutions. In this sense, it
is a cultural event and thus a historical phenomenon. And though it
can theoretically be quantified, it, unlike risk, resists being commod-
itized. Patterns of trust emerge, recede, and, most important, evolve.
The cultural inheritance around which trusting relationships are often built is meant, among other things, to harness baser instincts like
greed. This is part of our so-called moral side. Social virtues, such as
being frugal or honest, are translated into social capital.[2] Communities rich in social capital tend to be rich in trust. They also tend to be
rich.

A certain degree of trust is good. Economists have often noted
the strong correlation between high-trust societies and economic success and, at a lower level, between high-trust companies and commercial success. At the market level, an abundance of trust limits
transaction costs and litigation, both taxes on distrust. It is more expensive to do business when you do not trust your counterpart. At the
company level, a prevalence of trust permits an organization to adapt
to market changes flexibly and spontaneously. Free enterprise works,

some economists argue, because most people obey the rules; therefore, external reinforcement is rarely required.[3]

How do we come to be trusting? Some neurobiologists and evolutionary game theorists suggest our brains give us a head start. Human brains, they suggest, have evolved to favor collective, cooperative behavior. To work together is to fire synapses that give pleasure and fulfillment. Trust—even reciprocal altruism, evolutionary game theorists argue—can be highly advantageous, allowing us to reap the collective and individual benefits of working together. In our ambition to survive, it is something for which we have a natural desire.[4]

If we are indeed inclined to trust, why, then, do certain companies, communities, nations, and empires, both historically and currently, have such differing levels of trust? In sub-Saharan Africa, for example, trust levels along former slave trade routes remain lower today—though the trade disappeared in the nineteenth century—than at inland locations that were not involved in the trade.[5] Meanwhile, a shaded map of interpersonal trust levels, produced as part of the World Values Survey, shows extremely high levels of trust in Scandinavian countries and a low willingness to trust in South America.[6] Our evolutionary inclination to trust and cooperate (if indeed that is what it is) apparently needs to be protected and fed. Cooperative, honest exchanges improve our ability to trust and to be thought trustworthy—so says the argument put forward by academics and pundits who insist that commercial exchange improves our morality and thus our trustworthiness. Countries with McDonald's, a shorthand version of this argument once went, do not go to war with each other. Capitalism does not merely make us wealthier, healthier, and taller; it also civilizes. It allows virtue to grow, thus enabling trust.

This was indeed the great hope of capitalism's patron saint, Adam Smith, when he published *The Theory of Moral Sentiments* in 1759, ultimately followed and overshadowed by *The Wealth of Nations* in 1776. Today, Smith would hardly recognize the Scottish capital in which he studied and taught—or the British capital in which he dined, debated, and wrote. The emblems of empire would be familiar, but he would undoubtedly be struck by the prevalence of older people, by the size of his fellow Scots and Londoners, and by the comforts in which they live.

Such indeed are the spoils of capitalism. What's more, if he popped into the University of Edinburgh library or the grand British Library in London, he could find the World Values Surveys showing that, despite recent upheavals, Britons and Americans are, relatively speaking, trusting.[7]

By confusing where we are for how we got here, it would be easy to put all the pieces together. Commercial exchange over two centuries, building upon a natural inclination to trust, encouraged cooperative behavior that developed both morality and riches. Virtue, cooperation, and commerce together led to wealth. The picture is pretty, but it tells us very little. Instead of looking only at the *results* of trust, we should also look at *how* we trusted. And instead of considering a discrete moment, say, 1776 or 2007, we might consider a series of moments, a historical flip-book of commercial exchange. When we do this, we discover that the wealth and well-being wrought by capitalism are the result not only of cooperation and efficiency but also of more tenuous interactions among the vitality, creativity, and ambition required to develop a continuously expanding marketplace. And we encounter, again and again, the darker forces of greed and deception that prosper in new frontiers of commerce.

Throughout the nineteenth century, the vast uncertainty of Anglo-American capitalism tied to its financial crises, long-distance trade, industrialization, and urbanization rewarded creative and brave commercial endeavors. But this uncertainty also encouraged the marketplace to develop its own instruments for managing risk. Thus, a century that saw a remarkable explosion of global finance and trade also saw widespread attempts to manage the attendant risk, through insurance, principal-agent relationships, management techniques, hedging, and futures. Historians have widely acknowledged this concern and the expanding market for risk that accompanied it.[8] They have also pointed out, as we have so recently seen, how new types of risk management increased uncertainty in the marketplace and thus proved dangerous in unexpected ways.[9] If modern capitalism was built, at least in part, out of this drive for wealth, growth, and risk management, exchange still required an element of trust. Simply put, as capitalism and risk management evolved together at an astounding pace, trust had to keep up. This is why, in addition to speaking so often about risk, nineteenth-century commercial players also spoke just as much about fraud. It was not only the risks of the marketplace that needed to be managed but also the risks of human ambition and morality, what one insurance company called "non-natural or artificial risks."[10] As a result of new people, new assets, new technologies, and the drive to manage risk, the market was constantly forging new frontiers—places where capitalism demonstrated its cutthroat vitality and fraudsters hunted the excited and the credulous.

British and American novelists loved to portray fraud in the financial sphere. Charles Dickens's, Anthony Trollope's, and Herman Melville's greatest characters were not merely products of creative invention. The testimony and conduct of merchants, employers, insurers, financiers, and customers suggest a widespread fear of commercial fraud and crime. Those with money at stake did not presume the free market to be a moral place; as had been shown over and over again, it was a place where white-collar criminals posed a distinct risk. Yet capitalism did not decay from endemic distrust. The market continued to grow into new arenas, and into such spaces stepped those seeking to make the marketplace safe for trust as well as those seeking to abuse trust.

As we shall see, the intellectual forefathers of capitalism—most prominently, Adam Smith, David Hume, and Charles-Louis de Secondat, Baron de La Brède et de Montesquieu—understood that unleashing market forces would usher in changes not only in wealth but also in social exchange and politics. A thousand elegant phrases have been coined to describe these changes, none perhaps more lyrical than Marx's observation in 1848 "that all that is dissolves into air," and none more efficient and controversial than Joseph Schumpeter's description, almost exactly one hundred years later, of the operation of markets as "creative destruction."[11] Capitalism's critics have often focused on the "destruction" side of Schumpeter's coinage, but the energies unleashed by the promise of wealth and the challenges of competition have long made capitalism a dynamic, creative, organic system.

Throughout the nineteenth century, financiers created new types of financial assets, and insurance agents created new forms of insurance. Imperial expansion offered new commercial opportunities, and technology enabled new forms of trading at greater speed than ever before. Into these new markets stepped men and women seeking to make their fortunes. Some sought to do this legitimately, and some through crime, while others observed that it was difficult to tell one kind of operator from the other. In constantly reinventing itself, the marketplace also renewed not only its vitality but also its susceptibility to fraud. Often, we can best see the nature of trust from the nature of frauds. Fraud is the tax for creative capitalism, and like most taxes, it was not suffered quietly. If new forms of finance, commerce, and risk management were essential to capitalism's vitality, new forms of trust were needed to safeguard that vitality in a world of strangers and speed. The qualities that are most necessary for trust in any given era are precisely the qualities a sharp swindler is most likely to fake. As such, there emerged an arms race between the means of deception that enabled fraud and the means of verification that enabled trust.

What follows is a history of trust and fraud in a period of expansive capitalism, urbanization, and globalization. It is the story of new techniques of trust—often created to deal with new kinds of risk—in a creative marketplace. If Anglo-American capitalism were static, if it had not constantly created new relationships and destroyed old ones, if it had not pushed new frontiers of both assets and geography, the story of trust in the marketplace would be a static one of long-standing relationships and in-group bonds. While the rarified air of private banks and closed clubs is indeed part of capitalism's history, the dynamism of the marketplace constantly takes it outside, forcing players to find new ways to trust and confidence men to find new ways to defraud.

Just as our commercial players were acutely concerned with fraud, they were also abundantly aware of the advantages of trust. They spoke about it all the time, expressing concern over its distribution. They understood that it enabled wealth. But they never simply assumed that it would emerge, organically, out of commerce itself. In the almost completely unencumbered markets of nineteenth-century Britain, we find not simply a reliance on morality and capitalism's virtuous circle but repeated and evolving efforts to harness and encourage trust. It was a deliberate undertaking. You may have been able to look to the market to protect you from risk, but you had to look elsewhere for fraud protection. The stock trader in 1815, the insurer in 1860, the cotton financier in 1913 all trusted differently. As it was their money at risk, they well understood the important truth that just as trust can help make you rich, so too can it make you poor.

Part I
Status + Virtue

"All Trades and Places Knew Some Cheat"

O ne of the most influential legacies of the Enlightenment is the linking of commercial expansion and morality. From the beginning, the most profound thinkers on capitalism understood that the marketplace was not a system of mere mechanical exchange but an organic force that heavily influenced those who came into contact with it—and that required certain conditions to survive. The connection between capitalism and responsible, ethical behavior was central to the thought of the most influential economist of all, Adam Smith.

Smith made what remains the most profound argument for the positive effects of the pursuit of self-interest. It is the argument for which he is most famous. In *The Wealth of Nations* (1776), he observed that a merchant concerned with his "own security" will also "be led by an invisible hand to promote an end which was no part of his intention."[1] But he went well beyond that. Capitalism, he asserted, changes not only our material surroundings but also us. He believed that through ownership and exchange we come to appreciate not just wealth but moral improvement and government.

In *The Theory of Moral Sentiments* (published in 1759), Smith had laid the groundwork for the political economy he set forth in *The Wealth of Nations*. Smith argued that commercial exchange is a matter not only of states and empires but also of individuals and their codes of behavior. "The desire of becoming the proper objects of this respect," he wrote, "of deserving and obtaining this credit and rank among our equals, is, perhaps, the strongest of all our desires."[2] This concern, Smith believed, could be harnessed to encourage virtuous behavior alongside self-interest. Parsimony, authenticity, care for reputation, and the desire for knowledge could be encouraged by commerce while also checking its excesses. He presented a model of a prudent man who is sincere, industrious, and frugal, seeking not power or influence but reputation and respect. In a section titled "Self-command," he described the internal characteristics of the prudent capitalist: "Temperance, decency, modesty, and moderation, are always amiable, and can seldom be directed to any bad end. It is from the unremitting steadiness of those gentler exertions of self-command, that amiable virtue of chastity, that the respectable virtues of industry and frugality, derive all the sober lustre which attends them."[3] This hardly sounds like Fascination Fledgeby Gordon Gekko. Rather, Smith understood the market to work better when not corrupted by interests acting through government, and he envisioned capitalists pursuing self-interest harnessed by virtues gained through social exchange. In the political realm, favors and monopoly needed to be countered. In the commercial realm, reckless avarice and profligate behavior were to be checked. "Concern for our own happiness," he observed, "recommends to us the virtue of prudence: concern for that of other people, the virtues of justice and beneficence; of which, the one restrains us from hurting, the other prompts us to happiness."[4] Virtue and commerce came together, with commerce encouraging virtue and virtue harnessing commerce.[5]

Smith was in no way alone in making these connections.[6] He borrowed many of them from David Hume, twelve years his elder, a close friend, colleague, and fellow Scotsman. Born in a tenement in Edinburgh in 1711 and educated at the city's university, Hume would emerge as one of Britain's greatest and most controversial philosophers, tackling subjects ranging from economics to religion. A notable portion of his work was dedicated to the question of virtue and its role in social exchange. He would not deny the threats of indulgent self-interest, but he also recognized its beneficial effects. In his 1752 essay "On Commerce," he observed of trade: "Thus men become acquainted with the *pleasures* of luxury and the *profits* of commerce; and their *delicacy* and *industry*, being once awakened, carry them on to farther improvements, in every branch of domestic as well as foreign trade. And this perhaps is the chief advantage which arises from a commerce with strangers. It rouses men from their indolence."[7] In Hume's world, where commercial might was part of Great Britain's political stability and standing among nations, selfish indolence—not selfish interest—was a cardinal sin. Meanwhile, commerce bred good habits that encouraged greater commerce.

In a wonderful set of passages in his essay "Of Refinement in the Arts," Hume acknowledged the movement and tumult associated with capitalism and its towns and markets, but he also celebrated the social effects of bringing people into exchange with each other. Through luxury and production, minds are "roused" and put "into fermentation," while "profound ignorance is totally abolished." In such an environment, individuals "flock into cities; love to receive and communicate knowledge; to show their wit or their breeding; and their taste in conversation or living, in clothes or furniture. . . . Both sexes meet in an easy and sociable manner; and the tempers of men, as well as their behaviour, refine apace."[8] Here, in terms even more eloquent than Smith's, Hume offered a profoundly optimistic vision of capitalism's heightening qualities. Wealth and exchange were the route to improved manners, taste, conversation, and knowledge.

That was not all. Free commercial exchange, while encouraging good social behavior among individuals, would also check the power of despotism. On the continent, Montesquieu helped to develop this conception of exchange, most notably in his 1748 work *The Spirit of Laws*. Montesquieu wrote of *doux commerce*, an idea that celebrated not merely the economic results of commerce but the effects of such exchange upon manners and on sociability in general.[9] He praised the political effects of the movable wealth associated with commerce, believing that wealth not fixed to land, holding as it did the capacity to flee, could work as a check on political power.[10] The conversation was not simply about the merits of pursuing wealth but about what type of wealth was good wealth. New forms of assets, he suggested, created new social and political dynamics.

As the historian Emma Rothschild has shown, freedom of commerce was in part freedom from the fear of arbitrary control.[11] Liberty was buttressed by economic independence, and independence was enhanced by movable assets. "The effect of great commercial opulence," wrote John Millar, a Scottish historian and pupil of Smith, "is to produce caution and long-suffering under the hand of power, but to ensure ultimately a vigorous opposition to such acts of tyranny as are manifestly subversive of the fundamental rights of mankind."[12]

These ideas would echo through free-market economies for the following centuries. Capitalism held revolutionary capacities. It could check despotism. It could improve our taste, not to mention our wealth and well-being. And, of equal importance, it could improve our sociability—that is, it could make us be better to each other, improve our morality.[13]

But what the founding fathers of capitalism did boldly, they also did with noted apprehensions. In recognizing the potential benefits of self-interested behavior and the value of movable wealth, including paper credit, Smith, Hume, Montesquieu, and their allies had gone a good way toward solidifying two of the philosophical underpinnings of capitalism. But still they drew important lines, praising frugality and industry, criticizing greed and speculation. They had not simply endorsed self-interest; they hoped that self-interest would be checked by virtues polished through social exchange. Over the next century, the terrain separating harnessed self-interest from its unchecked version would be the battleground of what constituted commercial probity—as well as who was worthy of trust. Smith, for his part, understood how vulnerable the balance really was: "The man who associates chiefly with the wise and the virtuous, though he may not himself become either wise or virtuous, cannot help conceiving a certain respect at least for wisdom and virtue; and the man who associates chiefly with the profligate and the dissolute, though he may not himself become profligate and dissolute, must soon lose, at least, all his original abhorrence of profligacy and dissolution of manners."[14] Here was Smith's great gamble. He lived through a period in which economic life was in great flux. The rules of competition, or government intervention, and of the division between public and private, as well as the responsibilities of individuals, were being continually defined and redefined. We still live in the economic world that emerged from that period, where commercial exchange is the focal point of much of life.[15] But what if, in the world of commerce, men and women came across many of the profligate and dissolute whom Smith worried about? What would come of capitalism if its practitioners lost their abhorrence of greed, excessive self-interest, and even, to a degree, dissembling?

"Vicious Luxury"

At the beginning of the eighteenth century, a Rotterdam-born physician and pamphleteer, Bernard Mandeville, insisted loudly that he had seen the answer to such questions. In 1705 in London, he published a small six-penny pamphlet poem, *The grumbling Hive; or Knave turn'd Honest*, which presented a view of capitalism in which England grew both rich and corrupt. Mandeville would twice be brought before the King's Bench as a public nuisance, but try as the prosecutors (and, later, Hume and Smith) might, they could never fully extinguish his vision of commerce and riches.

In 1712, Mandeville republished his poem with an explanation in a work titled *The Fable of the Bees: or, Private Vices, Publick Benefits*. While the Earl of Shaftesbury waxed on about virtue, Mandeville saw a world where vice and commerce were intricately intertwined. His portrayal of commerce was almost Boschian: "Millions endeavouring to supply / Each other's Lust and Vanity."[16] In Mandeville's world, virtues had long fallen, and vice sat comfortably in the seats of power. Envy and vanity served as ministers of industry, while the arms of justice drooped under the weight of gold bribes. The streets of London looked little different, filled as they were with "Parasites, Pimps, Players, / Pick-pockets, Coiners, Quacks." No industry was exempt: "All Trades and Places knew some Cheat, / No Calling was without Deceit."[17]

What made Mandeville's work so controversial was not its observation of widespread vice but its linking of vice with commercial riches.
England's wealth, he proposed, was not a result of frugality or responsibility or liberty; it was borne of envy and greed:

Their Crimes conspir'd to make them Great:

And Virtue, who from Politicks
Had learn'd a Thousand Cunning Tricks,
Was, by their happy Influence,
Made Friends with Vice: And ever since
The Worst of all the Multitude
Did something for the Common Good.[18]

Just as Smith had Hume, Mandeville also had partners in vision.
Soon after the monumental collapse of the South Sea Company in 1720,
William Hogarth produced the print that would best capture the bubble's exuberance and danger.[19] In the print (fig. 1), the financial buildings of the city dwarf Christopher Wren's cathedral. Foxes fight at the
base of a column that declares "his monument was erected in memory
of the destruction of the City by the South Sea in 1720." A pickpocket
works in the foreground, while in the back greedy women wait in line
to enter a building promising newly enriched men. Fortune hangs from
a balcony dismembered. Hustlers roll dice. Honesty and honor are
whipped and beaten by self-interest and villainy. In its depiction of financial innovation fueling a collapse of values and wealth, Hogarth's
print portrayed precisely the dilemma that Smith, Hume, and other
Enlightenment philosophers worked to solve: how to reconcile virtue
and the public interest with the vices of self-interest.

Commerce could both civilize the masses and encourage the
"dissolution of manners," and it was precisely this multitude of outcomes that one of Smith's star students, the historian and philosopher
John Millar, explored in his multivolume *An Historical View of the English Government*, the first volume of which was published in 1787. Born
in a small town between Glasgow and Edinburgh, Millar had studied
under Smith at the University of Glasgow and absorbed many of his

The South Sea Scheme by William Hogarth, 1721. *(Reprinted with permission of the Trustees of the British Museum. ©The Trustees of the British Museum. All rights reserved)*

ideas, including the civilizing effect of commercial relations. "By a more intimate communication among the members of society," he wrote, "the manners of mankind are softened, their social dispositions are awakened, and they feel more and more an attraction which leads them to conform their behaviour to the general standard."[20] In volume 4 of his history, Millar dedicated more than two hundred pages to an historical examination of such effects. Undeniably, he observed, commercial exchange encouraged deference, respect, accommodation, concern for others, and the limitation of selfishness. "But this intercourse is often little more than a petty traffic, which aims merely at the purchase of reciprocal good offices."[21] In the process of socializing, Millar suggested, commerce and capital also alienated people from other emotions and connections. He envisioned a commercial world that would eventually be a threat to virtue.[22]

Millar did not live in a static world but, rather, in a time of intense commercial expansion of empires and cities. "By commerce and manufactures," he wrote, "the contracts and transactions of a country are multiplied almost without end; and the possessions of individuals are extended and varied in proportion." Whereas Smith acknowledged that virtue was fragile and might be corrupted in certain environs, Millar saw corruption as inevitable. "The pursuit of riches becomes a scramble," he wrote, "in which the hand of every man is against every other."

> Among an active and polished people, the desire of fame and distinction is production of competitions and jealousies yet more extensive. Neither age, nor sex, nor condition; neither wisdom, nor folly; neither learning, nor ignorance, is exempted from the serious, and the ludicrous discord which originates in this universal passion, or from the acrimony and malice which it often inspires.[23]

Virtue stemming from social exchange was a basis of trust and a tether upon excessive self-interest. But what if the same process that produced this virtue, when accompanied by more wealth, people, and distance, instead produced jealousy, rude competition, and excessive self-interest—in other words, vice? What if the multiplication "almost without end" of commercial transactions that was crucial to the growth of capitalism and the management of risk and uncertainty within it did not nurture virtue and trust?

Hume had in fact reconciled himself to this prospect decades earlier. Luxury, even "vicious luxury" that lacked in charity, frugality, and virtue and that proved destructive of relations, was still better than indolence. Vice accompanied by commerce was preferable to poverty and inaction: "By banishing *vicious* luxury, without curing sloth and an indifference to others, you only diminish industry in the state, and add nothing to men's charity or their generosity. Let us, therefore, rest contented with asserting, that two opposite vices in a state may be more advantageous than either of them alone."[24] Hume (Smith's friend) and

Millar (Smith's student) had acknowledged that vice was not an unlikely outcome and could even be a component of commerce.

In ways, all three were right. The pursuit of self-interest would lead to the expansion of wealth, while commercial exchange would result in a "scramble for riches" of remarkable energy, creativity, and ruthlessness. As individuals and companies sought wealth, they also sought safety from capitalism's risks. But while one could insure against all types of events (including movement in the marketplace), trust remained a problem the market could not always solve by itself. In this scramble, in one of capitalism's freest markets—with global capital movement, low entry barriers, massive movement of labor, and limited regulatory restrictions—it was not enough to put trust in moral probity. The rewards and dangers of creative destruction were often matched by those of creative deception.

Cities, Empires, and the Free Market

A history of capitalism, trust, and fraud must be a history of cities and globalization, of complexity, technology, and speed. In 1820, the population of the United Kingdom and Ireland was slightly more than twenty-one million. Thirty years later it had risen to over twenty-seven million.[25] The site of nonagricultural production had moved from the home (where both men and women were involved) to the factory or mill (the domain of men, some children, and unmarried women). Cities became crowded hubs for the passage of goods and people.[26] The population of Manchester, for instance, grew from under 10,000 in 1700 to 75,000 in 1801, to upward of 303,000 by mid-century. Glasgow and Birmingham saw similar explosions.[27] The population of London stood at nearly 1.4 million in 1851. Fewer than half of them had been born in the city, and many were young—meaning that, quite often, man was stranger to man, unable to know or recognize the people moving through the cityscape.[28] Never before had cities grown so big, so fast.[29]

Small wonder that the city, London in particular, gripped the imaginations of Victorian journalists, novelists, and playwrights. The young Dickens was obsessed with the city and ran about London collecting stories. Henry Mayhew, a London-born reformer, leading satirist, and cofounder of *Punch*, was a keen observer of the urban world, bringing to his descriptions of the capital both serious thought and humor. His 1881 *London Characters* was a veritable *wunderkammer* of the urban world. Cigar dealers, stockjobbers, and ex-convicts pass through the city streets. Coal shovelers and beer peddlers float down the Thames.[30] This was hardly the static society envisioned by evangelical economists and philosophers,[31] or a city checked by Malthusian limits. It was instead the world Millar had described, where information, social exchange, and goods increased in quantity and complexity: an imperial city of movement and commerce.

Like their capital cities, empires rose and spread. In 1860, the British Empire covered some 9.5 million square miles, expanding by 1909 to around 12.7 million.[32] With the rise of imperialism came a dramatic growth in global trade and finance, culminating in the unprecedented globalization of the century's last three decades. In his expansive 1843 study of metropolises, *The Age of Great Cities*, Robert Vaughan found himself observing the global movement of goods and money: "Even the mass of the people, in a great commercial city, are made to feel in a much greater degree than any other people, as citizens of the world. They see that their interests depend, not on themselves, nor upon their nearest neighbours, but upon relations which subsist between them and the ends of the earth."[33]

Meanwhile, between the time Vaughan published his urban observations and the outbreak of World War I, world trade expanded more than tenfold. The depth of Europe's financial markets and the global reach of its empires made its capitals the undeniable hubs of nineteenth-century finance, commerce, and globalization; of these, London was unparalleled in its reach and riches.[34] Between 1860 and 1914, the number of foreign banks with London offices went from three to seventy-one, while the branch numbers of London-based banks outside Britain went from 132 to 1,387. Companies involved in foreign land transactions or holdings swelled from 201 on the London Stock Exchange in 1885 to 1,566 by 1913. Walter Bagehot was the greatest financial journalist of nineteenth-century England. His 1873 masterpiece

Lombard Street provided a guide to the functioning of what was then the financial capital of the world: "There are very few civilized Governments that could not borrow considerable sums of us if they choose, and most of them seem more and more likely to choose. . . . No nation has ever had a foreign trade of such magnitude, in such varied objects, or so ramified through the world." By 1913, over half the value of stocks and bonds traded on the London Stock Exchange were of foreign origin.[35] Taken as a whole, the market had unparalleled depth, but also newfangled assets of all sorts, giving it remarkable complexity and demanding both expertise and heightened attention to detail.

Urbanization, transportation, imperialism, and population explosion meant more people, more *strangers*, interacting than ever before. By the second half of the nineteenth century, the market was freer than any market before it.[36] Regulation was expected to come from responsible people—compelled by interest in their shares or in their fortunes—who would be held liable should the company or bank not be able to meet its debt. By mid-century, prohibitive import duties on grain (the infamous Corn Laws) had been removed by Parliament, as had restrictions on company formation. The ease with which one could establish an insurance company, a bank, or a joint stock company led to a dramatic increase in the financial and commercial options available to consumers. To take the measure of capitalist exchange from 1815 to 1914 is to see how economic expansion and risk management evolved together in an increasingly free and globalized marketplace. This environment of fierce competition and gamesmanship was as promising for the confidence man as for the capitalist.

"Vice Smiles and Revels"

In 1828, George Smeeton published *Doings in London: Or, Day and Night Scenes of the Frauds, Frolics, Manners, and Depravities of the Metropolis*, in which, in the style of Virgil and Dante, an older man leads a young lad from the country through London's various squares and markets. Like Virgil's guide, Smeeton's warns his charge of the vision ahead: "You will find it a sea foaming with tempests, and boiling with whirlpools: you will be sometimes overwhelmed by the waves of violence, and sometimes dashed against the rocks of treachery. Amidst wrongs and frauds, competition, and anxieties, you will wish a thousand times for quiet, and willingly quit hope to be free from fear."[37] Smeeton's focus in this picaresque tour of London's streets and markets was not on the characteristics for which the early Victorian city came to be known—smog, horse dung, the challenges of sanitation—but on another ill endemic to nineteenth-century commercial life: fraud. Everywhere he looks—among the meat mongers of Smithfield, the fruiterers of Covent Garden, the publicans and the barmen at gin joints—he sees cons and frauds. Labyrinthine though this vision of London is, there is also a simplicity to it. Everybody is a bad actor. Nobody is trustworthy. A sherry salesman mixes Cape wine with his sherry and calls it a pure *fino*. At the fishmonger's, "cod, haddock, and whiting, are *blown*, to make them appear large and plump; a quill, or the stem of a tobacco-pipe, being inserted into the orifice at the belly of the fish . . . the breath is blown in." In the alleys around the Stock Exchange, traders "bang," "rasp," "waddle," and "ear-wig."

Smeeton may have been cynical and aggressive, but he was not paranoid. His depiction of fraud, forgery, and theft as commonplace in commercial exchange is borne out by the data. During the second half of the nineteenth century, crime rates in general declined, but they declined least among the middle class. Convictions for low-level forgery and fraud seem to have increased. In 1815, ten individuals were convicted of fraud at the Old Bailey, the nation's central criminal court. In 1847, convictions rose above one hundred for the first time and remained above that number for most of the second half of the nineteenth century.[38] Crime patterns, according to the historian Rob Sindall, followed the opportunities provided by work. More than 25 percent of crimes committed by people in military, law, medicine, or religious professions were some sort of fraud, while clerks tended toward embezzlement and larceny. "There seems to be more danger from the trusted officer and the employee than from the burglar," wrote the American bank inspector A. R. Barrett at the end of the century in an essay titled "The Era of Fraud and Embezzlement," and his cousins across the Atlantic were well proving him right.[39] Public policing presented a serious problem when the criminals looked so much like the clerks, merchants, and financiers in whom trust had been deposited.

Edward Bulwer-Lytton, the great dandy, playwright, and novelist, proclaimed in his 1840 play *Money*, "There are two rules in life—First, Men are valued not for what they *are*, but for what they *seem* to be. Secondly, if you have not merit or money of your own, you must trade on the merits or money of other people."[40] Trading on the qualities of others and *seeming* to be hardly correspond to the sociability meant to keep self-interest in check. Bulwer-Lytton saw these practices for what they were (i.e., vice) and understood them to produce what Hume predicted (i.e., vicious luxury). "The extremes in this life differ but in this," he wrote, "*vice* smiles and revels; below, *Crime* frowns and starves."[41]

As the concern for fraud advanced through the century, commentators on commerce—finance especially—increasingly pointed to an additional phenomenon: in a world of expanding speculation, it was ever more difficult to distinguish legitimate exchange and wealth from their criminal forms. The differences between fraud and law-abiding capitalism, some suggested, were clear only in their outcomes. Mayhew guided readers through a city in which it was difficult to read people's past from their present state. Many fraudsters and deceivers, he observed, are people of station and trust: "The forgers; they are not ordinarily professional thieves; they are usually people holding situations of greater or less responsibility, from bank managers down to office boys: well, all the forgers who are to be tried at all sessions and assizes for the next twenty years, are walking about among us freely as you or I. Then the embezzlers—these are always people who stand well with their employers and their friends." He described an old eccentric who is presumed by some to be a disgraced clergyman, by others an escaped convict, and by many a fraudulent banker.[42]

No one drew out the interplay between trusting sociability and greedy fraud with greater affect than Anthony Trollope in *The Way We Live Now*, published after serialization in 1875.[43] Trollope drew an extended network of complicated social relations, including good-for-nothing baronets, malaprop farmers, and American financiers. At the heart of the novel lies a juxtaposition of two men: Augustus Melmotte and Sir Felix Carbury. Melmotte is presumed to be one of the more powerful men in Britain, perhaps Europe, and possesses ambitions to represent Westminster in Parliament. His name is synonymous with wealth, and also with mystery. Carbury is an attractive dilettante of respectable name but little wealth, who passes his days drinking in his club and gambling away money he does not have. Both come to regrettable ends. Melmotte is sunk by his fraudulent railroad endeavor, the South Central Pacific and Mexican Railway, and commits suicide. Carbury, gambling into debt in a club where he is often drunk and often cheated, is forced to flee to France. The behavior of the gentlemen is shown to be very much that of the criminal capitalist. Trollope draws the connection between fraud and financial capitalism explicitly. "Nobody really loved Melmotte," he writes, "and everybody did believe. It was probable that such a man should have done something horrible! It was only hoped that the fraud might be great and horrible enough."[44] Great and horrible enough that the fraudulent railway would have become real wealth. Eustace Clare Grenville Murray, bastard son of one of England's greatest landowners, understudy of Dickens, and biting satirist, made much the same observation in his portrait of English life, *Under the Lens.* "Now and then," he observed, "a man of name becomes a defaulter for several thousands, and retires to France or America, where he begins his old games afresh, and in the majority of instances lives pleasantly enough. . . . It is with the turf adventurers as with other kinds of money-hunters, the little rogues who try for small gains, generally have a worse time of it when they do shabby tricks, than the big rogues, whose mal-practices involve the gain of thousands."[45] For Trollope, as for Bulwer-Lytton and Murray, in the dynamic marketplace it was a sterling line between the grand capitalist and the disgraced fraudster.

A History of Trust

It was one thing for Adam Smith to couple morality and capitalism, but quite another for the members of the London or New York stock exchanges to do the same. And what tales tell the traders, the shoppers, the shareholders? Capitalists in the world's freest market may well have believed that commerce had the potential to improve moral behavior. But in a growing marketplace, where trust could not simply be built upon old bonds, this was a dangerous bet to take. Instead, those with money on the line more often tried to strengthen traditional means of trust, while developing new techniques of trust to match the contours of the changing marketplace.

A history of vice and capitalism, then, must also be a study of trust—or at least its absence. Such questions were never far from Walter Bagehot's mind. The Somerset-born Bagehot was, as John Maynard Keynes would later point out, not so much an economist as a psychologist of businessmen, financiers, and politics. He took the question of trust to be central to the functioning of London's commercial world. His greatest work, *Lombard Street*, achieved unrivaled precedence as a guide to business and finance in Great Britain. "It has become the one book," Keynes would observe, "in the whole library of economic literature which every economic student, however humble, will have read, though he may have read nothing else."[46]

Confidence, Bagehot asserted in *Lombard Street*, can only be earned over time. Credit had to "grow"; it could not be "constructed." Stability and past behavior were key: "Great firms, with a reputation which they have received from the past, and which they wish to transmit to the future, cannot be guilty of small frauds. They live by a *continuity* of trade, which detected fraud would spoil."[47] Bagehot held a particular fondness and admiration for the Bank of England, an institution that owing to its status was able to keep extraordinarily low capital reserves for the amount of money it lent. In repeatedly drawing attention to the Bank's importance, Bagehot showed it to be one of the pillars of commercial confidence in London and beyond.

But outside the hallowed walls of the Bank of England, Bagehot was forced to acknowledge a more complicated economy, within which worked a more complicated version of trust. The South Sea bubble, as well as numerous nineteenth-century bubbles (including those in Latin American bonds and railway shares), drew his attention, as did the world of spurious stock sales and the buyers who jumped to grab the shares. "All people," he wrote, "are most credulous when they are most happy; and when much money has just been made, when some people are really making it, when most people think they are making it, there is a happy opportunity for ingenious mendacity. Almost everything will be believed for a little while."[48] In nineteenth-century commerce, almost everything was.

Theorists of trust like to discuss "bonding trust," which tends to be rooted in small groups and communities, and which is often homogeneous and exclusive. Late nineteenth-century finance, according to P. J. Cain and A. G. Hopkins, sometimes operated as a closed world, open only to gentlemanly capitalists who shared social and educational backgrounds as well as positions in Parliament, the Foreign Office, the Treasury, and the Bank of England. In what they call "Gentlemanly Capitalism," the important links became those between government and imperial agents and the City, rather than industry. These men were able to use the levers of the state—economically and militarily, in both London and the British Empire—to advance a shared set of interests, as well as manage the risks associated with long-distance investment. At home, however, trust focused around London's well-established institutions and seats of power. In this world, trust was constituted in traditional ways by the interlocking social networks of education and marriage. Whether through education, private clubs, or the intermarriage of prominent banking families with the aristocracy and gentry, networks were an undeniable aspect of the *haute* side of financial capitalism. Such closed networks testify to the compromised nature of nineteenth-century commerce, but they are far from the only story.[49]

Theorists of trust also like to talk about "bridging trust," which unlike "bonding trust" tends to be more inclusive—cutting across larger groups and allowing for more diversity. By the late nineteenth century, according to Cain and Hopkins's own estimates, "the City," London's financial hub, had become crowded, filled with strangers and specialists, including upward of 40,000 firms (few of which lasted long), employing some 350,000 workers.[50] Youssef Cassis's networks, described in *City Bankers, 1890–1914*, were composed of key City figures and high-ranking employees, but a teeming world of capitalism operated below and beyond them. And in this teeming world, the supposed neutrality of the state was at times another challenge to trust in commercial exchange. In this less gentlemanly financial capitalism, forgery, fraud, theft, bankruptcy, and speculation were frequent and usual concerns.

If polite Victorians—honest, sexless, Christian—still live in your historical cupboard, throw them out. We don't like them anymore, and they never existed anyway. When authors like Thackeray, Dickens, and Trollope placed capitalists at the center of major works, the thieves were often difficult to distinguish from the legitimate. As we shall see, consumers of financial news, investors, insurers, and customers were similarly confounded.

This history begins and ends with the world at war, stretching from the Napoleonic Wars to the onset of the First World War. As should become clear, commercial men paid serious heed to character, moral behavior, and reputation. These concerns were the cornerstones of "usual" or "regular" business, to which Adam Smith paid so much attention. And of course, as today, the vast majority of capitalists were not criminals. But enough of them were, especially in the new frontiers of capitalism. In the second half of the century, limited liability may have protected shareholders and directors from impoverishing lawsuits, but it protected neither group from fraud. Commercial men voiced their concern over fraud, embezzlement, and deception with great frequency. When they protested that business should be conducted judiciously and fairly, it was often in response to the darker, criminal side of exchange.

What follows is the history of that other capitalism: the one described by Dickens and Trollope, composed of agents, clerks, speculators, jobbers, brokers, lords on the take, knights on the make. It is a different meeting of capitalism and morality from the one Smith optimistically envisioned. In this version, participants in the market are increasingly forced to refine their means of trust and their protections against fraud. Trust as we know it today is an evolving legacy of our repeated ability to rise to capitalism's challenges—and of capitalism's failure to save our souls.

T • W • O

Unreliable Virtue

ometime on February 20, 1814, the Napoleonic Wars came to an
end. Napoleon, rumor held, was quartered, or maybe torn to bits—
reports differed. Allied troops, including British, Spanish, Prussian,
and Russian soldiers, entered and sacked Paris. Russian troops, the
burning of Moscow not far from their minds, were particularly vengeful.

In Dover, less than thirty nautical miles from Calais, the landlord
of the Packet-Boat Pub and guests at the Ship Inn were awakened, early
on the morning of the 21st, by knocks from a stranger asking for writing paper. He was hurried, frantic, and he claimed to be carrying the
most important news to hit England in two decades. It was an environment eager for such an arrival. London newspapers had dispatched
agents to the southern coast of England for news from France. Enterprising financiers of the City had done likewise.

Removed from the dark of the street, the man could be seen by
the light of two candles. He looked, a witness would later testify, "like a
stranger of some importance." A German sealskin cap, festooned with
gold fringes, covered his head. A gray coat covered his red uniform,
upon which hung a star. A red sash hung down from his waist onto
gray pantaloons. His official-looking appearance was furthered by his
apparently determined and disciplined manner. Neighbors and residents of the inn stirred and peered in as the visitor penned a note. Some

had still been at the pub when he arrived. Quickly finished, he summoned the inn's boy and had the letter immediately dispatched to Admiral Thomas Foley at Deal, a Kentish town eight miles from Dover and first home to the Royal Marines.

The letter, signed R. du Bourg, Lt. Col., announced with all expected excitement that "Bonaparte was overtaken by a party of Sacken's Cossacks, who immediately slaid him, and divided his body between them. General Platoff saved Paris from being reduced to ashes. The Allied Sovereigns are there, and the White Cockade is universal, an immediate Peace is certain." The letter was delivered to Admiral Foley's maidservant, who woke the admiral around 3 A.M. Before daylight, the stranger headed off toward London.

The stranger who claimed to be Colonel du Bourg, aide-de-camp to Lord Cathcart, was actually Captain Charles Random de Berenger—a slippery confidence man, a Prussian aristocrat who was simultaneously in His Majesty's Service and a prisoner of the King's Bench for debts undelivered. He was fond of the violin and the trumpet and was frequently referred to by friends and enemies alike as a man of science and skill when it came to sharpshooting. De Berenger's inheritance in North America had disappeared when his family sided with the Crown in the Revolutionary War; therefore, having some military talent, he had made himself useful to the British Army.[1]

Britain had been at war with France, with only brief interruptions, since 1793, first against the French Republic that emerged from the 1789 revolution and then with the empire that spread under Napoleon's rule. In the worst of the war years, like 1806, Britons felt themselves standing and sailing nearly alone. Napoleon ended the Holy Roman Empire, marched through Prussia, and threatened even Russia. William Wordsworth, once an enthusiastic supporter of the French Revolution, observed in verse in "November, 1806":

Another Year!—another deadly blow!

Another mighty Empire overthrown!
And We are left, or shall be left, alone;
The last that dare to struggle with the Foe.

Since 1808, the cost of the war to Britain had become immense. The scales of the battles were unprecedented. Three hundred thousand participated at the Battle of Wagram (1809), 500,000 in the Battle of Leipzig (1813), during which roughly 150,000 were killed or wounded. By war's end in 1815, the French had lost around one million soldiers; the British had three hundred thousand dead or missing.

De Berenger's news was therefore of obvious interest. Upon his arrival in Dover, he had been reluctant to share the details of his news. He had hoped that Admiral Foley would use the optical telegraph to send news to the Admiralty in London and, in particular, to the City of London. He was relying upon the latest in technology, the telegraph message that would travel from hilltop to hilltop, covering the 108 miles from Dover to London far faster than any horseman. But fog rendered the semaphores useless, and de Berenger set off to deliver the message himself. As he was leaving the Ship Inn, he declared with confidence: "The business is all done; it is settled."

"How?" an onlooker asked.

"He is dead!"

"Who is dead?"

"The tyrant Bonaparte," replied the colonel. Playing his role, he traveled up to Dartford, changed carriages, and passed along his account. An innkeeper asked the traveler if he had any good news to report. "Yes, Bonaparte is dead," he answered; "the Cossacks fought for pieces of his body as if they had been fighting for gold."[2]

The tyrant was not dead. Nor was the business over, as de Berenger had claimed. Napoleon did not fall in battle in his capital, but probably of stomach cancer six years later on the isolated island of St. Helena. The war would continue until June 1815, when the Duke of Wellington (rather than the Cossacks or the deserving Prussians) would claim fame for the ages. Nonetheless, de Berenger and his co-conspirators had set in motion a fraud that would alter the prices of financial assets that stood at the foundation of British wealth and power. By ten o'clock, de Berenger was in London, and by noon his news had let loose the bulls at the London Stock Exchange. The stampede would not last long, but the fallout would bring down a British hero and force the Exchange itself to take public recourse to restore trust in its assets and confidence in capitalism.

The Cochrane Residence, London: 10:00 A.M.

The next morning, February 21, Richard Barwick, a clerk to the bankers Paxton and Company, left home for his office in Pall Mall a little before 9:00 A.M. Passing near the Marsh Gate, he saw a man in military dress changing from a post chaise with four exhausted horses to a hackney coach. An onlooker told Barwick the gentleman was a general officer arrived from the coast with news. Barwick did what any man with an interest in the news would do: he followed the hackney coach. He followed it as far as the Little Theatre on Haymarket, but the officer never left the coach—so Barwick abandoned the pursuit. Asked later why he stopped trailing a man who might have vital news, he gave a clerk's response: "It is nine o'clock, and I must be at the office by that hour."[3]

The hackney coach Barwick followed was carrying de Berenger to no. 13 Green Street, just off Grosvenor Square. He had traveled from Dover to Canterbury, then Rochester, Dartford, and Bexley, ending his journey in London at the door of Lord Thomas Cochrane, later Earl of Dundonald, a famed master and commander in the British Navy. Cochrane was out visiting a manufacturer who produced navy signal lanterns, which Cochrane was trying to patent.

Cochrane was born in Scotland on December 14, 1775, to a father with a talent for invention but no ability to manage his finances. When his father was made Lord Dundonald in 1778, Thomas was granted the courtesy title of Lord Cochrane. Along with his father's earldom, he could expect one day to inherit the family's house at Culrose Abbey on the Firth of Forth, on the east coast of Scotland, and the estates that went with it. The elder Lord Dundonald, however, seemed to have nothing but patents and papers. He attempted to produce synthetic soda, to make alumina from silk, and to extract coal tar by a special process. After years of developing, proposing, and tinkering, he was left with many debts and few assets. In 1793, the young Lord Cochrane's inheritance was put up for sale, and his army commission was canceled. A

claim to naïveté in financial matters would one day be a cornerstone of
the younger Cochrane's courtroom defense, but during his upbringing,
his father's failings caused his life to veer somewhat off the traditional
track. He was left to pursue a career in the navy.

Cochrane's associates would prove his making and undoing. At
the beginning of his naval career no figure was more influential than
his uncle, Alexander Cochrane, who had fought in the American War
of Independence, bombarded Baltimore, and played a part in torching
Washington in the War of 1812. Alexander had significant influence in
the Admiralty and had been entering Cochrane's name in the muster
books of four different ships since 1780, when Thomas was five years old,
thus expediting future possible promotions.[4] As a result, when he entered the navy he had thirteen years of service, and with the continued
help of such connections, he took command of his own ship seven years
later. Such were the advantages of patronage. "I shall conclude [by] saying that I wish there was a war," the lowborn, fourteen-year-old Alexander Hamilton had written to a friend in 1769.[5] Cochrane missed the
war that made Hamilton, but he would have his own opportunities
during the extended conflict that engulfed Europe between 1792 and
1815. During the French Revolution and the Napoleonic Wars, he would
pass through Halifax and sail the Chesapeake Bay. He would hunt in
Virginia and in Morocco. He would meet Lord Nelson in Palermo,
guard convoys off of Cagliari and Genoa, raid off of Elba, Bastia, Capri,
Sardinia, and Barcelona.

Cochrane's monument, were there to be one in Trafalgar Square,
would be to bravery and controversy, daring and greed. After taking
command of his first ship, the HMS *Speedy*, in early 1800, he enjoyed
successes that are less noteworthy for their influence on the war's outcome than for sheer bravado—and for their ability to bring him personal wealth. Cochrane was a master of deception, or what were known
as *ruses de guerre*. These were well within the tradition of the ocean,
and he often tried to draw enemy ships into his confidence. On more
than one occasion he flew misleading flags—including that of the
young United States—and even painted his ship in the guise of other
neutral powers. He described one engagement some fifty years later in
his autobiography: "I had the *Speedy* painted in imitation of the Danish

brig *Clomer*; the appearance of this vessel being well known on the Spanish coast. We also shipped a Danish quartermaster, taking the further precaution of providing him with the uniform of an officer of that nation. . . . And to add force to his explanations, we ran the quarantine flag up the fore, calculating on the Spanish horror of the plague, then prevalent along the Barbary coast."[6] The *Speedy* would eventually be captured by the French in 1801, but before that Cochrane frequently used disguise and bravado to take prizes and, in certain instances, bigger and more heavily armed ships, such as the Spanish frigate *El Gamo*.

As the war dragged on in fits and starts, Cochrane concentrated his energy on two issues. The first, his concern for riches, drove much of his conduct in the Royal Navy. His second concern, reform of the navy and particularly its treatment of sailors, led him to Parliament as a member of the House of Commons for Westminster. As a raider, Cochrane had been entitled to a sizable share of the booty he claimed off of Spanish and French ships, not to mention the sale price of the captured ships themselves.[7] As an honorable lord, but one without means, he would remain centrally concerned with income for much of his life.[8] He would eventually become wealthy enough to live a comfortable and even, at times, extravagant life.[9] Until the late 1820s, his search for means would drive him to controversy after controversy.

One naval engagement in particular stands out. At sea in 1809, Cochrane managed to achieve perhaps his greatest tactical victory while effectively ending his naval career. Seeing the French fleet growing, the British Admiralty attempted to destroy it before it broke out of the British blockade at Basque Roads, a bay on the Biscay shore. On the night of April 11, 1809, Cochrane led a small flotilla of ships that were to be lit aflame and crash into the French fleet. The flotilla included one "exploding ship" of his own devising. Packed on the bottom with logs, the exploding ship carried fifteen barrels of gun powder in casks bound with hemp rope, several hundred shells, thousands of hand grenades, and, if his autobiography is to be believed, a dog. The blast was immense: "The sea was convulsed as by an earthquake, rising, as has been said, in a huge wave, on whose crest our boat was lifted like a cork, and as suddenly dropped into a vast trough, out of which as it closed upon us with a rush of a whirlpool, none expected to emerge."[10]

The point was not to destroy but to dissemble. Cochrane hoped that the French would think all the fire ships were exploding ships and would overreact accordingly. "They would," he wrote later, "in all probability, be driven ashore in their attempt to escape from such diabolical engines of warfare, and thus become an easy prey. The creation of this terrorism amongst the enemy's ships was indeed a main feature of the plan."[11] It was a ruthless, modern tactic and not thought by all to be worthy of a gentleman. The British may have erred by igniting many of the fire ships early, but chaos amidst the enemy fleet ensued nonetheless; all but two French ships ran aground. Despite this seemingly advantageous situation, Lord Gambier, who was directing the engagement for the British, decided against a more widespread general attack. Cochrane disagreed; the French fleet, in his opinion, was vulnerable to destruction. He spent the next several days destroying French ships in the bay, even using his own vulnerability to draw additional British ships into the engagement in his defense.

It was a courageous and reckless performance by Cochrane, and an overly conservative one for Lord Gambier. The incident prompted a legal dispute over which memories of battle were more trustworthy and less prone to the influence of self-interest—those given time for reflection or those recorded immediately.[12] The battlefields and bays of the Napoleonic Wars provided opportunity for fame and riches and thus became a contested terrain of virtue, interests, and corruption. But while wars allowed these ideas to be tested and strained, the true battlefield between virtue and interests was that hive of commerce and credit, the City of London, where Cochrane would soon make his reappearance.

The Monied Interest

The years between England's "Glorious Revolution" and the French Revolution were not peaceful. Between 1688 and 1789, the competing empires of England and France, one Protestant, the other Catholic, engaged in at least five significant wars on three continents. Among other places, they fought in Ireland and Holland, Canada and the Ohio River Valley, Mysore and Madras. These wars cost them dearly, in lives and in treasure.[13] It was to meet the demands of one of these wars, between 1689 and 1697, that England developed the political and financial institutions that would shape its political debates and forge its wealth for centuries to come—enabling a form of financial capitalism that was at once ruthless and expansionist, resilient and creative.

In 1688, the Dutchman William of Orange, along with his wife, Mary, accepted an invitation from a faction within Parliament to land in Britain and assume the throne then held by Mary's father, James II.[14] This event, known as the Glorious Revolution, was as messy as it sounds, and for most of the next decade, from 1688 to 1697, England, France, and allied powers fought what would be known in Europe as the War of the Grand Alliance or the War of the League of Augsburg, and in North America as King William's War. William III, a Protestant, fought his French and Catholic enemies on the continent, as well as James II in Ireland. Though major questions of continental succession remained unsolved at the war's conclusion, England had undergone more than a political revolution. "The whole period of English history from the accession of James the First to the present," wrote John Millar, the historian and pupil of Adam Smith, "may be divided into two branches: the one comprehending the occurrences prior to the revolution in 1688; the other occurring posterior to that great event."[15] In usurping the throne and raising taxes to fight his wars, William III had to accept a fundamental limitation upon his power, relinquishing, in the *Declaration of Rights*, significant control over the financial levers of state. A Parliament dominated by landowners now controlled spending and borrowing, and the monarch no longer had recourse to arbitrary taxation or expropriation of land.[16] The ultimate importance of this compromise has been the subject of much debate, but it is clear that with the Glorious Revolution came a strengthening of private property—as well as the groundwork for two centuries of debate on the relationships between land, political stability, and government finances.

The first of William's wars saw the birth of another pillar of English finance: the Bank of England. The Bank was established in 1694 in the City of London by Charles Montagu, first Earl of Halifax, based upon a plan proposed earlier by the Scotsman William Paterson. One and a half million pounds sterling had been raised for the government's

war effort from private investors in exchange for the privilege of forming the bank and the promise of interest payments from special taxes.[17]
Thereafter the Bank would serve all the government's banking purposes, issue its own shares, and be a consistent source of debt financing
for the century plus of wars to come.

At this point, the great political rupture that felled France's ancien régime and dragged Europe into more than two decades of war lay
nearly a century in the future. But many of the paths upon which history would move forward had been cleared. Britain refined the "fiscal-
military state" through which an expanded empire would rise, along
with the Royal Navy and the public debt.[18] The French, meanwhile,
taxed at lower rates that nonetheless created higher unrest, and they
borrowed more expensively.[19] This, undoubtedly, is part of the story of
how a small windswept island off the coast of Europe grew to govern
the largest empire since the Romans.

In what would be a recurring pattern, however, financial innovation and development brought new social and financial challenges. As a
leading historian of finance points out, financial markets were inade-
quately prepared for the innovation and enthusiasm that accompanied
early eighteenth-century credit.[20] In 1710, barely two decades removed
from the Glorious Revolution, the government found itself, drowning
in unsecured debt, "an oppressed and tangled state" as Jonathan Swift
described it—with long-term obligations around £20 million.[21] Credit
had become a central attribute of British commerce and government
spending. For English merchants in the sixteenth and seventeenth centuries, burgeoning systems of credit overcame limitations upon trade
over distance and even a lack of coinage.[22] The government, meanwhile,
increasingly relied on debt to fund its foreign wars. Whiggish commentators like Daniel Defoe could look around and see a nation of
expanded wealth and influence. In his 1724 *Tour through the Whole
Island of Great Britain*, Defoe describes the view from a riverboat on
the Thames: "A Luxuriance of Objects presents itself . . . : Where-ever
we come, and which way forever we look, we see something New, something Significant."[23] The perception of "new" wealth and "new" trade
prefigures the dramatic commercial and financial developments of the
nineteenth and twentieth centuries. Capitalism, it was understood, had

the capacity to change both its participants and the objects that surrounded them—whether rich or poor. With such changes came new
uncertainties. Even those who celebrated such new wealth were wary of
the extremes of credit, particularly speculation in stocks and bonds.

The stock and bond traders of London, as well as the Bank itself,
became targets of vitriolic attacks from the likes of Swift (and even Defoe) for their supposed usury, vicious self-interest, and disregard of the
public good. Along with financial developments came a profound distrust of credit, debt, and financial innovation—a position that came
to be known as the "country" ideology. This position saw luxury as a
menace to virtue, and war and commerce as potentially destabilizing
of a political balance built around land and agriculture. Over the
eighteenth century, as the usefulness of credit continued to make
itself clear, a distinction developed between credit for commerce and
speculation.

Credit extended England's influence and grew its wealth; speculation, on the other hand, was parasitic, producing nothing but instability
in interest rates and politics—and risk, commercially and socially. One
hundred years after the Glorious Revolution, this tension surrounding
financial assets was still very relevant. When an even more dramatic
set of wars with France loomed, the notions of virtuous commerce and
vicious finance made themselves heard. London quickly became the
safest and deepest financial market in the world, but with this turn
came renewed criticism of those who profited from it.

The massive expenses of the continental war threatened to over-
whelm the financial capacities of France, Britain, and their respective
allies. The warring parties incurred huge debts. By 1814, Napoleon had
built up an internal debt of 1.27 billion francs. Britain's national debt
stood at £834 million in 1815, or 222 percent of its national income. A
decade later, it was still more than £800 million.[24]

For European aristocrats and merchants, English assets had
proven a safe haven from the tumult of the continent. The English capital market was relatively well prepared for such an infusion of cash.
Compared with the French market, the English one was both broader
and deeper, having developed over the eighteenth century through
government bonds and shares in joint-stock companies like the East

India Company and the South Sea Company. Meanwhile, capital fled bloodshed. Those with money in the exchanges of Paris, Hamburg, and Amsterdam moved much of it away from Europe's war to the London Stock Exchange. These capital movements foreshadowed a century of international and imperial investment. The "crowding in" of capital to London fueled domestic investment in canals, waterways, and industry while altering the face of stock market listings by widening the options on offer. As so often happens, war provided opportunities for profit for those who could position themselves correctly, whether at sea or in the City of London.[25]

The City of London's boundaries have remained largely the same for centuries. In 1814, as now, it was bordered by the Thames River to the south and Westminster to the west. The borough of Hackney is to the City's northeast, and the boroughs of Islington, Camden, and Tower Hamlets also brush up against it. At the end of the eighteenth century, London had two financial centers, each serving different clientele. In addition to those in the City, banks in the West End specialized in serving gentry and the aristocracy, dealing with overdrafts, mortgages, and rents. A character from a Jane Austen novel, needing financing for a country estate or a town house, would probably turn to a private bank in this district. The City's alleys and shops, meanwhile, were home to merchants, insurers, and players in the Stock Exchange. The City was a diverse place that thrived, in part, because it was willing to embrace or at least accept exiles who brought links to networks of trade and finance.[26]

In 1815, the City's one square mile was home to 120,000 people and some 8,500 firms. Most of these firms, suggests David Kynaston in his history of the City, were small and family owned. The more successful merchants, like the Rothschilds, might move from more traditional exchange into merchant banking. As was so often the case, Dutch merchants led this transition in the eighteenth century, followed by British merchants in the nineteenth.[27] The trading world of London was thus something of a paradox: small, family-owned firms were crucial, yet expatriates and their international networks were increasingly important. The City's merchants, brokers, and jobbers became targets of financial capitalism's harshest attacks.

Attacks on money interest came in myriad forms during the Napoleonic Wars and immediately after, including parliamentary speeches, histories, and pamphlets.[28] The critiques were not all similar, but some recurring points stood out. William Cobbett, a critic of both governmental and financial corruption, often drew attention to the ways in which financial interests were destroying rural England, and with it England's "ancient constitution." In this vision, rural estates were the loci of independence, freedom, and virtue, whereas London, the City, and other provincial towns were hotbeds of the "Old Corruption." He thus targeted not only traders in the Stock Exchange but also pensioners, appointees, sinecurists—anybody who benefited from the expanded power of the state and the financial reach that went with it, including taxes, patronage, and credit. Writing in the chaotic period after the end of the Napoleonic Wars and before the Reform Bill of 1832, Cobbett romanticized country life in his *Rural Rides*, a travelogue of trips around the countryside. He set off, he claimed, not to see inns or turnpike roads but the country: farmers at home and in the fields. "Went to Weyhill-fair," he writes, "at which I was about 46 years ago, when I rode a little poney, and remember how proud I was on the occasion." Such rural innocence is set against the detrimental effects of industrialization and credit. "I hope," he observes, "that the time will come when a monument will be erected where that mill stands, and on that monument will be inscribed '*The Curse of England*.' This spot ought to be held accursed in all time henceforth and for evermore." But if mills were the "curse" of England, it was the City and its vicious men that were destroying the nation's country estates. "It is now manifest," he writes, "even to fools, that it [i.e., the City] has been by the instrumentality of a base and fraudulent paper-money, that loan-jobbers, stock-jobbers and Jews have got the estates into their hands." Cobbett's antisemitism was typical of anti-City criticism, as was the belief that everything produced in the City—paper money and shares, in particular—was somehow fake, the product of financial alchemy.[29]

An anonymous author who went by the name "Practical Jobber" published a pamphlet in London in 1816 that drove home many of these points. He promised to expose "the ground of the art, secret maneuvers, tricks and contrivances"—this position, taken to an extreme, merged fraud with finance, or more specifically credit and speculation. From the anonymous author's perspective, whatever benefit was gained from expanded opportunity was more than lost in the threat posed to honest work. The interests the men of the City served were theirs alone. For the jobbers that abounded in the City, according to the author, "there is nothing *real* but the prices they establish in favour of themselves, and to the loss of the community." The pamphleteer did not attack all credit but, rather, that particular type of finance in which capital was detached from labor and production and value seemed merely the product of speculation in the exchange.

The Practical Jobber lamented the "new era" in which performance and appearance mattered more than integrity, status, and morality. None of the men who worked in such an environment—alleys and coffee houses that welcomed bankrupts, retired brokers, and Jews—were to be trusted. Abolish the Exchange, he implored the government. Though the City may have given opportunity to some, it was fundamentally corrosive of virtue. It turned all men into deceivers.[30] When it came to financial affairs, no one in the Stock Exchange was trustworthy. The business lowered men; it allowed Jews to flourish; it was ruinous of character.

Here, too, the pamphleteer draws on a long history of corruption gazing. Cobbett's targets were not only loan jobbers and stockjobbers— men of the City—but also what he called pensioners, sinecure people, and "dead-weight."[31] His attacks on "old corruption" followed a long tradition of critics, beginning in the eighteenth century, who saw patronage and its tools of paid government posts and pensions as a threat to the distribution of political power and, ultimately, to morality, liberty, and virtue. Patronage fed dependence, and dependence led to concern for private interests rather than those of the public.[32] The criticisms of the City and of money interest advanced along much the same lines: paper money, credit, and shares were a threat to political balance and rural life. Most important, they threatened to corrupt public virtue in the name of private interest.

William Thackeray would later describe this morally compromised state as "Man-and-Mammon Worship." His novel *Vanity Fair*, though written later, was set during the period of the 1814 Stock Exchange hoax (the book also turns on news about Napoleon). Thackeray's wit, satire, and power of observation are frequently pointed toward men of the City. "Ours is a ready-money society," declares one character. "We live among bankers and city big-wigs, and be hanged to them, and every man, as he talks to you, is jingling his guineas in his pocket." One player has a simple mantra: "It's all fair on the Stock Exchange."[33] Such was the view from without, but what about from within?

The London Stock Exchange, in its modern incarnation, was founded in 1801 to provide a secondary market for the vast government debt emerging from the demands of the continental wars; it quickly became a home for the capital fleeing the wars' violence. The Exchange was divided between proprietors, who were shareholders in the Exchange itself, and members, who paid for the right to trade within its walls. Proprietors were limited to how much stock they could hold, and lacking a government-granted monopoly, they feared a competing exchange if they restricted membership or raised fees. Thus, to increase their profits and dividends, the shareholders of the London Stock Exchange—in stark contrast to the Bourse in Paris or, later, the New York Stock Exchange—had to enlarge its membership rather than raise fees. Whereas the predecessor to the New York Exchange started with twenty-four brokers agreeing to trade only with each other, and Napoleon limited trading in public debt to sixty *agents de change*, the London Stock Exchange opened its new building in Capel Court with 550 members.[34]

These members represented three discrete types of traders: jobbers, who sold stocks or bonds on their own account and could hold them in volume; brokers, who, much like agents, bought or sold on the account of someone else; and promoters, often less capitalized traders, who attempted to introduce new listings or companies for sale. Because new members could be continually added, Lance Davis and Larry Neal note, "each class of members was compelled to innovate continually."[35] Jobbers tried to increase the volume of their trades. Brokers attempted to expand the variety of assets they offered or to gain new clients. Promoters expanded the number of listings or traded in unlisted companies. While one could never call the Exchange "inclusive," it nonetheless offered—and served—a particular brand of capitalism. In an expanding

City, at the hub of an expanding empire, it offered assets of increasing diversity and at enhanced depth. In the future of such expeditionary capitalism lay increases in the speed of trade and information, as well as even further geographic diversity. But even then, it was clear that the dynamics behind financial trade were challenging notions of proprietary, productivity, and confidence.

An environment that prized competition and innovation, the owners and members quickly discovered, was also in need of rules. London's Stock Exchange, like New York's, was essentially self-regulating. Parliament was more likely to enlarge the trading domain than to limit or regulate it.[36] In 1812, despite Thackeray's later observation, the Stock Exchange codified its rules for the first time; the *Rules and Regulations Adopted by the Committee for the General Purposes of the Stock Exchange* attempted to add predictability and even a degree of transparency to trades on the exchange. Concern with conspiracy or double-dealing was paramount. Any new partnerships had to be announced to the committee and then posted publicly.[37] Here was an entirely different approach to the interests and passions unleashed in a commercial society. Attention was to be paid to connections, networks, and partnerships. Private interest was assumed rather than scorned. Vice was to be policed not through neutrality or morality but through information. The men of the Stock Exchange feared corruption of their exchange through veiled interests, conspiracy, and misinformation. It is now worth asking what informed these fears?

Financial News

For all the diversity and growth under way and still to come, four rather basic assets provide the best insights into the state of the London financial market on the precipice of a century that saw ever-increasing financial integration. The prices of shares in the East India Company and Bank of England, as well as the prices of the Omnium and of 3 percent Consol bonds (consolidated annuities—a form of British government bond or "gilt" introduced in 1751), provided for the contemporary investor, as well as the historian today, the best gauges by which to evaluate the market. The Omnium was an aggregate stock, comprising the various stocks and bonds used in government loans. The 3 percent Consol was to the nineteenth century what the ten-year U.S. treasury bond is today: the safest, most reliable place in the world to invest your money. It had been developed in stages out of the wreckage of the South Sea bubble and was offered as a perpetual security paying 3 percent per annum; if the price rose above par, it was redeemable at the government's discretion.[38] For the investor, the Consol offered transparency, clear terms, and easy liquidity. It was a simple, reliable asset upon which the British war effort—indeed, for a time the British Empire—rose and fell.

In the eyes of men like Cobbett and the Practical Jobber, such assets were merely paper money, part of a credit system manipulated by City interests. While the men of the Exchange may have dreamt of such power, the value of these four assets during the wars with France was often determined by blockades, trade crises, and credit lines far beyond the City's control. The jobber or broker in the City, however, was more interested in immediate news that could swing the market in the short term, bestowing fortunes or destroying them. The great philosopher of capitalism in the eighteenth century, Adam Smith, had claimed that fortune was the "consequence of a long life of industry, frugality, and attention."[39] His counterpart in the early nineteenth century was David Ricardo, the author of *Principles of Political Economy* and a highly successful stock market speculator who understood the forces that moved the market. In October 1814, Ricardo wrote to Sir John Sinclair, a Scottish politician and writer with more than passing interest in finance: "The Stock Exchange is chiefly attended by persons who are unremittingly attentive to their business, and are well acquainted with its details. . . . They consider more, the immediate effect of passing events, rather than their distant consequences."[40] This was an age fixated with information. Whether in the form of private letters or books, newspapers or pamphlets, the acquisition of information was a widespread preoccupation.[41] What is more, the authenticity of such information was crucial not only to wealth and power but also to trust and confidence.

Members and associates of the Stock Exchange admitted as much themselves. Richard Gurney was a lawyer who represented the Exchange. In court, he would describe the machinations of the market's obsession with news about France and Napoleon: "The fortune of war was uncertainty in this age of miracles, no man could tell what would be the final event; and every one was waiting on breathless expectation for the destruction of him (or at least of his power) who had so long been the destroyer of species." Joseph Swearn, a broker, remarked that "we rarely enquire into particulars of news. It is enough that the facts are produced."[42]

At crucial moments in the wars, the price movements of Omnium and the 3 percent Consol support the statements of Gurney and Swearn. Bond prices reflect confidence, the price rising and falling based to a great degree on the public's collective faith that the debtor can pay the interest on the bond and, ultimately, the principal. During a major war, the value of a government's bonds often reflects its perceived chances in the conflict. Victors do not necessarily always honor their debts, but they are more likely to do so than vanquished governments. When the French invaded Russia in 1812, Russian bonds fell from 65 percent of face value, or "par," down to 25 percent. By 1814, with an Allied victory seemingly at hand, Russian bonds traded close to par while the French version of the Consol, the *rentes perpétuelles*, was selling 42 points below par. The tides of war ebbed and flowed, and with them the prices of European bonds. Information—especially early information—on the outcome of conflicts was of great value not only to governments and military planners but also to men in the City.[43]

Information moved slowly and unreliably, but when it arrived brokers and jobbers took immediate action. Admiral Nelson defeated the French fleet in Abu Qir Bay, near Alexandria, Egypt, on the first day of August 1798. News of the engagement, later known as the Battle of the Nile, sparked massive celebrations in London and across England—but not immediately. Napoleon's fleet was sunk and his forces marooned in Egypt for months before news of the battle's result reached London, on Friday, October 5. On the day of the Battle of the Nile, 3 percent Consols were reported in the *Times* at 49¾. Over the next months they stayed between 49 and 51; for the year, up to that date, they had stayed safely between 47 and 51. Once news of the victory spread through London—before it was reported in the papers—the price of Consols reached as high as 58. In 1803, when a brief treaty with France ended, and Britain faced war alone against France, the price of Consols fell to near 50. But it would never again fall below that point.[44]

The problem for the City was clear: news was unreliable and late, yet it significantly moved prices.

London Bridge, London: 11:00 A.M.

It was upon this fact de Berenger and his associates had bet when they falsely reported Napoleon's death in February 1814. Late though the reports might be, newspapers were nonetheless capable of moving the market, and the papers dispatched agents to acquire what served as breaking news. No sooner had de Berenger arrived in Dover disguised as Colonel du Bourg than he came into contact with an agent of a London newspaper. The agent, William St. John, was staying at the Ship Inn (almost exactly a year later, Lord Byron would gather at the Ship Inn with his longtime friends and confidants John Cam Hobhouse and Scrope Davies for a long night of claret, which would prove the final night he ever spent in England) on the morning of de Berenger's arrival, having traveled to Dover in the service of the *Traveler*, a London newspaper. His charge was to seek news from the continent and report it directly back to London, though he later admitted that had news of peace broken he would have returned to London and traded Omnium from his own account.[45]

Given the unreliability of such agents, de Berenger shrewdly turned to the optical telegraph when he arrived in Dover, dispatching a letter to the admiral at Deal in the hope that he would relay the message. The optical telegraph was the invention of two French brothers, Claude and René Chappe. In 1791, using elevated wooden panels, an established code, and synchronized clocks, the brothers transmitted a message over ten miles in northern France. By 1794, the newly established French State Telegraph was reporting news from the American and French revolutionary wars. One line stretched from Paris to Dunkirk. Another, comprising 120 stations, stretched nearly five hundred miles from Paris to Toulon and could transmit a message over its entire length in twelve minutes. Napoleon made extensive use of the system, establishing a line from the battlefront in Prussia to

St. Petersburg. Two hundred and twenty different stations were used over the 1,200-mile route. The British installed their own smaller system from the coast to London.[46]

Fog having undone his first effort, de Berenger continued on to London. By late morning, he was sitting in Cochrane's Green Street residence, waiting for the lord to return. Meanwhile, three men hired a post chaise at the Rose Inn at Dartford. The keeper of the inn guessed that they were going to the Admiralty. The passengers, Alexander McRae, Henry Lyte, and Ralph Sandom, went over London Bridge, down Lombard Street, along Cheapside, and over Blackfriar's Bridge, arriving within sight of Marsh Gate around 11:00 A.M. Two of the men were dressed as officers of different rank, with coats featuring braiding of flowers in worsted. They wore cocked hats with white cockades; one hat had gold tassels and a brass plate on each end. Their horses were decorated with laurel.

They were the second wave of the fraud. They yelled out memorized French phrases (learned in a coffee house), and their laurels spoke of the return of the Bourbon monarchy.

The City was eager for such news. The previous month, on January 15, an optical telegraph message had announced victory for Napoleon. Soon, newspapers reported a Cossack advance near to Paris. According to the *Times*, this optimistic news was "eagerly caught up, and repeated, without having been traced to any very distinct authority." This was a sort of information mania. The desire for news, good or bad, was itself a force of nature.

According to the *Times*, the reports of February 21 were widely believed. "Never, perhaps," the paper commented, "was a greater agitation produced in the Metropolis by any foreign news, than was yesterday occasioned by a fraud of the most impudent and nefarious description." The fraud was great, implied the newspaper, because the news of Napoleon's death had seemed especially reliable: "This statement, probable in itself, and attended with so many circumstances of plausibility as to the mode of its conveyance, easily obtained belief. The Stock Exchange was instantly in a bustle."[47]

When the Exchange opened at ten o'clock, Omnium was selling at £27½. Around 10:15, as rumors of the news from Dover began to spread, the funds rose to 28½. Their price reached 30 around noon. Just as doubt set in about de Berenger, causing the price to decline, news of the other post chaise hit the market. Again, prices rose: to 30, 31, 32, and peaked at 32½ before the actual news—that there was no news—was confirmed hours later at the Admiralty.

Had anybody done particularly well during the trading on that February morning? Had anybody traded in especially high volumes? Lord Cochrane would later swear that on the day of the fraud, he owned £139,000 of Omnium. He was not especially wealthy. He held the securities in a style known as "on account," meaning that rather than buy them with cash, he had promised to pay an agreed price for them on the next settling day. In the London Stock Exchange, such days occurred every two weeks, allowing traders to buy and sell shares in the meantime, or to use credit on settling dates. Unlike New York, where shares were normally exchanged one day and settled the next, this arrangement allowed fluidity and ease of trade; it also meant that speculators could face steep bills twice monthly.[48] Cochrane was obligated to pay up for his Omnium but in the meantime could sell future rights at an even higher price. Price movement was everything to him. If the price increased, he could cover the agreed-upon price and sell higher. If the price dropped, however, he had to cover the margin himself. He had accumulated his entire position in a few days of intense speculation, buying and selling over £206,000 in Omnium in less than two weeks. On the 21st, the day of the fraud, he sold well over half of that. Shares in the amount of £66,000 were sold at 29¼, another £8,000 at 29⅛, £58,000 at 29½, and the final £7,000 at 30½.[49]

The profit was not astounding; Cochrane later estimated it at £1,200. He had made that limited profit by selling higher than the price at which he had promised to buy. But what if news of Napoleon's death had not arrived to drive Omnium north? The Exchange later estimated that he would have lost upward of £10,000. Cochrane's interest was in avoiding a devastating loss, and in that he was successful. Some of his associates did much better. Cochrane's uncle, Andrew Cochrane-Johnstone, sold £510,000 in Consols and Omnium; Richard Butt, their broker, sold £392,000.

Whoever perpetrated the fraud had successfully created such a stir in the City as to move the market, even if only for a couple of hours. Nothing solid was known of the stranger who rode into London on the morning of the 21st, yet he passed the test of appearances, played on networks of rumor and gossip, and satisfied, if only briefly, the need for good news. The *Times* explained it in a phrase: "So many circumstances of plausibility" had served to convince the traders in the Exchange.

Napoleon's actual political end would come in June 1815, when Wellington defeated him at the Battle of Waterloo—only so many resurrections are possible, real or fake. Some had the Waterloo news early.[50] War updates were delivered through government channels, optical telegraph systems, pamphlets, newspapers, even homing pigeons. The Rothschilds would not sit in wait for scoops. Like the perpetrators of the fraud, they understood the relationship between information and moneymaking. Amschel Rothschild would have his brother Nathan dispatch multiple copies of the same letter from London. Letters routed through Dunkirk, Paris, and Amsterdam would race to Frankfurt. When news of Napoleon's defeat reached London, the markets again reacted. Consols rose from a price of 56½ on the day of Waterloo to 60½ a week later. The Omnium saw an even greater increase of eight points.[51]

Reaction to the real defeat mirrored, if more strongly, news of the fake defeat. Authentic and fraudulent news reports often took similar paths and had similar effects. The proprietors of the Stock Exchange knew this intuitively as soon as the hoax was proven. Theirs was a house where immorality in the forms of misinformation, deception, and conspiracy posed a great threat. It was also an institution left to regulate its own trading rules and membership, and to investigate and prosecute frauds made against it and within it. Jeremy Bentham notably wanted the government out of the commercial realm yet in the business of policing that realm,[52] but that world was still decades off. In this case, the Stock Exchange had to be its own watchdog against conspiracy and misinformation. It would eventually launch a proto–public relations campaign, as well as a trial, attempting to reinforce the safety of and trust in the Exchange, as well as to reaffirm exactly what type of capitalism was sound, usual, and worthy of confidence. But first it launched an investigation, discovering, among other things, that the hoax had saved Lord Cochrane a huge sum of money.

Vice on Trial

Though the market recovered from the hoax almost immediately, and though few would ever claim to have been irreparably harmed by it, the day's trading was followed by weeks and years of publicity and legal recourse that far exceeded the scale of the hoax itself. Lord Thomas Cochrane had his reputation and character to defend, and the London Stock Exchange, judging by its behavior, had even more at stake—namely, a standard of conduct in financial commerce and confidence in their institution in general.

On the morning of February 21, Charles Random de Berenger's responsibility was to spread "news." The job suited his temperament. In the weeks leading up to the fraud, de Berenger hinted to numerous people about the coming hoax. He informed a producer of military accoutrement that he was purchasing military clothes "for a person who was to perform the character of a foreign officer, to be sent into the country that evening."[1] He bragged to the former British military officer James la Marchant of splendid opportunities to come in exchange for helping Lord Cochrane in the stock market.

De Berenger's were not the only loose lips. On February 14, Alexander McRae wrote to Thomas Vinn, asking him to meet at the Carolina Coffee House to discuss a "very particular interesting business." Vinn was an accountant, failed broker, and francophone. McRae stated his business bluntly: he was looking for man who could use French to spread a rumor. Vinn would later testify: "On my asking if there was any thing of moral turpitude in it, he said there was none, but that it was practiced daily by men of the first consequence. It was nothing more nor less than biting the biters, or in other words, a hoax upon the Stock Exchange." Hardly the morality Adam Smith hoped would underpin capitalism. McRae was no subtler after the hoax had been accomplished. He had been poor. After the 21st, he was flush, and it showed. He flaunted paper notes. He bought a new coat and hat. By this point, the fraud was a topic of widespread conversation.

The Stock Exchange convened a committee to investigate the fraud. The gang of Lord Cochrane, de Berenger, McRae, and Cochrane's uncle had all emerged as the leading, indeed the only, suspects. Even before the two sides had an opportunity to square off in court, the Stock Exchange and Cochrane began a battle for public opinion, image, and reputation. The Exchange was in the business of prosecuting the perpetrators of the fraud. It was also in the business of maintaining codes of conduct conducive of trust and confidence in the Exchange in general. As such, the Exchange posted placards around the City accusing Cochrane of the fraud. Cochrane, for his part, delivered an affidavit that would be published in the *Morning Chronicle* and the *Times*, and he solicited a bookseller and part-time stock broker to sell it as a pamphlet.[2]

The public display of information regarding the fraud got to the heart of the trial's purpose. While it was nominally about meting out some form of privately enforced justice, both parties had greater concerns. The special committee formed by the exchange pursued the case with such vigor because they were eager to prove that the Exchange was an arena of sociability and character, a place for the exchange of credit that fueled commerce—and not a haven for roguish, credit-manipulating speculators. The growing numbers of members and the expanding number of assets traded, on and off the books, put the Exchange at the forefront of capitalism's creative financial frontier. Maintaining space for that energy alongside rules that made trade safe and worthy of trust was a dance that required both delicacy and vigilance. The fraud on the Stock Exchange was not the first time news was used to manipulate stock prices.

Nonetheless, it was likely the largest to occur in the Exchange since its reorganization, at the beginning of the century, into its modern form. And the scandal could not have made clearer the relationship between information and wealth, as well as the threat posed by misinformation.

If the committee was eager to present the Exchange as a place where private and public virtue met, Cochrane obviously had more personal concerns. He needed to clear his name, in court and in the realm of public opinion.

The trial began on June 8, 1814, in the Court of the King's Bench in Guildhall. Influential lawyers and legal figures filled the courtroom. James Park, later chief justice of the Court of Exchequer; Henry Brougham, a founder of the *Edinburgh Review*, who would later become lord chancellor; and Serjeant Best represented the defendants. None, however, was more important or renowned than the presiding judge, Edward Law, first Baron Ellenborough.

Ellenborough was the fourth son of the Bishop of Carlisle. His letters show him to be concerned with the minute details of self-presentation and perception—what wig, what outfit, when to arrive from the country. Self-possessed, ambitious, and perhaps a touch anxious, he was one of the most influential characters of his time. His well-timed career touched on some of the most important questions of the day. He counseled commercial and mercantile companies. He was an abolitionist and a friend of William Wilberforce, leading evangelical abolitionist. A Whig in his youth, Ellenborough had switched to the Tories after the French Revolution. His politics were much at odds with Cochrane's radical and reformist tendencies.

Ellenborough would have known especially well that trials such as Cochrane's were not merely about justice. In eighteenth- and nineteenth-century England and France, trials were often bigger than the individuals involved; they were spectacles that established or destroyed reputations, settings where political battles were allowed to play out in the courtroom. One of England's most closely followed and fiercely debated trials had been the seven-year impeachment, beginning in February 1788, of Warren Hastings, who was charged with corruption in his time as governor general of India. In his opening, Edmund Burke accused Hastings of being a despotic prince who had violated the natural order and law of God. "I impeach him," Burke declared, "in the name of human nature itself, which he has cruelly outraged, injured, oppressed, in both sexes, in every age, rank, situation, and condition of life." Accusations of rape and violence were voiced as questions of financial conduct, and financial enrichment fueled the fire. Ellenborough, despite having just eight years at the bar, represented Hastings.[3] At issue was not only Hastings's conduct but also the future of the British Empire. Westminster Hall filled with spectators to hear Burke declare at the trial's opening in February 1788: "It is not only the interest of India, now the most considerable part of the British empire, which is concerned, but the credit and honour of the British Nation itself will be decided by this decision."[4] Burke could easily have been speaking for the Stock Exchange in 1814, with its ambition to draw stark contrast between a speculative Cochrane and a financial market deserving of confidence and credit.

Cochrane's case involved a naval hero and flashy reports on the largest war to confront Europe in centuries. As the flashiest and most dramatic fraud trial of the early nineteenth century, it clearly demanded that the Exchange and Cochrane both aggressively defend themselves. Opening for the prosecution, Richard Gurney urged the jury to dismiss from their minds everything they had heard on the matter before entering the jury box. He also attempted to defend himself in the newspapers. "It does also sometimes occur," he stated, "that they who are accused, industriously circulate matters which they consider useful to their defense and even on the very eve of trial, force them into public notice."[5] For the defense, James Park similarly attempted to counter what Cochrane and his supporters felt to be an unfriendly pretrial bias. This, it soon became clear, would not be easy. Cochrane had placed his affidavit in newspapers and in pamphlets; the Committee of the Stock Exchange had placed his name, and those of the other accused, on placards on the Exchange doors.

Thomas Worthington was a hatter from Dover who had been in the Packet Boat public house the morning of de Berenger's arrival. Upon taking the stand, he was asked: "You have heard a great deal about this transaction?"

"Yes," he replied. "It has been in every body's mouth."[6]

"To Puff a Quack Medicine"

Despite the onslaught of information, Cochrane himself managed to miss the trial.[7] Later in life, he would suggest that he did not attend because he thought the charges ridiculous and conviction improbable. There is good reason to doubt this. He had rushed to London to publish an affidavit defending his name in the *Times* and the *Morning Chronicle* and had followed these up with letters to the editor. On March 23, a little more than a week after the fraud, he published five more affidavits, including statements from his servants and from the lamp manufacturer he had been visiting on the morning of the crime. Furthermore, in advance of the trial and owing largely to the fraud, he had been dismissed from the *Tonnant*, the ship on which he was going to serve as flag captain for his uncle, Alexander Cochrane, in North America. During the trial, he was represented in his absence by his affidavit, which was entered into evidence.

As this was the only moment the jury would hear from the naval hero in his own words, both the prosecution and the defense gave it due attention. Cochrane's defense was obviously reliant upon the affidavit. Serjeant Best, Cochrane's attorney, treated it like a witness in absentia, and one that came with an honorable history. "I say the oath of Lord Cochrane makes the evidence offered on the other side kick the beam," he declared in his opening. "There is nothing to put in competition with the affidavit which my learned friend has himself given in evidence." Assess his status, assess his history, argued Best, and surely the affidavit must be of the highest value.

> What reason has my learned friend given you today? What reason can you collect from the former life of this noble person, for he has been before you, and has lived in the view of the public, that can induce you to believe he is so completely lost to all sense of right and wrong, to all sense of what is due to himself, as to go before a magistrate to make an affidavit, in which he must know he was deposing to that, which at the time he was making the deposition absolutely false?[8]

Gurney, for the prosecution, dismissed the affidavit as irrelevant. What weight had it, he asked, if its author faced no punishment for lying? Affidavits served only those who sought "to puff a quack medicine" or were of "a suspected character." Flying in the face of accepted law, and anticipating the reform work of Jeremy Bentham some years later, Gurney dismissed oaths to God in favor of statements that, if delivered falsely, would bring social and criminal punishment for perjury: "Although he who makes a voluntary affidavit attests his God to its truth, he renders himself amenable to no human tribunal for its falsehood, for no indictment for perjury can be maintained upon a voluntary affidavit." It was the threat of punishment for perjury that made the balance of one's interests clear, he argued. And that was a deal an affidavit did not offer.[9]

Ellenborough was more practical, understanding that both affidavits and witnesses had the capacity for truth and falsehoods. At various turns, he advised the jury to be wary of testimony. In a number of instances—"let me advise you . . . not to witness again"—he all but declared a witness's testimony corrupt. Of James la Marchant, the witness likely involved in an attempted blackmail of Cochrane, he stated simply: "There is a great deal he says which is no evidence to anybody." Most of the time, however, Ellenborough was satisfied to be more ambiguous, leaving it to the jury to decide what pieces of evidence and what witnesses were credible. Evidence, he told the jury, was "subject to your consideration . . . as to its truth."[10] Some further guide to assessing honesty, information, and trustworthiness was needed. In such an environment, it was not simply information—as there seemed to be so very much of it—that formed the basis of judgment but also social status, morality, and reputation.

"Honest Judgment Could Be Warped"

The case against Cochrane hinged on three questions: Why had he sold all of his Omnium almost immediately upon the market's rise? Why had he met with de Berenger that morning and even provided him a change of clothes? And why, upon the morning of his capture, had de Berenger been found attempting to escape with bills that had originated with Cochrane?

Cochrane's defense attempted to answer all these questions in turn. De Berenger had not arrived dressed like a Frenchman, they insisted; he left without promise of favor, the relationship being largely in de Berenger's head. As for the shares, Cochrane claimed that his broker acted under a standing order to sell once the market moved one point—which it did, that morning. The bills in de Berenger's possession, he claimed, had come from third parties: they were in no way a direct payment from Cochrane to de Berenger.

But the trial was not only about Cochrane. While it concerned his social standing, it was also about the reputation of the Stock Exchange, about the relationship between responsible dealing in credit and the vice-filled world of speculation. The lawyers and Ellenborough well knew this, as did Cochrane. The jury was presented with competing visions of Cochrane. The affidavit and defense attorneys drew attention to his heroic history, highlighting his honor and pattern of selfless service. The attorneys for the Stock Exchange had to acknowledge this history, but *that* Cochrane, they insisted, was a different man from the one on trial. *This* Cochrane socialized with speculators. He did not use credit for useful means but speculated recklessly. He was an embodiment of vicious finance, far removed from traditions of virtue or restrained self-interest. These were not merely contrasting portraits but, rather, references to controversial—and combustible—historical and moral questions. At the time of the trial, the war with France continued, and Cochrane's service had to be considered in light of the long, difficult fight with Napoleon. It was the ideal setting in which to play the hero card. But the jury's City merchants would have been well acquainted with the link between speculation and war profiteering and would have seen both as harmful to commerce in general (as they made credit more expensive and less predictable). De Berenger's identity came down to the clothes he wore, but Cochrane was of higher standing. For him, the question was whether he was a man of virtue or vice. It was their answer to that question, as much as the evidence offered in court, that would likely swing the jury. For a trial in which information was shown repeatedly to be influential but unreliable, a crucial question loomed: Did Cochrane seem sufficiently in control of his self-interest that his information was reliable? Or, as the prosecution would have it, did his engagement in speculation demonstrate a reckless, vicious self-interest that brought his character and affidavit into serious question?

In his opening, Serjeant Best attempted to lay out the good standing of Cochrane's honor as clearly as possible: "Gentlemen, you have been told, and truly told that Lord Cochrane is a public character." That he had served in the navy and in office was reiterated. "Is a man so circumstanced likely to commit so sordid a crime as that with which he is charged? . . . No prospect of gain could hold out any temptation to Lord Cochrane to put in hazard what he now possesses."[11] Best appealed not only to Cochrane's heroism and reputation but also to something more fundamental: his status. A "man so circumstanced," he suggested, could not possibly engage in misinformation and reputation. Such circumstances had associated values and virtues, which precluded Cochrane from such nefarious endeavors.

It was precisely this idea that was behind Cochrane's attempt to separate himself from the Exchange entirely. In his affidavit, he spent more time trying to play down his connection to the Stock Exchange than he did explaining his trades: "I did not hold on that day any other sum on account, in any other stock, directly or indirectly," he wrote, adding, "I further swear, that the above is the only stock which I sold, of any kind, on the 21st day of February." The affidavit contains repeated references to his naval duty and public service. He distances himself from the elements that would have been involved in pulling off such a crime. Then he goes further. The affidavit reads like that of a gentleman aware of the direct threat to his name by association with the crime, but also of the more subtle threat to his honor created by association with stock speculation. "Further," he added, "I do solemnly depose that I had no connection or delaying with any one, save the above mentioned, and that I did not at any time, directly or indirectly, by myself or by any other, take or procure any office or apartment for any broker or other person for the transaction of stock affairs."[12]

For the prosecution, Gurney acknowledged that Cochrane was a gentleman whose name was "associated with the naval and military glories of his country." The jury, he sensed, may have started with a predisposition to believe the man. Gurney himself had, admitting: "That Lord Cochrane would have been incapable of deliberately engaging in any thing so wicked some time ago, I am sure I as earnestly hope as I am desirous to believe." It would be easy to see an anti–Stock Exchange sentiment behind Gurney's conduct of the trial. But a closer look reveals that he and the other attorneys, including even Cochrane's, were not discussing the market for credit; rather, they were discussing speculation in that market. Such capitalism was risky, a danger to morality and the nation. It was to be discouraged. That at least three witnesses who had engaged in speculation declined to answer questions so as not to implicate themselves in time-trading—a form of futures trading—reinforced this image. Cochrane's own attorney took care to proclaim, "I am not at all conversant in those things, never having speculated in stock at all."[13] In the end, it was de Berenger's attorney who, in trying to defuse suspicion against his client, acknowledged the connection most plainly. He conceded that Cochrane had entered into a time bargain. That, he declared, does not mean that he "is not to be believed upon his oath." His word stood, one defense attorney insisted: "I think the supposition is so shocking and so derogatory to him as a man, an officer and a Christian, that you will not come to that conclusion."[14]

But it was Gurney who drew the distinction successfully and clearly. He constructed a binary world of contrasts between chivalry and speculation, honesty and interest, the brave sea and the City's alleys, Parliament and the King's Bench. Thus he opened:

> They [the Stock Exchange Committee] discovered, to their utter astonishment, that this nobleman—this officer highly distinguished in the navy, then latterly appointed to an important command, and one should have supposed his whole soul engrossed in preparation for the active and important service on which he was going—this Representative in Parliament for the City of Westminster, bound by one of the most sacred of all duties, not to involve himself in any situation by which his honest judgment could be warped, and his

parliamentary conduct influenced—they found Lord Cochrane to have been a deep speculator in Omnium.

And thus Gurney closed: "You must see in what circumstances men are
placed, when they do these things. Lord Cochrane had first found his
way to the Stock Exchange, he had dealt largely in these speculations,
which my learned friends have so liberally branded as the appellation
of infamous. He had involved himself so deeply, that there was no way,
but by this fraud, of getting out."[15] This was the rise, decline, and fall of
Cochrane, and the process was clear: his involvement in the markets
was not investment but speculation—an undertaking worthy of no lord
or officer. The damage sustained by the nation and its commerce revealed Cochrane's irresponsible self-interest and thus brought his defense into doubt. Much of the information in the trial remained in
question, but Cochrane's compromised character, his pursuit of vicious luxury, was a point well made. Gurney summed up his unfortunate charge in a manner reminiscent of Burke, linking Cochrane's
behavior to the standing of his nation: "It is a duty in which it is impossible to feel pleasure; for every gentleman must feel degraded in the
degradation of gentlemen, and every Englishman must feel mortified
in the disgrace."

Jurymen in Cochrane's day generally answered to Adam Smith
and Napoleon's shared description of England as a nation of shop-
keepers.[16] Records for all twelve jurors do not exist, but we know the
professions of nine of them. While they all worked in the City, most of
them owned small businesses. George Miles ran Miles and Company,
a company of grocers and teamen. Lewis Lloyd, of Lothbury, was a
wholesale furrier, while John Peter Robinson ran his own merchant
house. Thomas Wilson Hetherington was a partner at Hetherington
and Maskew, a wholesale tea dealership. Richard Cheesewright was the
founder of Cheesewright R and Company Insurance Brokers.[17] Whether
any had funds in the market is difficult to know. To speculate as to how
each juror's occupation might have influenced their decision would be
futile. They were merchants engaged in the type of commerce that had
come to be understood as part of the public good. Whether they looked
merely to the evidence, sought to punish speculation in general, or were

suspicious of the large financial interests Cochrane had in the day's trade, we do not know. Two and one-half hours after the trial's end, they returned a verdict of guilty.

"I Submit to Robbery"

We do not know where Cochrane was when he heard the news. We do, however, know where he spent a good portion of the year following his June 21 sentencing. He was ordered to pay a £1,000 fine, serve twelve months in prison, and be set in the pillory outside the Royal Exchange (though he was ultimately spared this public embarrassment). He was duly removed to London's King's Bench Prison, a place surrounded by a forty-foot wall covered with cheval-de-frise and home to "Black-legs, Gamblers, Dandies, Greeks, Quaks, Chimney-Sweeps, Pimps, Bawds, Prostitutes, Bullies and Panders, Clergymen, Soldiers, Sailors, Thieves, Sprigs of Nobility, upstart Gentry; and last—and least—the Honest Unfortunate."[18]

Interest in the case did not fade quickly. Cochrane himself kept it in the news through his astounding insistence on retrying the case in public. He was stripped of the knighthood gained for his performance at Basque Roads, his coat of arms and banner removed from King Henry VII Chapel in Westminster Abbey. He was evicted from his seat in the House of Commons (though this would ultimately be restored to him by a politically agreeable electorate in Westminster). In March, he escaped over the walls of the King's Bench Prison; more than two weeks later, he was found near Parliament. When the Marshall of Westminster discovered him, Cochrane was said to have warned that he was a member of the House of Commons and that the marshall approached him "at his peril." The *Times* relished Cochrane's fall, depicting him as aggressive, dangerous, and somewhat pathetic, concluding: "It is strongly suspected his Lordship's mind has been affected by the late proceedings, and that all his conduct of late has been the result of insanity."[19] After serving his sentence, Cochrane reluctantly paid his £1,000 fine to Richard Gude, an officer of the Crown. On the back of the bank note he wrote: "My health having suffered by long and close confinement, and my oppressors being resolved to deprive me of property or life, I submit to robbery to protect myself from murder, in the hope that I shall live to bring the delinquents to justice."[20]

When freed from prison, Cochrane was still a reasonably young man, about to turn forty. With the same determination he had shown in the war with France, he quickly began the two undertakings that would occupy his remaining working life: the reconstitution of his honor and the pursuit of riches. As he had suggested on the back of his bank note, the effort at redemption focused first on the "delinquents" who had perverted justice, a project that took the form of attacks on Lord Ellenborough and the Committee of the Stock Exchange.[21]

Within six months of his conviction, Cochrane had published an extended attack on Ellenborough under the title "A Letter to Lord Ellenborough from Lord Cochrane." Cochrane claimed that Ellenborough was part of a conspiracy to convict him (fig. 2). He accused the judge not simply of showing bad form but of violating the law. Ellenborough knew well how fickle was reputation in a chattering London,[22] and Cochrane's letter, despite its obvious interests, surely provoked anxiety. Cochrane also went after the financial establishment. The money he briefly gained, he charged, was nothing compared with the scams of those at London's most prestigious houses. He singled out an "individual, who, in the hurry attendant on the execution of his various employments, as an East-Indian Director, Marshall of the Admiralty, and Member of the Parliament, forgot to pay his differences at the Stock Exchange, amounting to more than 40,000 pounds."[23] The City was a club filled with men as corrupt as he was accused of being.

Did Cochrane have a point? Ellenborough's friend, William Wilberforce, thought the judge's merging of partisan perspective and judicial responsibility inappropriate. That Ellenborough was tough on the defense is now evident. Though he spared some of his finest wit for the prosecution, his concluding remarks were rather blunt. Judges had significant influence upon the outcomes of trials; in Cochrane's case, Ellenborough left little doubt about his opinion. In his charge to the jury, he laid out these pieces of information as fact: de Berenger wrote the letter at Dover; Cochrane should have noticed de Berenger's dress; the defense witnesses, for the most part, were not trustworthy. These are things no modern judge in a British or American courtroom

A disgraced Cochrane shown holding his treatise against
Ellenborough. *Things as they have been. Things as they are now*, 1815.
(Reprinted with permission of the Royal Museums Greenwich)

would likely tell a jury; today they would be more appropriate in a prosecutor's closing argument. They also seem to have been true.

Cochrane remained convinced that his trial had been rigged. "No other Chief Justice," he wrote in his memoirs shortly before he died, "ever came hot-foot from a Cabinet Council to decide the fate of an accused person, politically obnoxious to the Cabinet." The conspiracy, in his mind, was clear: "That there was collusion between a high official at the Admiralty and the Committee of the Stock Exchange on this point, I do not hesitate to assert."[24] In the 1830s, Cochrane regained his naval commission; took on his father's title, becoming the tenth Earl of Dundonald; and, in 1847, was reinstated as a Knight of the Order of Bath by Queen Victoria herself. In 1815, however, much of that redemption lay in the future, following other wars on other seas—for those with Napoleon were coming to an end.

When the Battle of Waterloo came to a close on June 18, 1815 (just ten days after Cochrane was released from prison) and, with it, the final round of the Napoleonic Wars, Cochrane's rehabilitation seemed unlikely. France, defeated, posed no immediate threat to Britain. At Vienna, the victorious parties created a realigned Europe in which Britain, standing alongside Russia, would not see a continental land war until the Crimean War began in 1853. The political disputes to which Cochrane alluded would define the next era of British politics as radical; Tories and Whigs fought each other on the slow path to the Catholic Emancipation, the Reform Act of 1832, and eventually the abolition of the Corn Laws. But Cochrane had more pressing concerns. He had been relieved of his commission and his knighthood and had suffered significant financial penalty. Perhaps worst of all, he no longer held any public honor, and his character was considered by some to be corrupt and compromised.

But it was always morning somewhere in the growing British Empire. The Napoleonic Wars had laid to rest the Catholic threat from across the channel, but they also dramatically expanded Britain's imperial domains. Her colonies had nearly doubled, to upward of fifty, including crucial strategic areas such as the Cape Colony, the Gold Coast, and Malta. This was to be a new empire, cleansed of the corruption of the likes of India's former governor general Warren Hastings. It was to be an empire of liberty, holding at its core that values were not relative: that humans everywhere could be transformed, civilized, by law and education; that they were to be freed from the ancient chains of despots and priests, from hierarchy and patronage, in the name of free trade and self-reliance.[25] At Hastings's impeachment, in front of Ellenborough and the rest of the crowd in Parliament, Edmund Burke had placed a "radical universalism" at the core of this vision. "I believe, my Lords, that the sun, in his beneficent progress round the world, does not behold a more glorious sight than that of men, separated from a remote people by the material bounds and barriers of nature, united by a bond of a social and moral community."[26] That community, of course, was to be molded in the British image. Thus, in his "Minute on Indian Education," Thomas Macaulay, the imperial officer and historian, would famously write of forming a governing class that was "Indian in blood and colour, but English in taste, in opinions, in morals, and in intellect."[27]

Such a concern for liberty and the passing of corrupt institutions looked west as well as east. In 1808, when Napoleon engineered the rapid-fire abdications of Charles IV of Spain and, two months later, his son Ferdinand VII, they left their empire in disarray. The first republic of Venezuela was declared in 1810, and Simón Bolívar declared a second one in 1813. In New Granada, Cartagena declared independence in 1811 and was soon followed by other regions. When Ferdinand reclaimed his crown, early in 1814, he returned to an empire in revolt.

To British eyes, the struggles of these newly formed Latin American republics were a fight for liberty against an unenlightened, retrograde Spanish monarchy. But where Britons saw the potential light of liberty, they also saw money. New frontiers of empire, informal or formal, were also new frontiers of trade, opening up the possibility of new financial assets. After victory at Cape St. Vincent in 1797, Admiral Nelson had enacted a total blockade on Cadiz, long Spain's most important port for South American silver and gold. British merchants had previously traded with Spanish colonies—most notably in slaves. Before Nelson's blockade, merchants had funneled goods through Spain and Portugal or traded in contraband.[28] Now, with the colonies' access to Spain severed, an obvious partnership was born.

In the Latin American republics' wars against the Spanish Empire, a man could gain riches and honor in the service of liberty. Self-interest and good character could meet; reputations could be redeemed. What is more, the decades that lay ahead saw a lessening of the stigma associated with speculation. By the end of the nineteenth century, speculative investment would no longer be taken to impeach one's character and render one's information immediately untrustworthy. That was yet to come. In 1817, a Chilean envoy named Antonio Alvarez arrived in London with $100,000 to raise a navy. This was an opportunity Cochrane was made for. By 1818, "El Diablo Cochrane," as he was known to the Spanish, was back at sea, wreaking havoc upon the Spanish navy off the shores and in the harbors of Latin America. In November 1820, he slipped into Lima harbor and captured the Spanish flagship *Esmeralda*. It was classic Cochrane: cunning, brave, and successful. Even back in Britain, his reputation—at least on the sea—was far from total disrepair. "Mexico is in a state of insurrection," wrote a British surgeon tending to Britain's soldiers in Latin America. "The valiant army of San Martín is in Peru and before the gates of Lima, whilst the victorious fleet of Lord Cochrane rides triumphant on the fast shores of the Pacific Ocean."[29] Here was the hero of Basque Roads, not the stock market speculator and infamous hoaxer. When, in August 1825, it became clear that Cochrane was leaving his position as head of the Brazilian navy, a *Times* headline ran: "Brazil Stocks fell yesterday one per cent, in consequence, as is supposed, of Lord Cochrane's relinquishment of the naval service of that country."[30] Few would have missed the irony of a Stock Exchange reacting negatively to news of Cochrane's departure.

Even with this second shot at heroism, Cochrane would never fully escape the legacy of the Stock Exchange fraud. Over and over again, he proved incapable of serving his own interests in a way that did not put him at odds with the politically powerful. Immediately after his capture of the *Esmeralda*, Cochrane found himself in an extended dispute, over money, with revolutionary leader José de San Martín. For years, the Peruvian delegation in Chile would fight a public battle with Cochrane over his behavior and his monetary demands. The dispute, claimed the Peruvian delegation, would make Cochrane's "name forever abhorrent."

All the while, Cochrane served himself. It was this line—between acceptable self-interest and the appearance of greed—that he could never successfully navigate. His status carried with it associated values. Credit may have been crucial to the war effort and to commerce, but speculation was a wholly different matter. Cochrane was perceived by some as a threat to the financial exchange so crucial to British power and by many as behaving below his standing. Given that the capture of enemy ships was rewarded by prize money, he was not expected to possess a pure form of disinterested virtue. But the tradition of virtue and sociability was meant to constrain his commercial behavior, and his failure to abide by these traditions (or at least appear to do so) cost him dearly. In England in 1814 and then in South America, Cochrane's conduct regarding his financial interests was thought below his status, threatening to make his affidavits, testimony, and word untrustworthy.

Not unlike the financial world to come, Cochrane was speculative and global, taking bets and hoping for profits in the City and around the world. Though the fraud was simple, he was a man of remarkable complexity, whose ambitions and greed would become more acceptable as the century progressed. Survivor of so many battles at sea, Cochrane was hardly unlucky. But in this particular, singular way, he was unfortunate: his 1814 trial took place amid tectonic shifts in Europe and the greater world, but also amid more subtle ones—including the way interests were assessed and trust distributed. The Exchange had successfully made the trial about status and moral rectitude; in so doing, it implicated Cochrane and sought to reaffirm codes of conduct that were conducive to trust in financial exchange. Moreover, the Exchange endeavored to reestablish confidence in its own trade. Unfortunately for Cochrane, the Exchange's ability to play to the mistrust associated with speculation and indulgent self-interest spelled his courtroom doom. The Exchange would move forward, but such status-based ideals would not survive the capitalist habits that enabled it to thrive.

An Empire of Optimism

P ublic opinion, ever present in polls and the mouths of pundits today, has not always been around. In 1828, it received its first prominent treatment in the form of William Alexander Mackinnon's *On the Rise, Progress, and Present State of Public Opinion, in Great Britain, and Other Parts of the World*. His august bust, if not his book, should be on the mantles of the pollsters who today dominate campaigns and news cycles. The growth and advance of public opinion, as Mackinnon saw it, were not so much a product of literacy or democracy as a result of technological and commercial changes. He believed that the sources of public opinion were improved communication, increased access to information, religious feeling, and the private and public possession of capital and private property. Mackinnon wrote: "Let anyone who is not fully sensible of this, open a magazine or look at a paper, and observe the difficulty and delay that existed sixty or seventy years ago in procuring intelligence, and the little intercourse that existed in those days; let him compare the case of communication as it then existed, with the ease and celerity that it is experienced at present, even in so short a time."[1] The term *public sphere* would come later,[2] but its elements were clear to Mackinnon's contemporaries: the rise of "public opinion," the expansion of the press in the form of newspapers and journals, and the sudden increase in data and information based upon census taking and map making.[3] Information, whether regarding news, people, or the City itself, was increasingly democratized, discussed, and debated in public venues and formalized in government studies, censuses, journals, and newspapers.[4] It was in this expanded arena that the relationships between the public interest, self-interest, and trust were to be renegotiated.

If, as the historian Linda Colley has argued, it was during the French Revolutionary and Napoleonic Wars that Britons at last came to see themselves as a nation and a people, the absence of an enemy—a Catholic, existential threat at that—left a vacuum of cause to be filled and a host of politically divisive questions to be answered. Fundamental questions of religion, commerce, and government had to be addressed, including the questions of Catholic rights, the restrictive tariffs on grain imports, and the reform of "old corruption" in government.[5] Further financial questions also loomed, including how to address wartime debt and whether to end the paper pound and return to the gold standard. And there was a new, expanded empire to be managed, one that promised bounty but also came with the self-assumed responsibilities of liberal empire.

Latin America and Liberty

All-consuming though they seemed, the Napoleonic Wars did not completely monopolize Britain's attention. British soldiers, readers, and investors did not discover the Spanish Americas in 1815. Between 1799 and 1804, Alexander von Humboldt, the German explorer and romantic, traveled there with the permission of the Spanish crown. He was accompanied by a French companion but had frequent recourse to British help. Humboldt, perhaps along with Joseph Banks, would become the most famous traveler-cum-scientist of his age; in 1811, he published an English edition of his travels, *Political Essay on the Kingdom of New Spain*. Humboldt began the edition with the necessary homage to his host, Charles IV of Spain, but followed the letter with an extended geographical introduction, providing what he hoped to be the best maps and detailed routes of Spanish America from present-day Taos, New Mexico, to the Yucatan Peninsula. Previous maps had omitted some mountain ranges and put certain cities in the wrong location. Most important, they had overlooked crucial information regarding mines: "In vain do we seek in the greater number of maps published in Europe for the name of the city of Guanaxuato, which contains 70,000 inhabitants, or for the celebrated mines of Bolanos, Sombrerete, and Zimapan. None of the maps which have hitherto appeared show the position of the *Real de Catorce* in the intendancy of *San Luis Potosi*, a mine from which there is annually drawn nearly 20 millions of Francs." Humboldt's maps also included communication lines between the Atlantic and the South Sea, as well as details regarding future port plans. But it was the new details regarding access to mineral wealth that set his work apart from its predecessors.[6] Extensive reviews in the day's journals, which appeared almost immediately, treated the book as both a scientific achievement and a commercial guide.[7] Humboldt's influence would not soon subside: the English edition would remain the most important book on South America for the next two decades.

While readers in London and Edinburgh dreamed of securing the mining riches Humboldt described, enterprising merchants took advantage of the effects of the wars on Spanish sea power. After the battle of Trafalgar in October 1805, the Spanish merchant fleet became irrelevant, sailing unguarded in treacherous waters. In 1806 not a single Spanish ship entered Havana. The following year, not a single bullion shipment arrived in Spain from the colonies. Meanwhile, the Spanish monopoly on trade with her colonies had come to an effective end by 1801. According to one estimate, British exports to the Spanish colonies nearly doubled between 1807 and 1809 (at which point they reached a wartime peak of £18,425,614).[8] At war's end, Lord Thomas Cochrane would discover this world of revolution and contraband—far from London and from the massive land battles of Europe—where a man on the make could gain both a name and a profit.

Cochrane was preceded in this endeavor by a man named Gregor MacGregor. In some quarters, the 1820s were a decade of indulgent vanity and irrational exuberance, and such was the case of Sir Gregor. His scheme on investors involved the mythical South American colony of Poyais and demonstrated that financial innovation, ambition, and interest often won out in the battle against speculation. New types of financial assets and new locations for investment became increasingly important in London's financial circles. MacGregor's Poyais scheme, the quintessential fraud of Britain's first modern investment bubble, was carried forth by two paradigmatic historical forces. First, financial investment, even of the most reckless type, was still tied to public causes and fueled by a confidence of Britain's place in the world—a confidence that had spread the gaze of imperialists and investors alike to new locales and associated assets. Second, trust was now fought for and displayed in a more formalized public sphere. While the fallout from Cochrane's fraud took place on billboards and newspapers, it was decided in the courtroom; the Poyais scheme, on the other hand, was almost entirely arbitrated in a pitched public battle over reputation. Reputation had long been considered a protection against the risk of fraud in commercial exchange, and social rank maintained an integral relevance in trust relations, but as the commercial world expanded, it no longer remained enough to look toward rank as a check on the excessive self-interest associated with risk taking and fraud. The marketplace, resilient and adapting to the demands of the new, would more and more look to reputation. Rather than relying on abstract, elevated values, the marketplace looked to a person's reliability, good character, and responsible commercial behavior through his or her past actions—known and exhibited in public—as a basis for trustworthy relations.

MacGregor was born in Glengyle, Scotland, in 1786, the son of an East India Company sea captain. Having married well in 1805, he purchased a captaincy in the 57th Foot, an infantry regiment, with his wife Maria's money. His regiment began serving in the Peninsular War in 1809; by 1810, he had retired from military service. As his biographer points out, MacGregor was not present at the battles that made the regiment's name (and to which he would later frequently allude with pride). Instead, he took to fancy clothes, nice addresses, and rarified company. When Maria died in 1811, however, he inherited nothing and was left with expensive habits and few resources and without the option of actually making his name in the continent's wars. So he looked west—not to the young United States but to the even younger Latin American republics.

In 1812, MacGregor arrived in Venezuela to join Francisco de Miranda and later Simón Bolívar in their fight against Spanish forces. It

was here that MacGregor polished the persona that fed his later undertakings. Having offered his services to General Miranda, he led forces
into combat at Cerro Gordo and Los Guayos in 1812. He commanded
the military district of Socorro in New Granada. In 1815, he played a
chief role in the evacuation of troops and civilians from Cartagena after an extended siege by Spanish forces, and in 1816 he helped take the
fortress in Santa Rosa on the island of Margarita. In that same year, he
would be the first republican commanding officer to enter Barcelona,
Venezuela, having marched twelve hundred troops from Choroní. In
his attempt to become a hero of the cause of liberty in the Americas,
MacGregor had struck out on his own, and bravely so. He had fought
for the first republic. He could trade on the siege of Cartagena at dinner. He had been a friend of Miranda and an ally of Bolívar, who offered
him lavish praise.

In 1817, MacGregor sailed for Dublin and then England to recruit
a regiment to continue the wars in Latin America.[9] A number of agents
for the young republics were then working in London, recruiting unemployed soldiers or disgraced naval officers like Cochrane. The British press had taken a strong liking to the cause of the republics and
especially to Bolívar, who was being depicted in British periodicals of
all persuasions as a capable, brave, and bold military leader. Though the
circulation of the two leading conservative periodicals together barely
topped thirty-one thousand in 1820, their influence was considerable—or so observed James Hackett, who sailed from London in 1817
to fight in the Latin American wars. The subject of Latin America, he
would remember, was on the lips of guests at dinner parties and summer gatherings. Uniforms bespoke heroism. Newspapers hailed the
cause.[10]

By the end of the nineteenth century, free trade would become
inextricably associated with a larger social and international order,
promising its believers both consumerism and peace. It would offer a
vision of the world that linked cheap food and open markets to the
British story of liberty and freedom. But the alignment of liberty and
commerce had long preceded the zenith of free trade.[11] In Hackett's 1819
memoir, *Narrative of the Expedition Which Sailed from England in 1817*,
the cause about which Londoners spoke, as far as he could remember,

was liberty: "At the period of my departure from England, the tide of popular feeling ran strongly in favor of the patriotic cause." Another Englishman who sailed in 1817, a surgeon known in Hackett's memoir only as "Dr. Weatherhead," echoed this view. "Liberty," he wrote, "hath become such an innate principle in the breasts of Englishmen, that whenever an opportunity has occurred to evince this feeling, they have invariably shewn a warmth and devotion in its cause." Of course, like Cochrane, such soldiers were frequently looking for more than just service in the name of liberty. Hackett admitted as much: "The kind and earnest exertions of my friends having failed to promote my interest in any other capacity, I was led, in the month of September, 1817, to turn my attention towards the contest in South America."[12]

Hackett had been recruited by Luis López Méndez, the patriots' primary agent in London. Young men and soldiers were in need of opportunity, and López Méndez offered good pay and the potential for acclaim. One of nearly ten thousand British soldiers who would fight in the wars, Hackett sailed on the *Britannia* in 1817 along with an armorer, letters of introduction from López Méndez to Bolívar, and a printer with a hefty press for the leader's use. As Hackett headed westward, MacGregor settled back in London, hoping to convince López Méndez to back his regiment. It is unlikely the two men knew each other directly, but MacGregor could not have been a stranger to López Méndez, and he succeeded in winning the diplomat's support. The "liberator" of the Floridas, the hero of the march from Choroní, the leader of the retreat from Ocumare, got his loan from López Méndez and thus the funding for his battalion, the First Regiment of the Hussars of the Kingdom of New Granada.

MacGregor's First Regiment was largely British. Some of his troops had served under Wellington. Others were French and had served under Napoleon (one of whom was lost en route when he fell overboard while trying to bathe). A pair of memoirs provide colorful insight into the regiment's fate. The first is from the aforementioned Dr. Weatherhead, the regiment's surgeon; the second, from a soldier, John Besant. According to both accounts, MacGregor's group got off to something of a glorious start. In early 1819, the regiment, numbering somewhere between three and four hundred, landed near the Spanish port of

Portobello, in what is today Panama. Portobello was not necessarily strategically significant, but MacGregor had visions of taking the rest of Panama, grabbing a notable victory in the same territory where hundreds of Scots had perished during the Darien scheme of 1698.[13] The attack upon Portobello was led by Colonel Woodbine, who (owing to his experience fighting American Indians in the colonies' Revolutionary War) was, according to Weatherhead, "well calculated for this description of service." The soldiers spent the night holed up in the bushes. Wet from the night's rain, they awoke in the morning and charged what had overnight become an empty Spanish fort. John Besant would nonetheless write of "the little army which, in twelve hours after landing, overthrew three times its force, and captured one of the strongest and most celebrated fortresses in all Spanish America." Soldiers were issued ribbons and medals in an elaborate ceremony in one of the town's two squares. Performance was MacGregor's specialty. Some one hundred peasants and former slaves traveled from the country to form the Regiment of America Libre. MacGregor, continuing with the ceremonies, "addressed them in a speech, pointing out to them that he came to liberate their country from the oppressive and despotic government of the Spaniards."[14]

The glory was short-lived. The hussars had not received the riches they hoped for, nor even their promised wages. MacGregor attempted to pay in installments. He grew desperate and taxed the local inhabitants and merchants, repaying them in counterfeit coins. The merchants raised prices. The soldiers had traded cartridges and gunlocks for liquor, and everyone drank together. Soon everyone was drunk or ill. As the surgeon later observed: "All were as happy and merry as it is possible for any set of unthinking beings to be."[15] That is, until the Spanish returned, sneaking into town disguised as country workers. The next thing General MacGregor knew, he was jumping out the window of his bedroom. According to Besant, he ran through the town and swam to his ship in nothing but his shirt. Some British troops died fighting the Spanish, who had surprised the drunk or sleeping soldiers, but most were taken prisoner.

While MacGregor escaped, the prisoners were marched from Portobello to Panama, where they suffered from disease and abuse.

Most must have awaited their death. During their imprisonment, they were aware of only one attempt to liberate them. In September 1819, near Panama, a frigate, passing by an island home to a Spanish naval base, hoisted Spanish colors and approached the fort. Once the ship was close enough, she opened fire. From the spires and churches on land, the city's residents watched as two hundred Chilean troops landed and seized the fort. The ship, the *Rose*, belonged to the fleet of none other than Lord Cochrane. Rumors swirled in the prison camp. An attempt at a trade was made: the *Rose*'s captain, Illingsworth, offered captured Spaniards and his cargo for the British prisoners. The Spaniards rejected the trade.

In late 1820, after seventeen months in the prison, the remaining prisoners were released by order of the King of Spain. Dr. Weatherhead estimated that only 121 of the 340 prisoners had survived. Some had been executed for trying to escape. Many had succumbed to disease— ulcers, yellow fever, dysentery. The mortality rate of prisoners in his hospital was around 50 percent. "It seemed to be the intention of the government gradually to destroy them," he wrote.[16]

Weatherhead's descriptions of the brutalities and disappointments associated with the wars of liberty in Latin America were not unique. Most of the ten thousand soldiers never returned home, with as many as five thousand dying in battle or of disease.[17] Of those who sailed out in 1817 and were fortunate enough to return, many shared their experiences in memoirs. Hackett described "revolting and indiscriminate brutality."[18]

Many soldiers felt they had been sold a bill of goods. López Méndez, the patriots' agent in London, had promised resources and influence that he could not provide. The promised payment, as well as compensation for uniforms, saddles, and the like, was delayed or never delivered. Such were the risks in the ambitious, often uncharted areas of military service for hire, not to mention commercial expansion. But had they been conned? Hackett asked the question explicitly. "I could scarcely refrain from accusing myself of rashness and precipitancy, in having placed such implicit faith in the alluring expectations which had been so widely and confidently circulated in England, by the South American active partisans. But on cool reflection, I felt, that I was rather the victim of deceit, than the dupe of my own folly and want of prudence."

MacGregor scarcely fared any better. Weatherhead, perhaps sarcastically, dedicated his book to MacGregor and to revolutionary leader José de San Martín. He had a hard time sugarcoating the Portobello incident's effect on MacGregor's reputation:

> There were associations excited in the public mind by the very name of MacGregor, which were not only favourable to the character of the general, considered as an individual, but gave an impulse to the expedition itself, from his being a highlander. Everything, therefore, which had gone abroad of the scenes in which he had engaged in South America, was readily believed and favourably reported; but as soon as the recapture of Portobello became generally known, the character of Sir Gregor sunk in public estimation forever.

Like his fellow Scotsman Cochrane, MacGregor seemed to have a talent for finding scandal. Also like Cochrane, he had a knack for resurrection. MacGregor should never have had prospects in London after the Napoleonic Wars. As Weatherhead suggested, his prospects should have been sunk forever (again) after the Portobello affair.[19] Nonetheless, when he returned to London in 1821, he had a new title, new plans, and new bonds, land plots, and army commissions to be sold. His challenges were twofold: to sell excitement in the investment opportunity and to renew trust in himself. Not entirely unlike the Stock Exchange in 1814, he had to inspire trust in his particular offerings and confidence in the larger endeavor that was investment in Latin America. To do so in the 1820s required publicity and that nineteenth-century version of a business plan, the prospectus. He would parade his bona fides in a public sphere, peddling opportunity to investors eager to send money, instead of lives, to Latin America.

The Roaring (Eighteen) Twenties in London

In 1821, Gregor MacGregor and his new wife, Josefa, née doña Josefa Antonia Andrea Aristeguieta y Lovera, a close relative of Bolívar, returned to London from South America, leaving behind a war-torn region that would soon become a thoroughly attractive destination for colonists and foreign capital. The couple took up at Oak Hall, a small estate in Essex, with their son and daughter. MacGregor set to rebuilding his reputation through public performance and through the press. No longer was he merely a hero of Cartagena or the antihero of Portobello; he was now Gregor MacGregor, Cazique of Poyais, Prince of the Mosquito Shore.

The Mosquito Coast, a stretch of Central America's Atlantic coast from southern Nicaragua down through what is today Honduras, was not unknown to Britons. Colonists had settled there in the mid-eighteenth century before quitting the settlement a few decades later, following a treaty between Britain and Spain. MacGregor was recruiting colonizers, investors, and soldiers for a small stretch of Mosquito Coast called Poyais. This action—the recruitment, the publicity, and most important the financing—took place in London and Scotland.

Operating, he claimed, with permission by treaty from the King of Mosquito Coast, MacGregor appointed a chargé d'affaires at the Legation of the Territory of Poyais, in the United Kingdom of Great Britain. He named William Richardson Commander of the Most Illustrious Order of the Green Cross. He opened offices in Glasgow and Edinburgh to sell Poyais land tracts. He opened the Office of the Legation from Poyais, in Dowgate Hill in the City of London. An official reception was held for MacGregor nearby in Guildhall, a centerpiece of the City. A former British army officer named Hall was named lieutenant governor of the town and district of St. Joseph, the capital of the Poyais Republic; another former British naval officer was appointed both admiral of the Poyaisian navy and count of Rio Negro.[20] MacGregor named a head to the Bank of Poyais, as well as to its national theater. His potential colony had all the required institutional seeds: a bank, a theater, a military, a government. Thus, he quickly established himself as a figure in the City and in the press.

Equally important to the reconstruction of his reputation and the selling of Poyais was a travel guide-cum-prospectus produced in support of the Mosquito Coast. The author was Thomas Strangeways, almost surely MacGregor's invention, as was his title, K.G.C., Captain

First Native Poyer Regiment and Aide-de-Camp to His Highness Gregor, Cazique of Poyais. The book—*Sketch of the Mosquito Shore, Including the Territory of Poyais, Descriptive of the Country, with some information as to its Productions, the best mode of Culture, and Chiefly Intended for the Use of Settlers*, published in 1822—sought to replicate the buzz that previous guidebooks had created for places like Mexico. It had the intricate detail to which early readers of Humboldt had grown accustomed, as well as Humboldt's sense of romantic adventure.

Sketch of the Mosquito Shore relied heavily upon previous authors whose names or positions carried a degree of respect. The author drew on three key works about the Mosquito Coast: Captain George Henderson's 1811 book, *An Account of the British Settlement of Honduras*; Thomas Jeffery's influential *West Indian Atlas*, published in 1788; and Bryan Edwards's *The History, Civil and Commercial, of the British West Indies*, published between 1793 and 1798. Strangeways never hid his borrowing—quite the opposite. He introduced an author and let him carry the weight of the description for pages. The passages can be tested against the originals, as Strangeways was true to the authors' original words, if not their meaning. Old names were called upon to assure the risk-averse reader that this place was not new, that it had a history.

The author also knew the value of scientific authority. The first fifty pages, dedicated to topography, go on and on with descriptions of latitudes, measurements of leagues, details of fathoms, and a thorough accounting of the way the wind blows. The next fifteen pages are devoted to minerals and soil, and more than one hundred to trees and wildlife. Of gold, he wrote, "The mines that have been discovered are very rich." Of lapis, he observed, "The importation of this ore into the United States of America, is free of duty; it may perhaps therefore merit the attention of some of the settlers." Coffee and indigo were said to grow "amply." The soil produced with "perfection." Sugarcane thrived with "luxuriance." Pine, cedar, mangrove, sapodilla, palmetto, and Santa Maria trees would all provide wood worthy of export.[21]

Some of these details were vague. Others, as befitted a prospectus, were buttressed with plausible detail.[22] For example, a new sugar plantation with £1,896 in investment capital would likely return £655 per annum profit (a 35 percent return) almost immediately after the land was cleared and the sugarcane was planted. With a proper storefront, profits could jump to £1,200, "free of all taxes whatsoever." Labor should not be a problem as the local Indians "possess[ed] modesty, docility, good faith, a disposition to friendship, and gratitude."[23] Poyais was not only a place to make a fortune but also a place to retire with one. The weather was unrivaled, wrote Strangeways, quoting from previous guidebooks.

The idea of a new settlement at such great distance from Britain, in the wake of memoirs detailing the horrors of the wars in Latin America, could have fallen flat. Strangeways's details were intricate; his sources well known and seemingly reliable. Real or not, Poyais had to be imagined before it could be sold. In an environment of exuberant optimism, where riches rooted in a wider world were often paid out in London, MacGregor had made his pitch very well.

If potential settlers and investors were to see in Gregor Mac-Gregor all the energy and dynamism of 1820s capitalism, his endeavor also embodied, even at face value, much of what was dangerous in expansionist capitalism. MacGregor had been just three years old when Adam Smith died, perhaps no more than a couple of miles from him. Yet Smith's concept of the prudent, frugal person was alive and well to the political economists and moral philosophers of the 1820s. What was fast and built on credit seemed illusory to William Cobbett—and to Thomas Chalmers, a theologian and leading figure in the development of a Christian approach to political economy. Chalmers published the first of three volumes of *The Christian and Civic Economy of Large Towns* in 1821; in 1832, he published *On the Political Economy in Connexion with the Moral State and Moral Prospects of Society*. In 1821 he declared forcefully that "we rejoice in the luxuriance of a rank and unwholesome overgrowth; and mistake bulk for solidity, do we congratulate ourselves on the formation of an excrescence, which should rather be viewed as the blot and distemper of our nation."[24] His language is not far from that of the City's opponents: separating the real and honest from the unwholesome and luxurious. Commercial ambitions, he advised, required moderation. Chalmers was hardly alone in this position. "Over-trading is *fast* trading," advised a contemporary, "is, in fact, the criminal folly which the Word of God so clearly warns us—the *making haste to be rich*, which is never innocent, but always culpable and baneful."[25] As the historian Boyd Hilton points out, the threat was not just fraud but greed. There was something untrustworthy, even fake, about excessive riches. Chalmers imagined an Elysian street where people served each other's interests, honored each other's reputations, and acted benevolently in their neighborhoods.

There is another vision of the London street of the 1820s, and it is filled with fraudulent food hawkers, strutting dandies, global goods, London men seeking capital for mines abroad, and foreigners seeking capital for their newborn countries. This world was interested in the maximization of everything, from mines to waistcoats. These 1820s were well suited to the speculator in Mexican mines and future prime minister Benjamin Disraeli, who believed the decade represented a turning point in history. When as a young dandy he took his tour of the Near East, he wrote excitedly to his father, Isaac: "It is the fashion among the dandies of this place, that is the officers, for there are no others, not to wear waistcoats in the morning," continuing, "I also have the fame of being the first who ever passed through the Straits with two canes, a morning and an evening cane. I change my cane as the gun fires, and hope to carry them both to Cairo."[26] In the words of Robert Blake, "Early did Disraeli discover the important truth that, up to a point, the world will take a man at his own valuation."[27] Disraeli and MacGregor had both grasped this lesson: public performance and public renown influenced reputation and, thus, confidence. Or as Blake observed, "Pose and sincerity are inextricably interwoven."[28]

These two Londons—one of Evangelical propriety and frugality, the other of profligate performance and stock puffing—were not disconnected. As we have seen, the former was acutely concerned with the latter. The 1820s provided many examples of indulgent self-interest and its destructive capacities. Over the decade, London's financial market added depth and liquidity, while the government loosened long-standing financial legal restrictions. In an attempt to consolidate its debt, the government reduced the interest offered on its 5 percent Consol by 1 percent. Those who did not want to accept the change could redeem their consols; many accepted the offer. By the end of 1822, the holders of at least £2.8 million were seeking new investment outlets.[29] Then, in 1825, Parliament repealed the Bubble Act of 1720. For over a century, the act had restricted the formation of joint-stock companies; its repeal saw a dramatic rise in the establishment of such companies. In the same year, the Country Bankers' Act allowed banks more than sixty-five miles from London to become joint stocks. The domestic economy boomed, while Britons consumed goods from all over the world.

The *London New Price Current* published the prices of British staples as well as major stocks. It broadcast Lloyd's rates for insuring to far-flung destinations like Brazil, River Plate, East India, and Honduras. (Rates to Africa resembled those to Honduras and Argentina, all of which were relatively cheaper than the rates to East India.) The *Current* catalogued prices of cocoa and coffee, balsam from Peru, bark from Cartagena, burwood from Angola, and goat skins from the Barbary Coast. Merchants and customers could find prices for Archangel tar, Riga flax, and Swedish iron.[30] London was becoming the capital of nineteenth-century globalization. The British press was particularly interested in Latin American prospects, and for good reason. According to Frank Griffith Dawson's detailed 1990 study *The First Latin American Debt Crisis*, the *Times* yielded 20 percent of its column space to Latin American issues.[31] Other papers took a decidedly bearish approach, but Latin America remained the subject: it was what investing readers wanted to know about. Liquid London was developing a penchant for the mineral wealth of the newly independent Latin American states for whose cause its countrymen had fought.

Government commercial interest in the newly independent states also reflected this sudden interest. In 1823, the British government dispatched consuls and consuls general all over Latin America.[32] Under George Canning's watch, the government committed to spending £21,200 per year to monitor trade in Latin America. In 1825, eight new consuls and vice-consuls were added. It placed consuls general in Mexico, Colombia, Argentina, Chile, Peru, and elsewhere and established consulates in Vera Cruz and Xalapa, Acapulco, Maracaibo, Caracas, Panama, Cartagena, and Montevideo. Two vice-consuls were placed in Chile, two in Peru, and two in Argentina.

Britain would be the leading investor in Latin America from the end of the Napoleonic Wars until the beginning of World War I. Loans to governments were the chief form of investment over that period, though direct investment claimed an ever larger share as the century progressed. Colombia was the first of the young nations to float a bond, which paid 6 percent annually on an initial offering of £2 million. Colombia's bonds were offered at £84; they would pay out at £100. (As Dawson points out, that was not far from prices of Danish and Russian bond issues in 1822.) Chile was next, followed by Peru.[33] Of the roughly £25 million invested in Latin America by 1825, nearly £21 million was lent to foreign governments, and only £4 million was invested in mines and raw materials.[34] It comes as no surprise that it was during the euphoric and manic periods of the Latin American debt bubble that some of the most spurious stock offerings took place. Confidence crept closer to credulity. Everyone sought to float bonds, from brewers to the Knights of Malta to confidence men. This had occurred before, during the Darien scheme and the South Sea bubble, and it would occur again with railway shares—and even bicycles: the dynamism that pushed financial capitalism outward brought moments when exuberance bested skepticism and trust was cheap.[35]

It was during one of these moments, near the end of 1822, that MacGregor sold his first bonds on behalf of the state of Poyais. To discount the bonds, he hired the respected firm of Sir John Perring, Shaw, Barber and Company. Perring had recently been lord mayor of London, and the company occupied offices in the middle of the action on Cornhill Street. MacGregor claimed that his right to sell land in Poyais came directly from the King of the Mosquito people, George Frederic. The land grant was registered at the High Court of Chancery. If the initial 1822 float was anything like that of the previous, it offered 5 percent, with a dividend payable every six months at the house of Sir John Perring and Company. The bonds, like so many floated during the 1820s, were secured against the revenue of the state. The 1823 loan promised that no additional loans would be undertaken until one-eighth of the initial loan was paid back.[36] As was standard at the time, and as any investor would have expected, announcements of the dividend payments were advertised appropriately on the front page of the *Times*, as well as other papers.

An amateur poet, Mary Anne Lloyd, self-published a poem that caught the spirit of the MacGregor phenomenon: "To the Gentlemen of the Stock Exchange. Lines on the Poyais Bonds." It began:

Ye gentlemen raise

The stock called Poyais . . . From mountains he came,
McGregor his name . . . at a fortune he aims.

To the poet, MacGregor was an enchanter with good timing. He made promises, offered hope, and carried himself with the air of a cazique. "He has," she wrote, capturing MacGregor perfectly, "flags and unicorns" but "no garter."[37] She could not have been more right. MacGregor had all of the trappings but none of the substance. Nonetheless, prior to his initial bond offering, a group of colonists sailed from Scotland for the promised land of Strangeways's Poyais. And they would eventually arrive.

"The Filthy and Almost Naked State They Were In"

In September 1822, the *Honduras Packet* sailed from Leith, near Edinburgh, to Poyais. The *Packet* sailed with five thousand banknotes for the Bank of Poyais, printed by the printer to the Bank of Scotland, and up to £6,000 worth of goods and materials.[38] They brought wheels, axels, cask beef and flour, rice, copper tools, tin, a small printing press, military supplies, and much more. It was perhaps a bad omen that for seventy initial residents and hundreds more to come, the ship carried only eighteen small casks of rum.[39] On January 22, 1823, the *Kennersley Castle* also sailed from Leith. In rough weather, it went north past St. Andrews and Aberdeen, turned west past John O'Groats, the northernmost point on the British mainland, and made the long trip to the promised land of Poyais.

MacGregor had given Lieutenant Governor Hall, charged with organizing the settlement, twenty-six precise orders on how to get the establishment up and running. Hall was to give directions in Mac-Gregor's name and to do so with authority: "I ordain, I decree, I command." He was authorized to issue microloans to enable settlers to build their homes. A $5 fee was to be charged for signing passports of departing merchant vessels. Order no. 4 allowed Hall to issue paper money from the Bank of Poyais. Order no. 11 mandated that every settler belong to either the yeomanry or the militia. Order no. 17 instructed Hall, immediately after landing, to "issue a proclamation, stating that no person whatsoever is allowed to purchase or obtain lands under any pretence from the Indians."[40] Hall and his staff were to bring bureaucracy, property rights, taxation, and fiat money. But when the *Kennersley Castle* arrived at the head of the Black River in April, the land the settlers found was not exactly what Strangeways had promised, a fact those who sailed months earlier on the *Honduras Packet* were already well aware of. Agents at the land office in Edinburgh convinced James Hastie, a Scottish farmer, that Poyais was the spot for him. There were already between fifteen and twenty thousand Scots living in the West Indies, and more in the United States. For a farmer like Hastie, the trip west was something thousands had made before him, including, as was often the case with Scottish emigrants, the well educated.[41] But Hastie did not find sugar plantations or developed colonies. Instead, he found sand, chigoe fleas, sand flies, and plenty of mosquitoes. "There were," he would remember, "two houses or huts there belonging to two persons who were cast away." The land held no more promise than England's rugged seashore.[42]

More detailed descriptions of the settlement come from a group of British colonial agents and merchants who claimed to have rescued the Poyais settlers. In April 1823, just months after the *Kennersley Castle* had completed its trip from London, Marshal Bennett, the chief magistrate of Belize, arrived at the mouth of the Black River to deliver to King Frederic his annual gift from His Majesty's government. Bennett described a scene of "sickness and wretchedness." John W. Wright described his fellow settlers as "miserable and suffering human beings." The most detailed description of St. Joseph would come from George

Westby, the keeper of the records at Belize, who traveled to the Black River with Bennett. "I think it scarce possible to witness greater misery than that which presented itself to us," he testified.

> Most of the people were lying on the ground, under a few leaves and branches thrown across some sticks, which it would be a violation of truth to call houses; many were in a state of fatigue and fever, and absolutely unable to crawl to the woods for the common offices of nature. The stench arising from this circumstance in the huts, the filthy and almost naked state they were in, the absence of cleanliness and comfort, the want of good nurses, nourishment and, above all, of good water, combined with the want of medicine, seemed to be accelerating the work of death.[43]

Over the final week of April and first week of May, nine settlers died. Most lay in makeshift tents along the beachhead. Some settlers attempted to build a store; others simply fled.

Investors had done the same. By the time the *Kennersley Castle* sailed, evidence of Poyais's troubles had appeared in London. As was common in that era, bonds and shares were purchased over time. Initially, one might buy a subscription to the share, giving the buyer the right to purchase; the purchase would be followed by a succession of payments in installments. Poyais bonds were structured this way. By January 1823, Perring and Company was already reducing the installment sizes—in other words, lowering the price. A January 15 *Times* advertisement informed those who did not want, on January 17, to pay their 35 percent of the initial share price that they could wait until February 10 and pay a mere 10 percent. On January 21, the *Times* announced the sailing of the brig *Alknomack* with "two-hundred tons of goods" for Poyais. It was leaving within days, and those seeking passage were urged to visit Wm. Walker and Company, ship and insurance brokers, on Old Broad Street. By mid-March, the *Alknomack* still had not sailed. The January installment payment was pushed back to late March and was dropped to a mere 5 percent. Investor confidence had turned on MacGregor. While the initial offering might have been a success, the installment payments were not being honored. Such were the whims of speculation and the speed of the marketplace. The market not completely sunk by the fraud, investors moved on, opting not to increase their exposure. But as with Cochrane's hoax, the fallout from the fraud continued long after the supposed crime.

The Court of Public Opinion

On May 6, 1823, Hall, the lieutenant governor and MacGregor's chief political agent, authorized the abandonment of the settlement to prevent what he called the "waste of human life." Their stores running low, overcome by fever and dysentery, the survivors boarded the merchant ship *Mexican Eagle* for the short trip to Belize. Two trips were necessary, the first one carrying sixty-eight individuals, almost all women and children. In Belize, the settlers were put in the hospital, with the overflow given shelter in the town's church and in British residents' homes. These residents formed a committee charged with fundraising for the settlers. The chief of Belize's public treasury claimed that more than $12,000 was dedicated to the care of the ill, with another $1,000 raised from donations. In August 1823, forty-nine settlers, mostly the young and old, orphans and widows, sailed homeward. A committee to aid the Poyais orphans was formed in London. As Lieutenant Governor Hall would make clear, however, Poyais was not just a human story but also a financial and commercial one.[44]

By August, London's newspapers would be engaged in a full-fledged debate over the tragedy of the Poyais settlers.[45] The airing of scandals, as we have seen in the case of Cochrane and of Warren Hastings, former governor general of India, was a British political and commercial tradition. It played a crucial role in buttressing the market against frauds that inevitably accompanied an economy that—while closed in certain circles—depended on trust of strangers. MacGregor was never tried for the Poyais fraud. He was likely bankrupt and would soon flee to France. Instead, the truth about Poyais had to be determined in the court of public opinion. Even when it came to cases as unambiguous as those of MacGregor and Poyais, the public sphere remained a space not merely for *receiving* but also for *contesting* information and judgment.

After the abandonment of Poyais, MacGregor and his agents rapidly began to defend the settlement. In August 1823, the *Times* published an affidavit sworn in by Henry Crouch, master of the *Kennersley Castle*. He claimed that he'd stayed in Poyais for twenty-one days and found the settlers from the *Honduras Packet* in good health. They had begun to work their land and had used fine tortoiseshells to kit out a schooner. The wood, especially the mahogany, rosewood, and cedar, was of exceptional quality. "I have no hesitation," he declared, "that [Poyais] is equal to the finest climate and richest soil I have ever experienced." Herman Hendriks, another of MacGregor's agents, purchased an advertisement in November claiming that the great success of Poyais was yet to come. The ad was an attempt to build confidence, assuring investors that their money was bound for the settlement, not for MacGregor's pocket. More settlers, arms, and silver, he claimed, were already on their way.[46]

Such puffery required explaining how two hundred settlers had ended up in Belize, and this meant attacking the credibility and honesty of their rescuers. William Richardson, MacGregor's representative and sponsor of sorts in London, wrote in a letter to the *Times*: "I unmasked to the world the secret enemy of Sir Gregor MacGregor—Mr. John Young, the Honduras Agent." Richardson and those in his employ would go much further. He wrote to the Earl Bathurst, secretary of state for war and the colonies, alleging that Belize merchants had seized goods at the Poyais settlement and sold them for profit. He demanded that the magistrates of Belize and His Majesty's superintendent there give Richardson's and MacGregor's attorneys—Usher, Fricker, and Usher and their agent, George Augustus Low—assistance in claiming upward of £10,000 worth of goods.[47]

Meanwhile, in London, the aforementioned Low published a tract, *The Belise Merchants Unmasked; Or, A Review of Their Late Proceedings against Poyais*, purporting to describe how the settlers in Belize had derailed and robbed the Poyais settlement. "Facts are stubborn things," declared Low on his title page. The "facts" he claimed were that Belize was a settlement with little or no commercial value, that the magistrates feared settlers would move to Poyais when it proved a success, and that the former settlers of Poyais, though skilled and talented, found no proper employment or opportunity once removed to Belize. Of the set-tlement that he claimed stole and sold tens of thousands of pounds' worth of goods, he wrote: "The laws are perverted, religion is made a laughing-stock, and vice reigns paramount in all her glory." It was, he argued, the Belize merchants who had doomed Poyais and its settlers.[48]

The truth was a question of honor and morality. In the inevitable uncertainty that potential investors and the reading public would have regarding what exactly occurred in Poyais, Low inserted the issue of the gentleman and trust. Colonel Hall "had betrayed his trust," while "*honest* men have been plundered, *honourable* men have been calumni-ated." Why was Low to be taken at his word? "I shall only add," he an-swered, "that, to the veracity of the statements here adduced, I solemnly pledge myself, as an officer and as a gentleman."[49] The language was high indeed, but the approach was of the gutter. Low and MacGregor might write of morality, law, and the rules of gentlemen, but they em-ployed blackmail, defamation, and intimidation in Britain's most pub-lic arena. Such were the gray areas exposed by a commercial energy that could forge new financial frontiers but also enabled the fraudsters who sought to people them.

Even the most honorable of acts, the rescue of the settlement, had been turned into a scandal. In newspapers and hearings, MacGregor and his agents squared off against Bennett and the merchants of Belize. The language invoked virtue and codes of status, but the battle was an ugly debate over reputation. The Belize party of Major General Edward Codd, Bennett, and Westby had to argue their case from afar. They wrote the *Times* with documents promising to "set the question of the Poyais Settlement at rest." They had been, they claimed, "informed by almost every tongue, that they had left their native country with the brightest and most flowery views before them, and had been deceived beyond belief." There simply was no city or sea of Poyais, despite its presence on maps long before MacGregor came around; it was all noth-ing more than a "baseless fabric of vision." For those who thought the land grants might still be worth speculation, they included an extra kicker: copied along with the letter to the editor was a note from King George Frederic II, King of the Mosquito Nation, declaring that "the grant given to Sir Gregor MacGregor is null and void."[50]

In response to this very public battle, and to the defamation and legal demands aimed at the merchants of Honduras, the superintendent, Major General Codd, called for an extended inquiry into the occurrences surrounding the evacuations on the *Mexican Eagle*. Hall, once MacGregor's man on the ground, was questioned by the superintendent of the Belize colony.

"Was not Sir Gregor MacGregor the only person you knew, or acknowledged, as the head of the Poyasian government?" Yes. "Did you," the superintendent continued, "consider the establishment of Poyais as a government, or merely an establishment for commercial purposes?"

Hall replied, "From the appointments made or projected, both civil and military, I considered it a government, embracing, as with all governments, commercial purposes."[51]

The inquiry appeared in print in London. In it, Codd named the purpose of the hearing and subsequent publication: "Laying open the true situation of the imaginary state of Poyais, and showing the sufferings of the unfortunate Emigrants to the Mosquito Shore." In so doing, they were in the business of defending their own reputations.

The World Is New?

This time, MacGregor's name would not recover. With the wisdom of hindsight, the Whiggish editors of the *Edinburgh Quarterly* compared Poyais to Darien, to the Mississippi Company, and to the South Sea bubble. "We had thought," they wrote, "that mankind, grown wise by experience, were perfectly on their guard against those deceptions which had been played off with such success on former ages. . . . But the success which has attended Sir Gregor MacGregor's scheme of a settlement at Poyais, in the Bay of Honduras, convinces us that we give mankind too much credit."[52] At the decade's end, MacGregor would appear totally undone in the work of George Smeeton, the chronicler of picaresque London. During a visit to a courtroom, two characters witness an innkeeper's complaint to the court. She accuses a customer of having stolen her bedding. Smeeton writes, "On Christmas eve, the person who she accused of having robbed her, called at her house, accompanied by two females: they retired to a room together, and, having remained in it for some length of time, she heard his two companions slip down the stairs, and, the street-door being open, they ran out of the house." Naked, and without his female companions, the man emerges: "McGregor came blubbering down into the room, wrapped up in a blanket, and complained that the women with whom he entered, had left him, taking with them the whole of his clothes, and not leaving even his trousers to go home in. He stole all the bedding, wrapped himself in it and charged out the door with the fireplace poker to clear the way."[53] The cacique had no clothes. MacGregor had not gone without a fight, but his constructed reputation was gone—and with it his hope of reviving Poyais. He would attempt something similar in Paris, briefly visiting a French prison before returning to England, where he spent his days destitute, trying to revive Poyais bonds. He died in 1845.

MacGregor's may have been the most spectacular and dishonest scheme in the Latin American debt bubble, but it was hardly the only one to crumble. Bond prices hit a peak in mid-1825; then, owing to the collapse of country banks and a shortage of gold, the bottom fell out. The Latin American republics received just 60 percent of the sums for which they contracted. The first Colombia loan of 1822, for example, issued bonds of £100, which were underwritten at £80 and issued to the market at £84. It offered an attractive 6 percent return and was oversubscribed. This meant that Colombia took on £2 million of debt for a £1.6 million loan. The underwriter assumed profits from the difference of four percentage points, while also charging Colombia for advertisements and legal expenses. The loans were never a great deal for young independent nations, but even less so for the bondholders. Of the more than £20.7 million lent to the seven Latin American nations, £19 million stood in default by 1829.[54]

The mines about which Humboldt had written so enthusiastically fared little better. Between 1823 and 1825, at least forty-six mining associations or companies were established, with a combined nominal capitalization of at least £36 million. British merchants, enticed by prospects of a postwar boom in demand, flooded Latin American cities with goods. But there was no demand. Nor was transportation cheap or sufficient. The first shipment into Lima following San Martín's victory exceeded demands for many goods. The merchants' eagerness could not overcome stifled demand, the continued production of local goods, the lack of capital, and the absence of Latin American exports to pay for the imports. Minerals were one important way to balance trade.[55]

Meanwhile the mines, another driver of the boom, proved difficult to open or reopen, with capital demands far exceeding initial expectations.[56] Political instability, lawlessness, and violence plagued some of the larger Mexican mines, as did disagreements over labor profit sharing. The Anglo-Mexican Mining Association launched in 1825 and was in financial trouble within a year. Like many other companies in the bubble, it demanded significant capital but ultimately could not fulfill the promised returns or attract further investment. The association operated twenty mines in 1825—a number that had fallen to eight by 1836 and, ultimately, to a single mine by 1848. At century's end, one historian points out, the mines still looked much as they had in the initial years after independence.[57]

Just as the Anglo-Mexican Mining Association was opening for business, the financial crisis of 1825 saw the failure of scores of Britain's country banks—threatening to sink the entire financial system. In an effort to provide merchants and country banks with the ability to pay bills and keep reserves, the Bank of England restricted credit rather than loosening access to cash. Though the bank soon followed with a complete about-face (lending in all possible ways), there first occurred, as journalist Walter Bagehot put it, "a period of frantic and inconceivable violence; scarcely any one knew who to trust; credit was almost suspended." In 1824, no fewer than sixty English banks stopped payment or defaulted. Average annual bankruptcies doubled from the early 1820s to 1826. Bagehot considered it the first crisis of his modern period.[58]

Nonetheless, the bubbles and banking crises of the 1820s did not bring stronger financial regulation. The repeal of the Bubble Act in 1825, combined with the Country Bank Act in 1826, had made the formation of joint-stock banks easier; by 1833, at least fifty such banks were registered outside London.[59] Laissez-faire was increasingly the norm and would only become more so. Over the next two decades, until 1844, no significant laws were introduced to regulate company formation or performance. Directors had no obligation to audit themselves or to verify the information they disseminated to the public. Not until 1857 could trustees be criminally prosecuted for pilfering a trust. Only in the wake of the Royal British Bank's collapse in 1856 did the government sponsor the trial of directors and managers.[60] In the absence of state regulation, the burden of risk and responsibility was borne by the individual. The individual could respond by managing risk (through action in the marketplace, often in the form of hedging or insurance) and by managing the techniques through which he or she distributed trust. Through these two courses of action, the market—and trust within it—would prove resilient, time and again. While the liquidity boom that drove the 1820s bubble would not be reproduced exactly, the energy to create new assets, to explore new places, and to trade at greater speed did not diminish. Thus, the public sphere remained a space of contention and debate. Meanwhile, the ugly side of expansion was visible to all—exposing capitalism's frauds and enabling further creativity.

For decades, the name Poyais would symbolize the reckless, exuberant, and irresponsible behavior of the 1820s. It would become an enterprise against which even supposedly honest endeavors had to define themselves. The young Disraeli, erratic, eager for acclaim and riches, had seen in the Latin American bubble an opportunity to increase his means. He had speculated on the market's collapse, only to mistime it. Largely on margin, he invested heavily in the Anglo-Mexican Mining Association and the Colombian Mining Association. By June 1825, he was down £7,000—leaving him no option but to attempt in vain to renew confidence in Latin American mines.[61] Disraeli turned to his father's literary network for help. With the help of John Murray—the seemingly ubiquitous publisher—he published three pamphlets aimed at puffing up the mining market.

One of the first published works by one of the century's most prominent politicians and writers was a pamphlet aimed at driving up the prices of his own stocks. Disraeli's "An Inquiry into the Plans, Progress, and Policy of the American Mining Companies," published by Murray in March 1825, was more than a mere pamphlet. Running well over a hundred pages, it resembles Strangeways's fable in its absorption in the dry minutiae of mining. But it lacks the romantic flair that makes Humboldt still readable today.

Trying to drum up business, Disraeli defended the character of the investor in shares. In the past, he wrote, there was "something invidious in the character of a stock-jobber, there was something disreputable in the character of a loan-monger, there was something, in short, *in watching the turn of the market,* that would never have suited Upper Brook Street or Grosvenor Square." No longer. The 1820s, he asserted, had fundamentally altered the social makeup of investors: "There was nothing invidious in the character of a mine-jobber, there was nothing *ungenteel* in watching the turn of a *mine* market; it was compared to purchasing an estate, and it was called patronizing infant liberty and liberal principles." As the Stock Exchange had attempted to prove in 1814, it was responsible investment—not speculation—that served both public and private interests. "We must not confound the spirit of enterprise, which arises from knowledge, with visionary speculation. The enterprise of the present day arises from knowledge; that knowledge has been gained by the extent of its international relations."[62]

Disraeli's would become a standard approach in the expeditionary capitalism of new locations and new assets. It promised that the mistakes of the past would not be repeated; the present offered new information, knowledge, and wisdom. The world was different, even new.[63] A decade after Napoleon's defeat, Disraeli wrote not for "disoriented" Britain but for a triumphant, confident nation that he saw as increasingly unrivaled on the world stage. He had been part of a spectacular decade that saw an entrenchment of the public sphere, unrivaled public political activity, and, in its first five years, a liquid and booming economy. He assured the reader that the world was new, inasmuch as the British investor understood it better than ever before. This age, he insisted, has nothing to do with that of the Mississippi and South Sea bubbles. Those were "the unnatural efforts of an impoverished people" and "grew out of the *poverty* of the times." By increasing knowledge, the expansion of British interests around the world had decreased risk taking: "Now in proportion as international relations become more extensive, more numerous also become the means and opportunities of employing capital."[64]

Disraeli's three pamphlets would not rescue the Mexican mines—or his finances. In fact, the disasters of 1825 lay just ahead. But he was half right. The investment patterns of the first half of the decade showed just how important and appealing the world was to British finance and trade. But they had also shown the limitations of Britons' knowledge and their extreme exposure to risk and fraud. Over the following decades, the British commercial community turned to both of these problems, attempting at once to expand commercial opportunities and to limit exposure to risk. Fraud was a threat to both efforts and was to be countered by building a more responsible version of trust: trust centered upon the shared social knowledge of others—that is, reputation. New approaches to trust had to be developed, and the old ones strengthened. After all, it had become clear to many that the market was an abundant but dangerous place, where neither status nor morality could be relied upon safely, but new riches could always be found.

Part II
Reputation

Principals, Agents, and Their Mutual Friends

A s a performer, Charles Dickens could have given Gregor Mac-Gregor a run for his money. Dickens was an extraordinarily productive literary genius; he was also protean. He did not simply resemble some of his characters in his capacity for shape-shifting. He was the most popular Anglo-American novelist of his age and became so, in part, by holding up a mirror to the manipulation of identity. His public readings to packed houses across Britain and the United States made him wealthy and famous by midcentury. At these readings, he would assume the identities of the characters he read. At home, in private theatrical productions, he would step into myriad roles. While writing, he would assume his characters' voices and facial expressions.[1]

In February 1864, when he learned that his eldest son, Walter, had died in Calcutta, Dickens was at work creating the many characters that would compose *Our Mutual Friend*. This novel, which appeared in nineteen installments between spring 1864 and fall 1865, displays all the tropes we associate with Dickens. There is London fog and Victorian stuffiness. There are orphans. London's inhabitants are grimy, boot-strappy, hard done-by, and overdrawn. But some are also deceptive, performative, chameleon-like, and mercurial. As Dickens scholars have observed, his characters were practiced in double-talk and adaptability, faking their names, their identities, even their own deaths.[2] In *Our Mutual Friend*, which most explicitly deals with these qualities, fortunes and histories are all forged. There is Fascination Fledgby (a "kind of outlaw in the bill-broking line") and John Harmon (who goes by the name of John Rokesmith and by the alias Julius Handford). Early in the narrative, Mr. and Mrs. Lammle—recently married after having been introduced in London by the Veneerings, new arrivals to society— further acquaint themselves during a walk on the beach on the Isle of Wight. It is their honeymoon. After a little more walking and a little more silence, Mr. Lammle breaks the latter.

> "You shall proceed in your own way. You claim right to ask me do I mean to tell you. Do I mean to tell you what?"
>
> "That you are a man of property?"
>
> "No."
>
> "Then you married me on false pretences?"
>
> "So be it. Next comes what you mean to say. Do you mean to say you are a woman of property?"
>
> "No."
>
> "Then you married me on false pretences."

Players at the same game, they recognize the situation immediately. "We have both been deceiving, and we have both been deceived." Tricked, but not stupid, Mr. and Mrs. Lammle move forward:

> "We have pretended well enough to one another. Can't we, united, pretend to the world? Agreed."
>
> "Yes. Agreed."[3]

The pair had duped each other, but they were also duped by the third party that introduced them: the aptly named Veneerings. *Our Mutual Friend* is a study in introductions and reputations, constantly probing the uses and abuses of society as agent. Trust is not merely a two-party game, played out in letters or through an established contact, but a multiparty game. The Lammles' courtship was not unlike the commercial and financial world: it involved strangers, it included an increasing number of parties, and it relied on reputation as an arbiter of trust.

Agents, clerks, brokers, and middlemen played an ever larger role in the development of trust in the mid-nineteenth century. The size and scope of capitalist exchange expanded opportunities for riches and access to goods, but it also brought notable challenges. Expanded exchange brought new frontiers, new assets, and new people into the marketplace. Not unlike capitalism itself, the principal-agent dynamic needed new forms and checks. All of this was necessary for healthy exchange and trust to develop in an environment fraught with fraud and risk.

Of course, there were those still in religious and political circles who disapproved of the expansion and alacrity of commerce. Nonetheless, the "*fast* trading" that Thomas Chalmers looked down upon was becoming all the more common, and in unexpected places. For stock-jobbers and brokers, for government agents, insurance agents, and British commercial agents, the speed, distance, quantity, and frequency of exchange had all increased. New risks, new ways of managing risk, and new spaces for fraud had materialized. A comparison of numerous industries and commercial relationships reveals that by the mid-nineteenth century, "overtrading" and "fast trading" had become the norm. Bills of lading were borrowed against with notable frequency, while exchequer bills were traded faster—and insurance policies issued with greater quantity—than had been the case earlier in the century. And that merely involved paper. Partly as a result of market competition and partly as a result of risk management, insurance companies found themselves with growing numbers of agents. The quantity of information, not just the quality, had to be managed. Trust had to be built. Gentlemanly behavior and status remained relevant, but in a commercial environment where even the most respectable affairs took on some of the attributes of speculation, better approaches to trust had to be found. If commercial exchange was to be a space of creativity and excitement, it needed also to prove hardy and pliant.

Lord Thomas Cochrane may have been judged for betraying the expected behavior of his status, but a few decades later it was no longer beneath an aristocrat to be playing in the markets. More and more Britons invested in stocks and bonds and employed financial services. While status remained supremely important, it could not be relied upon to ensure good behavior. The binary notion of moral commerce versus vicious commerce, as had been posited in the Cochrane trial, became increasingly blurred. Yet trust survived. Meanwhile, how one engaged in commerce became more important than the arena in which it was done. Reputation based on past behavior was supposed to speak to the ability of merchants to control their self-interest, as the morality of strangers was considered too risky a bet. In the most fundamental of commercial relations, that between principal and agent, employer and employee, it was during the middle decades of the nineteenth century that reputation—already important—became preeminent in commercial affairs. Trust was built around reputation, as risk was redistributed away from anonymous relationships that had repeatedly proven to be moral roulette.

The Third Man

Managing employees at a distance was one of the great challenges of nineteenth-century commerce and governance, but it was hardly a new problem. In medieval times, the difficulties of long-distance trade were countered by closed networks, a practice that continued into early modernity. Networks of émigrés, particularly from minority communities, could cross-monitor each other. By keeping a community closed to outsiders, by encouraging literacy and thus letter writing, and by exacting heavy penalties for the breaking of rules, small networks could limit the problems associated with far-flung agents. This model, however, did not transfer to larger, faster, or more diverse marketplaces.[4]

For the directors of the East India Company, for instance, the managing of far-flung factors was one the most challenging aspects of their business. In the 1620s, just two decades after the company's inception, the Crown began issuing proclamations in support of the East Indies trade. These proclamations evince an acute awareness of the apparent damage caused by "side dealing." A 1632 proclamation allowed company officials to search ships en route to and from India and even in port in London. Goods were to be seized, and any "rebellious" persons could be detained and handed over to the government for trial.[5] This concern with the loyalty and intentions of company employees in India continued until the nineteenth century. Writing from the Cape of Good Hope in 1798, during his outward voyage to assume the governor-generalship for India, Richard Wellesley wrote to Henry Dundas (then president of the Board of Control, responsible for overseeing the East India Company): "I much fear that many British subjects might be found in India whose spirit of adventure would rather direct them to seek a new order of things, than to contribute to the maintenance of our power."[6]

With the expansion of credit in the seventeenth and eighteenth centuries, a new dynamic entered principal-agent relations, one that became indispensable to questions of trust and fraud in the nineteenth century. In its bare form, the principal-agent relationship is fairly simple: under some agreement, one party (the principal) delegates decision-making authority to another (the agent). This authority can be broad or circumscribed, but operating over distances, principals in the eighteenth and nineteenth centuries often gave their agents considerable freedom.[7] To compensate for the slow pace of long-distance trade, agents often had to borrow against goods. An agent could borrow against a commodity in transit or sitting in a warehouse waiting for market by using a bill of lading, which represented the commodity and, when exchanged for credit, could be used as collateral. This practice was commonplace and was done by agents from New York to Bombay, but from the principals' perspective, the frequent need of agents to borrow involved an obvious risk. An agent could use a bill of lading to borrow cash for his own purposes, not just those of the principal for whom he worked. An agent, or factor, as they were known, might borrow to cover his own debts and then repay the loan without the principal ever knowing. But if the agent went bankrupt, the lender held the principal's bills of lading—essentially the right to the commodity itself—and the principal was left trying to reclaim his goods from the lender.

    English courts addressed this issue in a series of trials prior to the
1820s. Though critics would later attack the rulings and the subsequent
interpretations, as a group they acted to limit the exposure of principals to risk from agents. In the 1743 decision *Paterson v. Tash*, the chief
justice of England, Sir William Lee, held that agents could not use
property as security against their own debt, making side trading with
the principal's credit expressly illegal. Agents could use their principal's goods only to raise cash in service of the principal. The 1794
case of *Daubigny v. Duval* established an even stronger precedent.
When a factor pledged goods, the principal might recover them from
the pledgee (the lender who provided the cash)—meaning that if an
agent borrowed and then absconded, the principal still held the right to
recover the bills of lading against which the agent had borrowed. This
ruling shifted risk from the principal to the lender. In 1805, the case of
Newton v. Thornton reaffirmed the restrictions upon agents borrowing
against bills of lading or endorsements.[8] In his judgment decision,
Lord Ellenborough (the same judge that presided over the Cochrane
trial) observed: "The Symbol [the bill of lading, for example] then shall
not have a greater operation to enable him to defraud his principal than
the actual possession of that which it represents."[9] With a telling justification, Ellenborough limited the legal standing of the bill of lading.
Once the paper received the same treatment as the commodity it represented, he worried, fraud would become easier. For all involved in
establishing and reforming principal-agent law, fraud was among the
chief concerns.[10] To today's reader, the three rulings are somewhat ar-
cane, but together they established a powerful precedent: risk was not
born by the principal, who employed and presumably knew the agent,
but by a third party, the lender who issued cash on loan to the agent. In
other words, risk was redistributed away from the presumably familiar
relationship.[11]

    The principal-agent dynamic, then, actually entailed two different
relationships: that between the principal and agent, and that between the
agent and other parties. In the eighteenth century, a series of judicial
rulings established a risk distribution that very much favored the principal. But this arrangement, favoring ownership of the actual material
over the functioning of credit and exposing lenders to pronounced risk,

would not hold. Between the 1820s and the 1840s, English merchants, financiers, lawyers, and politicians renegotiated this arrangement through a series of bills and rulings that put reputation at the center of the principal-agent relationship. Agents could not be done away with—in fact, they were proliferating—but the dangers they brought were becoming increasingly unacceptable, exposing principals and lenders to fraud, loss, and liability. A new dynamic was needed to allow such relationships to succeed.

"The Vast Extension of Modern Commerce"

In 1819, William Paley, a barrister at Lincoln's Inn, published a new edition of his *Treatise on the Law of Principal and Agent*, among the most influential English books written in the nineteenth century on the problem of agency.[12] A focus on trust and the widespread occurrence of fraud, the most human of risks, permeates the work. Combined, the words "trust" and "entrusted" appear fifty-five times, and "fraud" appears forty-eight times.

An agent, wrote Paley, was not responsible for losses occasioned by respectable or convincing fraud. That is, the agent did not have to compensate investors for goods lost by frauds or failures when the transaction was conducted according to custom or regular practice. Crucial here were the twin concepts of the regular course of business and reputation. Trust built on those two concepts was held to be "responsible" trust. If an action could be shown to be irregular, however, or if the third party could be shown to be of bad reputation, then the agent could be held liable. As Paley summarized: "If he sells to a person of good credit, he is discharged, but if he sells to a person of discredit he is liable."[13] Agents were also liable for failing to insure, for neglect of precaution, and for breach of orders and incompetence.[14] Paley employed a very powerful idea that had also been a focus of Adam Smith, the usual or regular course of business. Losses, even owing to fraud, could be considered part of normal business, but only if they were incurred in an exchange that appeared responsible. Theoretically, this could distribute risk way from responsible trading and toward fast, frontier speculation.

For the most part, the agent was held to be a full representative of the principal. Delivery of goods or money to an agent was the same as delivery to the employer. The same was held for information. "It must be taken for granted," wrote Paley in his 1819 edition, "that the principal knows whatever the agent knows."[15] In cases where statutes of limitations were relevant, the admission of an agent was commonly held to be that of the principal as well. That is, when it came to the transmission of information, the agent was considered a full proxy. This should come as no surprise. The slow speed of communication required agents to be empowered. And as one might expect, the first half of the century was a boom time for agents and agency houses from Calcutta to Buenos Aires. According to Paley, something of a golden rule existed, requiring only that agents take care of a principal's goods as if they were their own. That golden rule, however, did not license agents to use bills of lading as collateral without exposing lenders to great risk, and in the decades following the 1820s it was this precise problem that interested parties in London had to grapple with.

Two features, both products of an emerging nineteenth-century globalization, help explain the sudden impetus to renegotiate the risk distribution. The earlier statutes, which had put the risk in the hands of lenders, had been intended to encourage foreign merchants to do business in London. These investors were to feel confident in trade with London because the risk fell upon the third-party (British) lender. Increasingly, however, as London emerged as a global hub, risk was reallocated to protect its lenders, who helped fund trade all over the world. London's merchants and financiers sensed, as well, that that world was growing faster and bigger. Paley saw the principal-agent dilemma as one of beguiling simplicity: "The law of Principal and Agent appears at first view to be founded upon principles so few and simple, and in general so easy of application, that a treatise upon such a subject may seem altogether superfluous." But commerce was complicating things. "The vast extension of modern commerce," he wrote, "both foreign and domestic, the novelty and variety of the channels through which it is carried on . . . have given rise to new situations and questions upon the subject of commercial agency."[16] The regular and usual course of business was shifting, at least in terms of its players and places.

In May 1823, a select committee convened to review the principal-agent problem. Alexander Baring, founder of Baring Brothers and Company and president of the Board of Trade, and the economist David Ricardo both sat on the committee and offered testimony, as did Nathan Rothschild. Witnesses from Hamburg, Trieste, Konigsberg, Antwerp, and elsewhere answered questions. London merchant houses were also widely represented: William James, of Jameson and Aders, spoke about trade on the continent; George Larpent, a partner in Paxton, Cockerell, Trail, and Company, testified about trade in the East Indies; John Henry Freese, of Blackenhage and Company, discussed trade in Brazil. The proceedings opened with a statement from the representative of the Committee of Merchants, Bankers and Others, the lawyer James William Freshfield. Like Ellenborough's career, Freshfield's is a study in the permeable line between the political and legal worlds. In 1825, only two years after the commission convened, he entered Parliament as a conservative member. He also founded one of England's most influential law firms, Freshfields, which remains in operation today. He served as solicitor to many of the prominent firms and institutions of mid-century London, including the Bank of England and the treasury, and his work on the legal aspects of the principal-agent problem would remain notable among his accomplishments.

Freshfield would himself question the witnesses, but first he provided his own summary of the problem. Like the array of witnesses who followed him, he couched the problem in international terms, drawing attention to imperial trade in the West Indies, international timber trade in Danzig, and the global coffee business. The committee's report acknowledged the effects of growing international trade, stating: "In the rapid and multiplied circulation of merchandize in this country, it appears to be indispensible that some easy and simple mode should be adopted for guiding capitalists in this respect."[17] Within this global trade, the committee recognized two potential commercial situations:

I. *Bona fide* Advances made in regular course of Commerce to Agents or factors, upon the security of merchandize, in ignorance of their not being the Owners of the property.

II. Purchases of Merchandize from Agents or Factors not invested with the power of sale, although the fact is unknown
to the purchaser.[18]

A simple and powerful assumption underlay the committee's concerns:
in the course of business, merchants and bankers often dealt with people
they did not know, leaving them vulnerable to fraud. William Bridge-
man, an East India goods agent for Inglis, Forbes and Company, illustrated the point. He was asked by the committee: "Upon consignment
made to your house of East India produce, is it usual to draw part of the
value?"—that is, to take a loan or an advance.

"Very usual," he responded.[19]

"Have you any means of knowing to whom the goods really be-
long so consigned to you?"

"None whatever," he answered.[20]

If he could not know whether he was dealing with an agent or a
principal, a lender did not know to what type of risk he was exposed—a
fact of which British lenders were increasingly aware.

"Do you think," Nathan Rothschild was asked, "that the British
capitalist will advance his money as freely as he has hitherto done,
when he becomes acquainted with the risk he runs in making an
advance?"

"Certainly not," Rothschild answered. "When a man lends his
money, he wants to be safe."

The committee's report, issued in 1823, drew much the same conclusion. Risk was passed on to the third party, but that party could
not always know who was an owner and who a factor. "It is impossible,"
the committee declared, "for the purchaser to ascertain which of those
characters apply to the factor, and yet upon that distinction his title
may depend." Something needed be done: "In the rapid and multiplied
circulation of merchandize in this country, it appears to be indispensible that some easy and simple mode should be adopted for guiding
capitalists in this respect."[21] For the principal-agent relationship to remain useful to those with money on the line, its dynamics had to prove
not only rewarding but also adaptable.

Making Money Safe

Parliament first sought to address the problem in the Factors Acts of 1823 and 1825. According to the acts, a third-party banker or merchant might be protected on an advance only "provided such consignee or consignees shall not have notice . . . that such person or persons so shipping in his, her or their own name or names, or in whose name or name any goods, wares or merchandize shall be shipped by any person or persons, is or are not the actually *bonâ fide* owner or owners."[22] This is as confused as it sounds: agents could borrow against goods provided the lender did not know them to be agents. The new legislation made matters worse by encouraging a dangerous incentive scheme. Agents, as they had long done, would borrow against consigned goods. Should they fail to meet their obligation, they need only claim to have informed the lender of their status and the goods would be returned to the principal.

Arguments in favor of the new legislation continued to echo throughout the 1830s and early 1840s. While a shift in the political balance of the cabinet of Lord Liverpool, the long-time prime minister, had helped push through the 1825 act, interest groups played a crucial role in the subsequent legislation.[23] The Commercial Association of Liverpool—which included representatives from the American Chamber of Commerce, the West India Association, the Cotton Brokers Association, and the Mexican and South Brazilian Association—proclaimed in a pamphlet published in 1842: "The owner who confides his goods to an agent ought to bear the loss arising from his unfaithfulness or insolvency." The insolvent agent, the pamphlet noted, "has strong temptation to magnify some casual remark in conversation into a notice of agency."[24] Association members bemoaned a lack of confidence, a general feeling of insecurity that "had materially restricted the employment of capital in advances upon goods."[25] Two years earlier, James Cook, a broker in the City for Trueman and Cook who had testified in the 1823 hearings, had published his own pamphlet on the subject. The principal, he argued, was responsible for character judgment. It was he who should take on that risk. "Does the foreign merchant want security! Let him choose an agent of uprightness, propriety and high character—this must be his security." The third party, he insisted, just as he had two decades earlier, deserved the protection.[26] David Ricardo had said as much in 1823, noting that it "was not desirable that either party should lose: but one must suffer, and the sufferer ought to be the individual who did not use proper caution."[27] Risk was to be redistributed toward relationships that could build trust, based either on past commercial exchanges or on social knowledge, including reputation. The 1842 Factors Act at last made this a reality, decreeing: "That from and after the passing of this Act, any Agent intrusted with the possessions of goods, or of documents of title to goods, shall be deemed and taken to be owner of such goods and documents."[28]

The complaints of the merchants and bankers who testified at the 1823 hearings were not about the definition of credible or usual actions. They complained not of the risk taken on by a principal in employing an agent, or the risk taken by an agent in selling on. These things were supposed to be policed by reputation and the "usual course of business." The concern was that, in a world of quickened commerce and greater credit among more people, third-party buyers faced greater exposure to risk than ever before. In the triangular relationship of principal, agent, and lender, trust could now be built along two lines: via repeated transactions and reputation, as so often occurred between principal and agent, and through legal statutes that reduced the risk tied to anonymity.

The legislation on risk and the principal-agent problem was meant to guard against some of the challenges associated with long-distance trade by redistributing risk away from strangers and back to "usual" and "regular" interactions built around reputation. In a way, the Factors Acts, particularly that of 1842, reemphasized the importance of social exchange in financial and commercial interactions. The men who testified before the select committee repeatedly drew attention to the threat of fraud and made clear that the morality of the stranger was not a safe location for the placement of trust. Instead, they suggested trust should depend on relations gained through repeated social and commercial exchange. The solution to the challenge posed by trust and fraud was to place the burden of risk squarely on social knowledge and reputation. Just as these relations now bore more of the weight of risk, so too would they become the targets of fraud.

The historian David Sunderland has written of "reputational mechanisms" for middle-class trust during this period, and the economic historian Joel Mokyr has described a "signal economy" of presentation and reputation. Robin Pearson and David Richardson have shown how social relations, including religious, cultural, and political associations, helped buttress relationships initially formed in commercial spheres.[29] Even as it affected business, reputation became a product not only of the commercial but also of the social sphere. It became a mechanism through which trust was meant to work, affirmed repeatedly by merchants and politicians as a basis for responsible commercial exchange. Reputation-building mechanisms included home furnishings, etiquette, manner, dress, and the location of one's home. Shortly after mid-century, a group of diplomats and officials from the Foreign Office testified before Parliament as to the importance of presentation. Edward Hammond, the British undersecretary of state, described the importance of appearance for Britons in America: "In North America, the English consul ought not to be in a position of comparative poverty; he is living in an expensive state of society, among a very rich people; even as regards the dress of his children, if they go into the society of the place, which a consul's family can hardly keep out of without discredit, the expenditure is very great."[30] W. R. Holmes, the consul in Diyarbakir, a great Ottoman seat in Anatolia, observed of British consuls: "Much of their influence depends upon the nature of the appearance which they make in the eyes of the natives. If a man is seen to live in a miserable house, and cannot afford to move about with the same sort and number of attendants, which even common persons employ in Turkey, he cannot expect to be treated as the representative of a powerful nation."[31] Though Hammond and Holmes spoke of locations thousands of miles away, they might as well have been speaking of London.

Personal presentation was crucial, as were networks and introduction. It was precisely to these mechanisms that Dickens's Veneerings turned to build their reputations. "Tremlow had first known Veneering at his club, where Veneering knew nobody but the man who made them known to one another, who seemed to be the most intimate friend he had in the world, and whom he had known two days."[32] The Veneerings turned acquaintances into friends and friends into buttresses of reputation within days. Of course, as Dickens knew, the importance of reputation was also its weakness. The fates of those with reputation almost inevitably became intertwined with those lacking in respectable pasts.

It would be a mistake to describe the commercial environment of the eighteenth century as tranquil. The historical forces unleashed by credit and expanding commerce were remarkable and made the later part of the century especially exciting and chaotic. As the 1820s had shown, the forces of self-interest, profit making, and commercial expansion had returned with renewed vigor after the Napoleonic Wars. Building and distributing trust were challenges for which traditions of virtue and the values associated with status were not, by themselves, adequate. Indeed, reputation as a basis for economic exchange was in no way new, but in this environment, its usefulness and subsequent prominence became more apparent.

As eighteenth-century moral philosophy gave way to nineteenth-century political economy, the mechanics of exchange assumed a prominence over its morals. To allude to reputation was to employ a rhetorical device that justified an exchange. Reputation was not simply held but frequently discussed. It was a key point separating responsible and credible business from reckless exchange, and the investor from the speculator. Investment could still be virtuous or moral, but more important, it had to be responsible. In an arena fraught with new faces and fraud, commercial exchange demanded that the social dynamics of capitalism be as open to change as the marketplace itself—and in such a space, reputation, long a part of trade, achieved new-found preeminence.

Reputation Contagion

In the autumn of 1841, as members of Parliament grew nearer to finally codifying reputation as the basis for regular exchange, a new
financial crisis hit London. In early August, rumors had circulated
in the City that a large number of fraudulent exchequer bills were circulating in the City's banks and the government's financial institutions. The *Times* reported that the fakes were of such quality that
"some of the bills have been shown to Government officials, and have
been pronounced to be genuine documents." The fraud was not an affair
of back-alley traders and men of low credit; instead, it struck to the core of
the age's financial and commercial practices.[1] "We are not," the paper observed, "at the present moment at liberty to state the names of the parties
given to us who have ignorantly or otherwise been the agents in this fraud,
but it is sufficient to say they are more than well known in the city."[2]

Exchequer bills were a fundamental financial instrument of the
government, second perhaps only to the Consol—thus the shock of the
Times at rumors of foul play in the exchequer bill market, and the shock
of the City and the government when it emerged that Beaumont Smith,
a reliable clerk from a notable family with connections to the navy and
the government,[3] had run a huge fraud out of the Exchequer office. The
newspaper reports of summer and fall 1841 were the beginning of a case
that gripped the capital's attention for the next year.

As we have seen, a number of notable frauds occurred in the first half of the nineteenth century.[4] Some of these, such as the small-bill forgeries in the century's first two decades, involved many small, scattered transactions; others, like Rowland Stephenson's defrauding of the bank Remington and Company of £300,000 in 1828, were large and localized.[5] Smith's fraud had gone unnoticed for more than four years, during which time he produced £377,000 worth of fake government bills.[6] This was the largest fraud involving government securities yet to occur in nineteenth-century Britain; in terms of victims and geography, it was both substantial and diffuse. Its vehicle, the exchequer bill, was a simple enough instrument, but the great attention the government and the press devoted to the fraud revealed the complex dynamics of the financial world in which these bills circulated. The usual course of business encouraged the use of reputation as a means for managing risk, as well for addressing the challenges of asymmetric information in a competitive and increasingly anonymous marketplace. As this fraud shows, once reputational mechanisms became the primary vehicles of trust, they also became the targets and unwitting facilitators of fraud.

"The Irreproachable Character"

Unlike the Consol, which worked as long-term debt, paying interest in perpetuity to the holder, exchequer bills were interest-bearing notes that were used by the government for short-term debt, being issued and redeemed or exchanged often within a twelve-month period. They had been introduced as a form of government debt, underwritten by the Bank of England, in the decade after the Glorious Revolution. The bills had proven an astounding success, with the yield dropping from more than 7 percent in 1697 to just over 3 percent by 1710. As one commentator points out, they were seen as an alternative form of money and were likely the cheapest form of debt available to any government at the time.[7] The standing of exchequer bills increased through the crises and wars of the eighteenth century and had risen still higher by 1840. They were as good as notes from the Bank of England itself and were circulated in much the same manner. It was precisely this confidence that made the reports in the *Times* so disturbing, suggesting as they did that some of the good names of the City, as well as the bills of the government, were in fact compromised.

Beaumont Smith had been born into an adventurous family with a recognized name. On his father's side, one of his great-uncles had died in the South American port of La Guira in 1743, and another great-uncle and his grandfather had fought in the Seven Years War in North America. Beaumont's father, Colonel Charles Douglass Smith, served in the West Indies, fought in the American Revolutionary War, and ruled as lieutenant governor of Prince Edward Island before standing down in controversy.

Of all the Smiths, however, it was Beaumont's uncle Sir Sidney Smith who achieved the greatest fame. In 1788 he entered the naval service of Sweden, fighting against the Russians in the Russo-Swedish War of 1788–1790. At the outbreak of the French Wars, he was a volunteer in the Ottoman navy at Smyrna. Joining the Royal Navy, Smith was eventually captured and imprisoned in Paris in 1796, only to escape two years later and command the fleet that helped hold back Napoleon's siege of Acre—encouraging Napoleon to abandon his army to its fate in Egypt and pursue his political ends back in France.

Sickly at a young age and rheumatic, Beaumont Smith had a successful if less illustrious career.[8] His was the realm that financed the empire rather than traveled and soldiered it. In 1822, owing a creditor £30, he was sent to debtors' prison. If his later letters are to be believed, it was a scarring experience, owing both to the shame of the imprisonment and to an absence of help from his family. Seven years later, he wrote to his sister Fanny with the hurt still apparent: "In the year 1822 with *your* knowledge + Henry's also I was allowed to go to *prison* for £30! It is truth my health at that time was such my *life* might not have worth £*30* + it was of course your joint or several opinions that there was no prospect of my ever being able to any good for the family therefore my character."[9] By that point in 1829 he had (most likely through family connections to the Grenvilles) righted his career path: the former debtor was now a junior clerk at the Exchequer.[10] He had not forgiven his family. When his sister wrote asking for a contribution to a charitable foundation, he responded curtly from his office at Palace

Yard: "I will not enter into any engagement or arrangement for a provision for *any one*. I have been left to shift for myself + I will do what is *right* + *be free in mind and purse* before I enter into any arrangement of the sort."[11] Having seen debtors' prison, he further explained, his current debts must remain his chief concern. "I hope I have now come to a port where I can ride safely and anchor," he wrote, and only then might he be of service.

Less can be deciphered about Beaumont's finances over the following decade, but it is clear that money remained a preoccupation of the entire family, including Sir Sidney, and that Beaumont's uncles, cousins, and sisters often went to him for financial support. Sir Sidney, owed money by the Crown but owing more to creditors, spent the 1830s in Paris. In 1834 he wrote to his nephew complaining of "knock down blows" of creditors and of having been "barely saved from discredit."[12] Three years later, he complained, "It is hard to be stung by the flea bites of small demands and discrediting attacks."[13] Just before Christmas in 1838 he wrote Beaumont again to say that he had acquired cheaper lodging in Paris, allowing him to discharge a carriage and devote more of his income toward his debts. The same letter suggests that by this time Beaumont had taken on more responsibility in the family.[14] By June 1840, Sir Sidney was dead in Paris, and one of his sons wrote to Beaumont hoping he might continue to support family members, as the son's hopes of becoming a rector had left him entirely dependent upon his father.[15]

In Beaumont's correspondence with his family and with Sir Sidney in particular, two undeniable bonds emerge: family and debt. By the late 1830s, Smith is a figure of responsibility. Responses from his family members, it being their turn to deal with debt, are polite and grateful. This Smith of duty and responsibility was the employee whom his superiors at the Exchequer knew. As Lord Monteagle later said, Smith "had been senior clerk of the department at the time I was Chancellor of the Exchequer. He was continued in the discharge of the same duties, and in possession of the same office, on the ground of his previous services, and of the irreproachable character which up to that period he had borne."[16] Such comments give little hint that his peers and supervisors were aware of his previous debts. Instead, over years of repeated interaction, Smith had won for himself a reputation as reliable and honest. By 1840, he was a member of the Parthenon, a club on Regent Street located in the former residence of the great architect John Nash.[17] At work his colleagues tended to speak well of him, even to confide in him. At home, he was the foundation upon which his sisters and his extended family relied. He was in every way an image of responsibility, dedication, and trustworthiness.

On October 19, 1841, a trader in London had attempted to borrow £10,000 against exchequer bills at the Stock Exchange at a rate of 6 percent. The rate seemed unusually high to a member of the Exchange who had recently issued a loan on similar bills at just 4 percent. He soon addressed a letter to the chancellor of the Exchequer, and rumors of foul play in the bill market circulated through the City and the office of the Exchequer.[18] On October 29, the chancellor, acting on the tip, issued an advertisement in the *London Gazette* announcing that all bills sent into the Exchequer for redemption or subsequent interest payments would be checked against their counterfoils (a copy of the original) for genuineness.

One can imagine Smith closing the door to his office that evening, knowing the game would soon be up: the bills would eventually, inevitably lead back to him. He could look up at three drawn prints of actions in which Sir Sidney Smith had distinguished himself, and a framed print of his family arms and its motto, "Forward," which likely stood next to two family portraits. He had many books to which he could have turned for distraction—four volumes of *Percival*, a copy of *Robinson Crusoe*, the works of Homer, Robertson's history of Scotland, the works of Cicero and Horace, and *The Lives of Admirals*—and other books for guidance. In his office he kept a large prayer book, four smaller prayer books, and a Bible. He may have opened a bottle. The tally for his office alone, when he left it for the last time, was ten cases of port, sherry, and marsala.[19]

Smith's role in the scheme unraveled so quickly that by December he was in the Central Criminal Court, where, in front of an audience that included his wife, he confessed to forging two exchequer bills. The punishment for one forgery was the same as for a hundred—or in Smith's case, for 377 (the total number of fake bills that bore his signature). According to news reports, he trembled. Unable to look at his friends and family, he offered a statement: "I am born of a family upon which disgrace never lighted till now; educated in principles of integrity and honour, I have lived respected, and I believe esteemed and I have enjoyed the confidence of many highly honorable persons. I am now, by my own confession, a guilty criminal."[20] In a statement that lasted a full twenty-four minutes, he explained:

> I humbly call its [the court's] attention to circumstances which are calculated to show that I have not become altogether debased in my feelings and principles. Pecuniary difficulties, arising from misplaced confidence, and unconnected with discredit and of very limited extent not exceeding a few hundred pounds, although beyond my means to meet, first exposed me to the suggestions of those who tempted me to obtain temporary relief by the fraudulent fabrication of Exchequer Bills. . . . I yielded to the temptation, but without obtaining the promised relief; and once committed, I became in the power of the tempter, and my retreat has been prevented. Allured and beguiled by plausibility, power and talent, which I could not resist, I became entangled beyond escape.[21]

Following the verdict, the judge spoke of the pain of "his being obliged to pass sentence upon a man whose ancestors had reflected honour on their country."[22] He sentenced Smith to lifetime transportation to Australia. Smith had gone from a highly respected clerk to a convicted criminal in just six weeks.

It was a massive fraud, and one for which only one man would sail. In his statement, Smith had alluded specifically to a tempter, a party who, wielding a financial power over him, had encouraged his reckless behavior. But when given the opportunity to implicate his coconspirators, he confessed only to having pursued the fraud himself. Two separate parliamentary commissions had to construct the larger picture of how such an astounding number of fake bills had entered the market.

"Highly Superior Mechanism of Modern Times"

Two parliamentary commissions convened over the year following Smith's forgeries. More than two hundred witnesses were called, and the resulting reports totaled in excess of six hundred pages. One took as its subject Smith and his office, focusing on the fraud as a matter of procedure and forgery. Its authors cared little for questions of temptation, allure, and reputation; their subject was process. The second was all about milieu and context: what kind of people, economy, and marketplace could enable—even unknowingly—such a considerable fraud.

The office within the Exchequer that handled the production and issuance of the bills had changed little since their introduction in 1696. In production, bills were numbered in succession, meant to be signed by the comptroller or his deputy, and then cut from the counterfoil against which the circulating bills could be checked. Each bill as it circulated was meant to be signed, like a bank note, so that ownership could be tracked. Randall McGowen and Phil Handler have both drawn attention to the pointed concern with forgery in the early nineteenth century. Forgery was considered a particularly insidious crime that threatened the credit of the state and the integrity of the growing middle class, whose members were often the culprits.[23] In their discussion of the fraudulent bills, the first commission drew comparisons to the laws enacted to counter the forgery of bank notes, noting that the checks on fraudulent exchequer bills lagged behind those on bank notes.[24]

There had been small changes in the production and storage of bills over the nearly 150 years since their introduction. A number of these changes—the supervision of papermaking; the signing of bills during working hours; the in-house, rather than private, production of engraving; the abandonment of second counterfoils—occurred under Lord Grenville in the early nineteenth century. Nonetheless, the Exchequer's system of internal checks, which depended on a small handful of clerks, was relaxed in practice. Undoubtedly, this atmosphere had enabled the counterfeiting. What is more, as the senior clerk, Smith had access to the plates for engraving, as well as the seals and counterfoils. As the first commission put it, the entire preparation of the bills was "entrusted to the uncontrolled discretion and integrity of the Senior Clerk of the Department in which the Bills were prepared."[25]

The first commission, which included the prominent financier George Glyn, came to a simple conclusion. "These defects of the internal arrangement of the Office," wrote the commissioners, "palpable though they are when attention is drawn to them, had for nearly a century escaped observation and correction, and had led to no injury to the public."[26]

> Although we are fully aware that every mechanical process is capable of imitation, and consequently that none can be an entire security against forgery; yet it is in evidence before us, and we cannot doubt, that in the highly superior mechanism of modern times, may be found the means of materially increasing the difficulty of imitating Exchequer Bills of the present day, which differ very slightly from those first used nearly 150 years ago.[27]

The fraud had occurred as a result of "the absence of sufficient internal checks, and the incompleteness of general supervision."[28] Earlier in the century, in the case of small-bill forgery, £1 and £2 notes, the forgers and bills had been pursued out in the world, in what one contemporary called "the most extensive criminal operation of the day."[29] In this case, the solution was to be located in-house, at the point of production, and as so often happened after the beginning of the Industrial Revolution, technology and management were meant to play central roles.

Almost as soon as the first commission concluded, demands for a second, more comprehensive investigation appeared in the British press. "It is a curious question," wrote the *Times*: "How many millions of Exchequer-bills in all have been fabricated and put into circulation[?] . . . It is clear that a perpetual system of issuing, redeeming, cancelling, and replacing must have been in operation for the last dozen or twenty years; and it is a moderate supposition, to conclude the total amount to have been from *five to ten millions!*"[30] Though perhaps ripe with overreaction, the piece still rightly depicted the question of the fraudulent bills as a systemic one. The issue was not simply the system of signing bills or oversight at the small, antiquated Office of the Comptroller-General. It involved the manner in which bills moved through the market.

This was the charge to the Earl of Devon, Henry John Stephen, and Robert Mitford, the three men appointed by Parliament to oversee the second commission: "Find concerning the manner of the issue, circulation, deposit, or possession of every such document, and especially in what manner the owners or holders of such documents received the same . . . and also whether the owners or holders of such document received the same in the usual course of business, and whether they employed any and what means of inquiring into the genuineness of such documents."[31] How did the bill holders obtain the documents, and did they do so responsibly? The issue was not what traders were dealing in, but how they were dealing. This question went to the heart of commercial probity. To find the answers, the commission had to follow the bills' paths and interview their owners, reconstructing the cobweb of trades. As was becoming increasingly clear, though Smith conceived and executed the fraud in his small office, it lived out in the world. It was a story not just of stamps and signatures but of asymmetric information and market-making speed, of principals and agents, of strangers and networks.

The mapping of the bills' paths was an extensive and complicated affair. The commission called some 160 witnesses, who answered detailed questions about interest rates, bill redemptions, loan securities, and duration of possession of bills. It was clear that Smith had generally distributed his bills first to Angelo Solari and then Ernesto Rapallo, two brokers of Italian descent. Rapallo, from Genoa, was said to be the nephew of the governor of Bialta in Piedmont and had been naturalized by an act of Parliament. Solari, dead by the time the fraud came to light, was also said to be Genovese and to have once served as Genoa's attorney general. After Rapallo and Solari acquired the bills from Smith, they were in the habit of passing them on to three different parties: William and James Morgan, F. T. De Berckem, and William Mariner. These men would then distribute the bills into the market. The Morgans were stockbrokers in the City, while Mariner had traveled in the East on East India Company trading ships, clerked for a stock broker, and worked for the National Brazilian Mining Association—all before he met Solari and began trading exchequer bills. Smith's fraud might easily be told as a story of counterfeiting or conspiracy, of a small group working together to con the market. But the reach of the fraud had exposed something much more dangerous.

The Half-Life of Bills

There are four interacting explanations for the scope, size, and duration of the fraud. The first was the quality of the forgeries, which allowed them to escape attention and detection. The historian Mark Casson has identified a series of factors that affect the market for a good, including the complexity of the item, the time between payment and exchange, quantity and quality control, and ease of exchange.[32] While Casson examines commercial goods, the same tests can be applied to financial assets. The forged bills easily entered a fluid market. The number of bills that entered the market during the fraud, however, was no greater than the norm over the prior two decades.[33] Smith's bills did not create a sudden swell of numbers. Instead, the forgers and fraudsters took advantage of three interrelated phenomena that were all part or products of expeditionary capitalism: first, the speed and frequency of exchange in a secondary market allowed for greater risk taking; second, the approach to market making, common to the financial market, allowed and even encouraged asymmetries of information; and third, those who traded in fake bills, knowingly or not, were able to maintain good reputations—as long as the fraud was not discovered.

On the first point, the biographies of four sets of fraudulent bills, reconstructed from parliamentary commission testimonies, reveal a fast-moving, extensive, informal network of trade that connected roguish individuals with responsible ones and with some of England's finest institutions.

BILLS 6495, 6496, 6497

In October 1841, Alfred Bell and Samuel Steward, solicitors in Lincoln's Inn Fields, had the "occasion to lay out," or invest, £3,000. They turned to John William Cook, a clerk at Messrs. William and James Morgan who was allowed to do business on the side. Cook, not being a member of the Stock Exchange, had to turn to E. L. Morgan, a member, to make the purchase for him. On Cook's private account, Morgan purchased the bills from Harry Tompkins, who had received them that day from F. T. De Berckem. De Berckem had delivered the bills to Tompkins so they could be exchanged in order to raise money to redeem bills deposited with the Bank of England as security for a loan. De Berckem had received Bills 6497, 6496, and 6497 from one William Mariner, who had received them from Ernest Rapallo, who in turn got them from Smith.[34]

BILLS 7056, 8284, 8388–8400

James Anderson, magistrate for Essex and Middlesex and a major in the East Essex Regiment of Militia, was told by John Cook that "if he had money unemployed, it might be lent from him on the security of Exchequer Bills, at 4 ½ per cent, for a period of six months." Anderson, who had £15,000 in the Bank of Scotland at only four percent, purchased fifteen bills from Cook in April 1841. Cook had acquired them from Messrs. W. and J. Morgan, for whom he was acting not in his private interest but as an agent. "A few days afterward, Major Anderson having occasion for money," according to the commission, "gave an order to Messrs. C. and H. MacRea, his brokers. . . . The purchasers from Messrs. C. and H. MacRea were Messrs. Cooper and Co. who afterwards sold the bill to Messrs. Knight and Co., who sold it to Messrs. C. and T. Brown, who sold it to Messrs. Cole and Mullens." Cole and Mullens were in possession of bill 8284 when the fraud was exposed.[35]

BILLS 8725, 8276, 8278

Bills 8725, 8276, and 8278 were submitted to be funded by Alfred Cutting, a stockbroker, in October 1841. He bought them for funding on behalf of the bill discounters Bennison, Lennard and Company, who were acting on the account of John Mollett and Company. With the funds from the three bills, Cutting purchased stock in Mollett's name, which he sold later that day to a man called Maubert.[36]

In 1840, Cutting transacted a £20,000 exchequer bill loan for Bennison and Leonard. He then took twenty bills belonging to Bennison and borrowed on them from William Scott and Son, brokers in Russian bonds. Scott and Son then sold a number of the bills to the broker for the London and Westminster Bank, which sold them at a fee. When Bennison repaid his loan, he asked for the return of his original bills, which, of course, had been sold. Bennison claimed they were not Scott's bills but belonged to F. T. Berckem, who, unbeknownst to Bennison, had himself acquired them from William Mariner, who had acquired them from Ernest Rapallo, who had acquired them from Beaumont Smith. Eventually, Mariner and De Berckem hired Henry De Berckem, F. T.'s brother, to track down the bills. Though he thought "it to be a fact that all Exchequer Bills could be retraced," he succeeded only after three weeks, traversing half of London, and "after great difficulty and trouble."[37]

All the bills were held for varying lengths of time: some for a year, others for less than twenty-four hours. Interest rates on short-term loans, according to witnesses, changed by the hour, if not by the quarter-hour. Though not all bills traveled as far or moved as often as those described, it is clear that the frequent trading of some bills meant less risk for those trading in them—as long as they got rid of them quickly.

This, however, is not enough to explain the fraud's depth. Of crucial importance is also the breadth of the secondary market where asymmetries of information flourished. As numerous witnesses testified, the process of market making and trading required such asymmetries. And while reputation was considered a responsible protection against being victimized, it was precisely because of these asymmetries that fraud was able to spread through the system.

The Stock Exchange was meant to offer clear delineation of responsibilities—classifying traders as (a) jobbers, who sold stocks or bonds on their own account and in volume; (b) brokers, who bought or sold on someone else's account, much like an agent; or (c) promoters, who were often less well-capitalized traders and attempted to introduce new listings or companies for sale. But in reality, the lines were less clear.[38] Sometimes brokers represented principals, but sometimes they represented themselves. Sometimes they were members of the Stock Exchange; other times they relied on acquaintances who could buy and sell for them in the Exchange. The standing of the players varied immensely, ranging from the Bank of England itself to retired militiamen and magistrates.

The securities may have been those of the government, but this was a laissez-faire market, and regulation, as both James Taylor and George Robb have shown, was left to the market—a market that was open to informal trades, side dealing, and quick trades.[39] Most trades took place with only a limited amount of information exchanged between parties. Jobbers sold to agents but did not necessarily know whom the agents represented. Brokers did not need to divulge the principals for whom they sold. In fact, it offended Stock Exchange culture to reveal for whom you worked. Just as in market-making operations today, it was considered important that sellers and buyers not be required to reveal their identities, as this information might affect their capacity to work in the market.

William Knight was a member of the Stock Exchange and in business with his son. He was asked by the commission about bill 8284, which he purchased from Cooper and Company: "Did you tell Cooper and Co. for whom you were buying it?"

"Certainly not, we never do that."

"Did they ask any questions upon the subject?"

"Certainly not; they do not question us upon the subject, because they look upon the broker as the responsible person; they do not know our principal, and do not inquire about it."[40]

Another broker testified: "We never know any thing about the principals in our transactions," adding that "it does not come in the scope of our information to inquire the source from which a broker gets money."

John Hutchinson also seconded this approach: "If a broker borrows money off another broker, he does not, in the ordinary course, give the name of principals."[41]

William Dobson was asked about his acquisition of bill 7102: "Did Tomkins tell you from whom he got it?"

"No, he did not," Dobson replied. "That was an inquiry I could not make, and had no right to make; as a broker he was a confidential person, and it is a question never asked of a broker."[42]

As the frequency of transactions illustrates, this asymmetry of information both in the Exchange and outside it did not inhibit trade. The biography of the bills reveals a secondary market of frequent, rapid, and widespread exchange. The committee, however, was charged with more than simply tracking the movement of Smith's bills; rather, it was tasked with finding the mechanisms by which individuals had come into possession of or sold the bills. Its business was not only the paths of financial exchange but the nature of the exchanges themselves. Such questions inevitably brought up the ongoing tension between ideas of productive credit and investment, on the one hand, and speculation, on the other. It was clearly in the interest of bondholders that they appear as responsible investors rather than speculators. In trying to do this, in trying to show that they had made a responsible use of trust, the witnesses before the commission drew attention to reputation as the social basis for their financial exchanges. The existence and maintenance of good reputations—believed a safeguard against asymmetries of information and their associated risks—were in fact the final enabling factor of the fraud.

The Rhetoric of Reputation

Witnesses before the committee, ranging from confused to angrily defensive, tended to reveal two approaches to solving the problem of information in competitive markets. Buyers and sellers could reduce risk and cost either through repeated, specific interactions themselves or, more generally, through consideration for widely recognized reputation, good or bad.[43] The former approach offered the benefit of personal knowledge; the latter expanded opportunities to work with new individuals and interests. Traders used both approaches, and both were referenced by witnesses as evidence of the usual course of business.

Sir Edmund Antrobus, one of the early witnesses, suggested that despite the appearance of fast trading, he dealt only with individuals he knew or who were connected to his network of trusted individuals. "It was not at all usual with us," he testified, "to lend it to any person but those we knew or had in some way connection with."[44] Another witness observed that he never did business of any sort with strangers. Social capital, unwritten rules, and informal arrangements were dominant features of exchange. John Lewis Wolfe, of Wolfe Brothers, testified that reputation was indispensable in the Stock Exchange, where very large sums of money were often lent for as little as a day. People lent money quickly so they could get it back quickly, but they did so within a social arena that valued reputation. Wolfe, for example, was owed money by one William Scott, but rather than holding him in default, the Exchange and the interested parties negotiated an agreement where Scott paid all "he could conveniently spare."[45] Such testimony lends credence to the image of a civil, congenial approach to business. Nonetheless, Wolfe acknowledged, these exchanges were also complicated. He relied not simply on the institution but on a wider, diffuse notion of reputation: "All Scott's connections I knew were highly respectable, and I never observed that he transacted business with any speculative persons. We did not consider him to be rich, but thought him sufficiently rich to pay any loss which might take place in dealing in Exchequer Bills."[46]

Wolfe's statement adopts the rhetorical stance of the age of reputation. Long gone is the disinterested gentleman of virtue who needs nothing more; in his place is the man who has enough but probably wants more. He need not be rich enough to be honest, but he must have enough to cover his risk. According to Wolfe, it was the custom of the Stock Exchange to depend on reputation and behavior—from the conduct of the trades (with little or nothing being written, instead transacted on honor and memory) to the emphasis on Scott's respectability. Other witnesses echoed Wolfe's statement.[47] Sam Steward, a solicitor, testified as to his possession of three bills he had purchased through John Cook, clerk to Messrs. Morgan and Company. Steward was asked if he knew Cook's pecuniary circumstances. "I never supposed him to be a man of any considerable property," Steward responded. "But he was very much trusted. I know that persons put great confidence in him, in fact, the connections we are concerned for, we invariably pay their monies into his hands . . . we have always supposed him to be solvent, but never supposed him to be a man of property." It was as simple as that: "If persons wanted to make an investment, they would go up to him in the City, and make it through him. He was a man who appeared to gain people's confidence very much; he had mine most fully."[48] The sense of knowing a person through his past behavior and standing among others was central. Descriptions of routine, commonplace, and reputation-based exchange were standard during the commission's interviews. Benjamin Cole, a broker for Smith, Payne and Smith, dealt with men of "character" and "in the usual course of business." A solicitor at Lincoln's Inn Fields was very much in the "habit of trusting" Cole. All previous affairs with him had "been done with the greatest accuracy and correctness."[49] Sir Edmund Antrobus had unknowingly lent on forged bills in a way that "was a regular usual matter of business."[50]

Mariner and De Berckem had gone to great lengths to locate and reacquire wayward bills, demonstrating a crucial aspect of the fraud. The bills were not immediately redeemed for cash but used to borrow against, for speculation. The loans were very short term—sometimes lasting only one day—and the bills were quickly reacquired.[51] This was crucial for two reasons: first, the bills were not detected; and second, the reputations of those trading in the bills (knowingly or unknowingly) could remain intact.

This rhetorical positioning, of a proper use of trust built around reputation, took place not only in front of the commission but also in the public sphere. In his pamphlet *Exchequer Bills Forgery: A Statement*, published the year following the fraud, Mariner set to defending his name and his conduct in the transit of Smith's bills. "Character is power," he acknowledged. "I have found it to be so in every clime and under every circumstance of my chequered existence; to maintain the power derived from it, is the motive which now induces me to the publication of this pamphlet."[52] Mariner did not have to explain his relationship with Smith but rather with Solari—the Italian-born naturalized British citizen who had acquired most of the bills from Smith.

Solari died before the fraud came to light, while Rapallo fled to Boulonge after a brief imprisonment that ended when nobody could prove he knew the bills were fakes.[53] Even in death and exile, however, they remained figures against which investors had to demonstrate their

financial rectitude. In his pamphlet, Mariner did this in two recogniz-
able ways: by pointing to the well-respected figures who dealt with Solari and to the general respectability of Solari's past conduct. He had
met Solari while working for the National Brazilian Mining Association. "Early in 1838," he wrote, "I learnt that Mr. Solari was carrying
on large financial speculations, and that many brokers of long standing were seeking to obtain a share of his business."[54] Though the initial trust may have been built on network and reputation, Mariner's
trust in the pair, he also claimed, was also built on their regular conduct of business. "In his personal demeanour," Mariner wrote, Solari
"was attentive and exact beyond measure; he not only fulfilled every
contract to the hour, but to the second."[55]

He and Rapallo were figures of bourgeois frugality and sociability: "I beheld nothing unreasonable, nothing that denoted sudden
wealth in the possessors. I saw decency of apparel, decency of domestic
requirements; nothing further. The outward appearance of all that met
my eye brought to mind no idea, I say, of accumulated riches; but the
idea of respectability was forcibly impressed upon me: just the degree
of respectability that one might expect to find in a confidential agent—a
man not a *millionaire* himself, but acting for *millionaires*."[56]

Mariner knew the stakes. "I have been trusted and rewarded accordingly," he wrote. "The capitalist relies on one thing solely—gold; but
he who is without the treasure must, if he wants some of its advantages,
obtain the object of his wants through another medium—character."[57]
Because of his dealings with Rapallo and Solari, Mariner's character had
come under great question.

Nowhere was the suspicion of Rapallo and Solari (and whoever
dealt with them) more evident than in an anonymous 1842 pamphlet,
titled *The History and Mystery of the Exchequer Bills Forgery Examined*,
written by a member of the Stock Exchange and addressed to Henry
Goulburn, the chancellor of the Exchequer to prime minister Sir Robert
Peel. The author, ignoring how far the bills had traveled, felt that none
of the holders of the exchequer bills deserved to be compensated or
have their reputations repolished. "In the Stock Exchange and out of it,"
he wrote, "every body was apprised of all that I have stated; it was the
subject of general conversation. The name of Rapallo was mixed up

in these public accusations, and no man of respectability would conde-
scend to have anything to do with either of them."[58] In pamphlets and
newspaper articles, the Genoese pair had become pieces of clay that could
be molded to fit any author's interests. Having claimed that Rapallo and
Solari lacked reputation, the author of *History and Mystery* then set to
illustrating the type of conduct that could so damage reputations.

The author's Solari was a former vitriol manufacturer from Bat-
tersea who had been imprisoned for debt and declared bankruptcy in
1822: "He had scarcely a bed for himself and his family, and was very
often in want of bread." Lacking social respectability and presentation, Solari was also guilty of chronic speculation. By 1836, the author
concedes with disgust, he was a director in many companies and entering into transactions with Morgan and Price. This Solari would
have been familiar to Dickens, who wrote skeptically in *Our Mutual
Friend*: "As is well known to the wise in their generation, traffic in
shares is the one thing to have to do with in this world. Have no ante-
cedents, no established character, no cultivation, no ideas, no manners: have Shares. Have Shares enough to be on Boards of Directions
in capital letters, oscillate on mysterious business between London
and Paris, and be great. Where does he come from? Shares. Where is
he going? Shares. What are his tastes? Shares. Has he any principles?
Shares."[59] By 1838, Solari was a director in the Brighton Railways; he
would ultimately be sued by its shareholders. He had also, over time,
become a director in the United Kingdom Fishery Company, the Gal-
vanisation Metals Company, the British Asphalum and Patent Coal
Company, the French Patent Coal Company, the Brighton Cemetery
Company, and other concerns. Were it not for the ongoing efforts to
differentiate investment and stockjobbing from mere speculation,
this Solari would seem a paradox: notoriously unreliable and yet involved in numerous companies. At first glance, the author of the
pamphlet seems to implicate many of his colleagues and the companies in whose shares they traded in the City. Instead, the author
linked Solari to firms he claimed had failed to deliver for shareholders or in the production of goods. Solari traded in the unproductive,
even fake, portion of the economy. For that reason alone, he neither
possessed nor deserved a reputation.

The author of *History and Mystery*, on the other hand, continued a well-worn tradition of Exchange members, drawing a clear distinction between good and bad, real and fake investment. But his attention to Solari left much of the story untold. Not everybody in possession of Smith's bills had gotten them directly from Solari and Rapallo. Were the sins of the bill-holding magistrate the same as Mariner's?

The commission set to answering just this question, attempting to devise a system for differentiating the responsible from the reckless. It created four classes in which financial exchanges took place and then ranked them from responsible to irresponsible to reckless. The ranking system demonstrates just how important reputation was; meanwhile, the connections between the classes of behavior illustrate how increasingly inseparable investment was from speculation.

The language used to establish the hierarchy of financial conduct is familiar, descending from the "usual course of business" to "peculiar circumstances" to extreme "want of caution." Class I included parties who had "become respectively the holders of the bills with which they are connected, in the usual course of business, and without knowledge or suspicion that they were other than genuine."[60] Class II included players who had acquired bills in the "usual course of business" but under peculiar circumstances and with a want of caution. Such elements as large amounts deposited, extended duration of loans given and received, or unusually high interest rates made this class's conduct suspicious.

But it was classes III and IV whom the commissioners saw as operating outside the normal bounds of the economy. In these classes, want of caution was illustrated by the absence of due diligence on the sources of the bills and the backgrounds of sellers or lenders.[61] The "usual course of business" meant trading in interest rates that seemed reasonable and not only having regard for reputation but correctly assessing it.

Mariner, in his self-defense, divided up the bills into the four classes associated with their claimants. Class I, he guessed, included £193,000 of the forged bills. The bills held by class II players amounted to £49,000. The rest fell to classes III and IV. Which is to say, of £377,000 worth of exchequer bills examined by the Treasury, at least £135,000 appears to have moved around the market in ways that were defined as reckless. Mariner, however, dismissed the class IV transactions as these bills all belonged to F. T. De Berckem and had not yet fully entered the marketplace. Claiming to value reputation as a guide above all else, he attempted to show that classes III and IV were not relevant, that everything could be grouped into the top of the commissioners' hierarchy. He was right, in a sense. The categories, while useful to a normative conception of reputation, were not accurate—but not because almost everyone belonged in class I.

With the exception of four sets of bills, all the circulating bills traveled between at least one individual or party in class I or II and one in class III or IV. This is not to say, as Mariner tried to argue, that everyone was respectable; rather, those who valued reputation and those who merely traded at great pace to cover their risks inevitably became connected. Of the 324 bills that entered into circulation, 236 went through the hands of or ended up with reputable parties. Yet all of those 236 bills were also at some point in the possession of numerous so-called class III or class IV characters. There was a sort of reputation contagion: the failure of one party to properly assess background and reputation could allow for fake bills to enter the marketplace and then be traded out through normally desirable commercial relationships. Most bills, Mariner and the commissioners agreed, were traded in responsible fashion. Most were also, at some point, handled by those with an absence of caution and a disregard for reputation. In a laissez-faire environment, reputation was more important than virtue. It was a check on strangers and both a defense against and an enabler of increased pace in commerce and finance. As a system, however, it also had a notable flaw: reputation was prone to contagion. People who held reputation inevitably came into contact with those of lesser repute. Once a fraud entered this sphere, reputational mechanisms actually helped it spread. The problem, as Dickens knew, was the mutual friend. The reputation regime, like diffused risk, turned out to only be as strong as its weakest link.

With its attention to process and production, the first commission had left unanswered a fundamental question: what would happen to bill holders who had acquired the bills with no knowledge of their being false? This question surrounded much of the press coverage of the fraud and loomed as a central concern for those following and testifying in front of the second commission. Two-hundred thirty-six bills initially presented to the Exchequer were detained as fraudulent. The Bank of England held 76 such bills; 51 were held by James Capel of Coutts and Company; 26 by Messrs Price and Company; and another £50,000 worth largely by individuals. Somewhere between 61 and 115 had been rejected in additional examinations. In other words, a lot of money was on the table—all of it held by people claiming to have acquired the bills in regular trading.

Merely ranking the classes of conduct, the commission likely knew, was not enough. While the report and the witnesses' testimony buttressed the importance of reputation, they solved neither the short-term problem of determining who was liable for the forged bills nor the long-term problem of the dangers of trading on only reputation. A letter to the editor of the *Times* signed "A Bona Fide Holder of Detained Exchequer-Bills" raised this short-term question with regard to legal recourse: "The party I must commence my action against assures me solemnly that he is equally innocent as myself, and that an action against him would be a most unjust and oppressive act, as he can prove to the commissioners that he is as *bona fide* and innocent in the transaction as myself; I therefore feel my hands tied by every principle of justice and humanity."[62] Such were the uncomfortable options left to the bills' holders in the laissez-faire financial sphere. The holders of bills were left to pursue their grievances privately or in civil court, and their complaints, like Smith after his transportation, seem to have disappeared from the historical record. The first report had recommended strict new approaches to the production of bills. The second commission attempted to reiterate the importance of the "usual course of business" and respect for reputation. It chastised, evaluated, and even offered a model of responsible financial behavior and use of reputation. In this sense, the commission was consistent with the Factors Act of 1842 and the deliberations that had led up to it, all of which emphasized the importance of reputation and of social exchange as a buttress against fraud. Unlike the Factors Act, however, which altered the distribution of liability away from buyers and back to sellers and their agents, the second commission did not recommend or help usher in new legal measures or an approach to adjudicating liability for the bills.[63]

The exchequer bill market had become increasingly complex in the way it connected unknown investors and agents. Legislation like the Joint Stock Banking Act of 1844 and expanded global trade and finance would further open the market to new entrants, new assets, and new locations. Individuals and institutions were left to fend for themselves in a sphere where trust and risk were to be negotiated.

S • E • V • E • N

The Detection of Lies, Lives, and Agents

Nearly a decade after Beaumont Smith's antipodal exile, a new fraudster hit one of London's leading insurance firms, Globe Insurance Company. Like Smith, Walter Watts had been a clerk for years, had earned the confidence of his superiors, and used the knowledge gained in his position to exploit technical weaknesses in the financial exchange. Watts led two lives: one as an unassuming clerk at an insurance company, and the other as an extravagant theater owner with a penchant for champagne and women and a residence in a smart part of town.

A history of trust and fraud in the laissez-faire mid-nineteenth century cannot ignore insurance. The 1840s and 1850s for the insurance industry were not unlike the 1820s for Latin American bonds, a time when a change of the market dramatically altered the industry, opening it to new players and forcing old ones to adapt quickly. Dozens of new insurance firms entered the marketplace, squeezing the profit margins of well-established firms and forcing them to revise the usual course of business. Government legislation enabled an expansion of the market while offering little regulatory help. In an impersonal and increasingly complex industry, it was left to consumers and insurers to figure out how best to manage the risk of fraud. Like merchants, insurance companies had to have inspectors and agents scattered across the

world. Like brokers, insurance agents were discovering the challenges
and opportunities of an expanded market of strangers and potential
clients.

The nineteenth-century boom in insurance, in both Britain and
the United States, was driven in part by the uncertainty created by
capitalism, urbanization, and industrialization.[1] The market's development, however, unleashed its own associated risks, including rampant new opportunities for fraud. By midcentury, insurance companies
found themselves in an increasingly anonymous world where managing confidence, maintaining competitiveness, and limiting risk were
of the utmost importance. Reputation, familiarity, and the usual
course of business were the cornerstones of conduct for Globe's officers, firm bases for trust, and guards against fraud. But changes in
their offerings—both in location and in services—coupled with the arrival of new market players required that Globe also adapt to a more
widespread and dynamic insurance market. Maintaining the ability to
trust in this new environment demanded flexibility. By the 1850s, agents
were deployed increasingly often to inspect claims and bodies, not to
mention employees. Even as it approached its demise in the late 1850s,
the firm's adaptations would show the beginnings of the verification
and standardization that would be the norm by century's end.

In the eighteenth century, insurance was as much an intellectual
development as a commercial one, drawing on multiple strands of
Enlightenment thought, including crucial developments in the math-
ematics of probability, distribution, and inference.[2] Though versions of
life insurance existed before the mid-eighteenth century, they are usually dismissed as something akin to gambling. The establishment of
the Scottish Ministers' Widows Fund of 1744—operating on the "maximum principle," in which the contributions and interest on capital
were calculated to be enough to pay the maximum expected payout in
a year—is often identified as a watershed in the development of modern
life insurance.[3] The fund, which was open to Church of Scotland ministers and professors of the University of Edinburgh, was premised on
the ability to predict life expectancy and thus the number of future
beneficiaries, as well as the income earned from the capital. Similar
funds soon followed, including the establishment in 1761 of the first real

life insurance fund in America, the Presbyterian Ministers' Fund of Philadelphia. The two working premises of these funds—the capacity to predict life span and the ability to raise capital and then invest it at a positive return—were actuarial and mathematical. But there was also, inevitably, a messier human side to insurance that grew more complicated as the numbers of insured and insurers increased.

The question of how to maintain and encourage confidence, which pervaded nearly every corner of mid-nineteenth-century political economy, was particularly relevant in the life insurance industry. The issue of trust was fundamentally trickier for insurance companies than for merchant houses, banks, or governments. An insurer accepts not only physical hazard—be it life or fire—but also moral hazard. Insurers have to worry that the mere fact of their guarantee to compensate policyholders will encourage reckless if not criminal behavior. Perhaps even more important, as the historian of insurance Timothy Alborn has shown, insurers had to manage the problem of adverse selection. Put simply, insurance was more appealing to people who were more likely to need it. Insurance companies had to worry not only about people's actions once they were insured but also about how to screen and examine people's history and health before they received insurance.[4]

Trust was therefore a more crucial factor in insurance, at least in its beginnings, than in most other service sectors. The Widows Fund had nearly a thousand beneficiaries in 1745, but its insurance was still available to only a limited number of individuals in two communities.[5] In 1800, the number of life insurance policies in Britain also hovered around a thousand. By the middle of the nineteenth century, however, the world of known beneficiaries in nearby communities had been replaced by a world of strangers. The pooling of funds, the distribution of risk, the reliance on probability, and the networks and resources needed to make these strategies work all favored large organizations over individuals.[6] Fire and life insurance in particular experienced booms due to industrialization and urbanization. Partly as a result of the growth in English cities, fire insurance quadrupled between the mid-1780s and late 1820s. Meanwhile, the assets insured in life policies nearly quintupled in the first half of the nineteenth century.[7] This dynamic was intrinsic to the industry. If Smith's confederates Solari and Rapallo had wanted to trade with only one individual, they theoretically could have. Brokers and merchants could still trade with small groups, though as the exchequer bill fraud shows, they were increasingly unlikely to do so. But an insurance company had to reach out to large numbers. This was risk management on an industrial scale.

Beginning in the 1840s, the challenge for established insurance firms like Globe was not only the large number of customers they had to reach but also the expanding number of competitors.[8] Following the 1844 Joint Stock Companies Act—which allowed companies to incorporate as joint stocks without a royal charter or act of Parliament—a host of new insurance companies entered what had been a limited market. According to the *Post Magazine Almanack*, an authority on insurance, 131 new insurance companies opened in the first seven years after the 1844 act, 78 of which collapsed within that period.[9] An 1852 report to Parliament detailing the expansion of the insurance industry showed that between 1849 and 1852, upward of one hundred new insurance firms were in operation.[10] The result was typical of the mid-nineteenth-century laissez-faire economic order. Government legislation enabled new players to enter the marketplace, offerings of risk management begat new risks, and regulation of this marketplace was left to consumers and industry. In an environment with limited legal or regulatory recourse, one of these risks was fraud.

Trust was also especially important for consumers in the insurance industry given the long time scale associated with the business.[11] Even before the new joint stock companies entered the scene, companies like Globe were trying to separate themselves from competition by highlighting their history and reliability. Newspapers, pamphlets, and journals continued to be important media through which to demonstrate bona fides. An 1838 advertisement for Globe assured readers that it was a "traditional" company appropriate for those who "seek certainty and security, rather than apparent cheapness, or the chances of future profit."[12] A million in sterling, the advertisement claimed, was already paid up and invested. The attacks upon the companies formed after 1844 very much mirrored the values exhibited in this advertisement: young companies did not have capital; they did not have experience; they were not trustworthy. The *Morning Chronicle* and Robert Christie, a manager at Scottish Equitable Life, were two of the fiercest critics. The new companies, Christie wrote, were "founded and conducted, in many instances, by persons possessing neither capital, nor character."[13] They simply did not have the means, or perhaps even the intention, to honor their obligations. Beware the immoral firm, warned the old guard; trust our history and our money.

This was survival-of-the-fittest capitalism, and the new firms would respond. In an 1852 pamphlet, *The Facts and Fictions of the Life Assurance Controversy*, an anonymous author explicitly attacked the older firms and their defenders. At issue, again, was confidence. The author knew that pamphlets such as Christie's could damage a new company's prospects: "I am aware of how soon unchecked assertions, however wrong, however palpable the errors to persons acquainted with the subject, are apt to make an impression on those who, without knowledge of the particulars are addressed through the medium of their imaginations." Attempting to counter such assertions, the author claimed that insurance had become more widespread and dependable only after the 1844 act: "The changes which have converted Life Assurance into a great vehicle of national good are owing to the introduction of a new and superior class of institutions." It was the old companies that were rotting from the inside: "Beyond the precincts of the Board-room no human being is honoured with the distant adumbration as to the profit or loss on each year's transactions. They revolve in a region of cloud and obscurity, in an age when the test of soundness is candour and publicity." This final sentence is telling. The author of *Facts and Fictions* refers to virtue and morality and suggests that the new insurance companies offer a transparency not matched by the older firms. This was very much the economy of the public sphere, where individual investors were given the opportunity but also the responsibility to monitor their interests. Christie claimed the new firms lacked character; they, in response, pointed to their transparency. There was a further point implicit in the author's description of the established firms: they might not be turning a profit.[14]

The anonymous author understood that the success of insurance companies was not predicated simply on public confidence but also on successful operation. Confidence should be a product of a company's prospects rather than its age, he argued, and the young companies were better situated for the future. "The parading of a large paid-up capital is one of the most telling symptoms," the author asserted, "that the concern does not possess the qualities which would entitle it to the confidence of the public." That which the established firms saw as a strength, the young firms called a weakness. Rather than sitting on paid-up capital, the new firms reinvested their money in expanding the base of their business, thus spreading the risk. They also, he claimed, had more income coming. The author—who explicitly attacked Globe—may have written in service of the new firms, but he was undeniably right that the prospects of insurance companies were primarily a question of management and investment, not past performance.[15]

During the first decade after the Joint Stock Act of 1844, many of the old firms felt suddenly threatened by scores of new companies. One option, as we have seen, was to undermine confidence in the new enterprises. The other option was to improve performance. As the pressure grew and margins decreased, firms searched to find ways to improve profits—the threat of creative destruction prompting innovation. Competition from new firms prompted established firms like Standard Life Insurance Company to raise commissions for agents, establish more beneficial contracts, increase advertising, and introduce new types of insurance. Between 1840 and 1851, insurance companies established coverage for hailstorms (1840), livestock (1844), burglary (1846), personal accident (1848), and travelers' luggage (1851). Some of these would presumably have been useful in previous decades, even centuries. Burglary, personal accident, and loss of luggage, on the other hand, had grown more frequent with the growth of urban life, street traffic, and travel. The end of the century saw a second boom in insurance options, including insurance for bicycles (1883) and elevators (1888).[16] Insurance providers, in short, produced a changing market basket for a changing economy and a more connected world.

As part of this heightened competition, one had to come up with not only new assets but also new ways of managing principal-agent and employee relations. Older firms set to reforming the way they distributed their own trust: to employees and agents, and to policyholders.

For many, this was a question of improving assessment and measurement, making better tables, reading individuals with better accuracy, and managing the information provided by agents and employees. The trust needed to run a successful business was to come not from moral improvement but from improved methods.

The Strange Case of Mr. Watts

Walter Watts's midcentury fraud required no spectacular performance, only a long and simple history of competency and a workmanlike dedication to the usual course of business. His initial anonymity in the workplace and the City was a strength. Unlike Lord Thomas Cochrane or Gregor MacGregor, Watts wanted to blend in, to cause no waves. Thus, little can be said about his early life. He never elaborated on the subject, and no one troubled to find out. It is unlikely that he was married as there is no mention of a widow in a handful of the obituaries printed after his death. The little we know about him before the late 1840s comes from trial records and relates to his career at Globe. Watts worked for the insurance company for at least ten years and may have been employed there from as early as 1832, when he would have presumably done menial work fit for a fifteen-year-old. His family was also in the long-time employ of the insurance company, which is probably how he got the job.[17] One of the few places Watts shows up in the historical record, aside from his fraud and his career as a theater producer, is as a witness on Globe's behalf in a forgery trial.

In 1833, Watts testified at the Old Bailey against Robert Byers, who stood accused of eleven counts of forging checks and attempting to defraud. Adding an element of irony to his later crimes, Watts testified to the banking practices of Globe, as well as to the identity of its many clerks.[18] Though it is unlikely that he saw his future in Byers's conviction and sentence of lifetime transportation to Australia, the makings of his own fraud and fate were already clear. The same knowledge of the company's clerks and check-drawing process that made him suited to testify in court also allowed him to take advantage of it himself. Yet after 1833, Watts went quiet for over a decade. He probably lived with

his father somewhere in East London, attending penny operas and theater on the weekends. He did not appear in further trials, nor did he
rise beyond the level of a clerk. All this, however, was to change.

At the end of 1848, William Tite, the deputy chairman of Globe,
received a supposedly anonymous tip that his clerk Watts was connected with a pair of theatrical establishments. "I remonstrated with
him," Tite later testified, "upon the inconsistency of that profession with
his office." Such paternal scoldings as they pertained to lifestyle were
not uncommon between clerks and senior officials. Employers worried
chiefly, according to Gregory Anderson, about indebtedness and intem-
perance, both of which decreased reliability and increased the chances
of embezzlement or fraud.[19] Watts's job, as an assistant clerk in the accountant's office, was to collect and monitor the passbooks (collections
of checks paid out from and into the company), the company's internal
accounts, and the bank's ledgers as payments came in and out from
Globe and its various bankers, including the London and Westminster
Bank and Glyn and Company on Lombard Street. Watts's office sat on
the third floor, adjoining the country office that managed Globe's
agents in England and beyond. Every Wednesday, a messenger would
deliver to him the passbooks, ledgers, checks, and bills from the bankers at Glyn and Company. Watts, who had access to blank Globe checks,
was charged with the books before they went out to the banks and as
they came back, before inspection by company directors. It would later
be estimated that he used this position to embezzle tens of thousands of
pounds. Whatever the total, in March 1850, the cash transactions office
noticed that a £1,400 check was drawn from a Globe account by Glyn
and Company and paid into the account of Walter Watts by the London and Westminster Bank. Tite suspected not only Watts but his father, who also worked as a clerk. "In the presence of both," he testified,
"I stated that great irregularities had been discovered in the cash transactions of the office, and that before I took any step with respect to it I
thought it right to call them before me, because they must, I thought,
both be involved in it." Both pleaded innocence and, expressing indignation at the accusation, resigned their posts. "I have no alternative but
to immediately tender my resignation," Watts wrote his boss. "Should I
be required, I shall be at the Olympic Theatre throughout the day."

Indeed, they now knew where to find him. On the other side of town from Globe's offices, Watts was living an entirely different life, one filled with parties, toasts, and theater boxes. As an invisible, thieving clerk, he was a performer of the first rank; across town, he employed professional performers of similar skill. Today Watts might have bought a soccer team with his sudden wealth. In the mid-nineteenth century, he bought theaters. He kept a home in St. John's Wood and a box at the opera at Covent Garden, and he was an occasional noted visitor in the social circles of seaside Brighton. Though never featured in London directories of merchants or bankers, he was widely known as the owner of the Marylebone and Royal Olympic theaters. In October, the first plays produced under Watts's ownership began appearing, including *The Happiest Day of My Life, Hamlet,* and *A Winter's Tale.* In December, the last month during which he owned the theater, more Shakespeare appeared, as did, appropriately, *Stranger* and *Mischief Making.*[20]

But as quickly as he arrived, he was gone. News of Watts's arrest for stealing a check worth £1,400 began to appear in the London papers in April 1850, barely a year after he had purchased the Marylebone. In the section "Town and Country Talk," the *Examiner* reported his arrest on April 6 in matter-of-fact fashion: "Mr. Walter Watts, charged with stealing a cheque for £1,400, the property of the Globe Insurance Company, has again been remanded, till next Tuesday."[21] In his 1877 memoir, *First Nights of My Young Days,* the London theater critic Godfrey Turner described Watts's arrest as a theatrical event. He was set upon, suddenly, by a plain-clothed constable who quickly put him in iron bracelets. The Olympic was closed just as a five-act play had begun rehearsal and an historical tragedy had been accepted. "Poor, knavish, light whiskered, light hearted, convivial," wrote the critic, "Mr. Watts was called upon to appear on another scene, and to be the central actor in another tragedy."[22]

Supposedly suffering from delirium tremens, the thirty-three-year-old Watts soon hanged himself in his London prison cell. Following his death, he was remembered in a somewhat positive, if tragic, light within the theatrical community. The London rags would recall his elaborate home in Brighton and his horses in London. His cellar, it would be noted, was one of the finest in town, far exceeding the meager collection of marsala and port Beaumont Smith had kept in his office. "Nothing could excel the magnificence and liberality of the Olympic management. It seemed to make little difference, or none whatever, to Mr. Watts that the public rendered but poor support of the enterprise," remembered Turner.[23] Edmund Yates, a man of all seasons in the British theater community, similarly recalled Watts's days at the Olympic and Marylebone with fondness. "He was," Yates wrote in his 1884 memoir *His Recollections and Experiences*, "an excellent paymaster, very hospitable to all authors and critics, drove in a handsome brougham, and made elegant presents to the 'leading ladies,' whom he admired."[24] Watts was well liked. He paid his bills. He brought in good talent. To those who knew him from the theater world, his crime was secondary to his job as theater owner. The *Leader* wrote of his death: "At home the suicide of Walter Watts will have produced more pain than that of an ordinary criminal. . . . Many a man gets through life with impunity who commits far blacker acts; and Watts had qualities which make him liked."[25] Such was his legacy in a community where mimicry and deception were part fun, part art.

But Watts had a day job, and in that environment deception was a dangerous threat. "His turpitude," added the *Leader*, "was not that of a very deep dye, though very necessary to be checked in a commercial country."[26] The popped corks and stage props, the gifts to leading ladies, and payments to his St. John's Wood landlord stood as affronts to his employers. Above all else, they signaled the need of Globe's management to reform the way it handled employees, agents, and finances. His deception may have been a threat to "a commercial country," but it was also a reminder that to survive in a market plagued by asymmetric information and rife with associated fraud, one had to change, and such change would come in the form of increased attention to reputation, bolstered by expanded bureaucracy and processes of inspection.

The Detection of Lies, Lives, and Agents

Watts had particularly good timing in both of his endeavors. In his fraud on Globe Insurance, he understood that management and verification had not kept up with the increased financial and insurance activities of the company. At midcentury, even while doing business with more strangers and foreigners than ever, Globe still possessed rough life tables, poor internal management, and no developed means for investigation or verification of claims. The complexity of the marketplace and the company itself had outrun the habits of its managers. These problems were typical for a nineteenth-century firm with global reach: the company had to develop internal management capacity, a more secure way to assess the life and fire claims of global customers, and the ability to regulate its far-flung agents.

Watts's fraud corresponded with a sense within the firm that it was failing in all three areas. Though never mentioned in the committee reports, the recorded policies, or the summarized minutes of board meetings, Watts's fraud may exist as a shadow in the urgent tone in which reforms were discussed. The sense of vigilance in the company's records is that of self-reproach, of alertness to internal decay. Globe directors seemed to understand that it could restore its reputation not simply by recycling advertisements and pamphlets of its previous standing but by changing the way it did business.

At Globe's founding, by Frederick Morton Eden at the beginning of the century, the directors' responsibilities to shareholders were fairly routine, if detailed at length. General meetings were to be held semi-annually and advertised at least ten days prior in the *London Gazette* and other major London newspapers. Long before the government required companies to publish their balance sheets, directors and shareholders communicated in the emerging public sphere. Any change to internal regulations, according to the Globe constitution, had to be published in the *Gazette* as well as two or more London morning newspapers.[27] Yet the company's founding constitution dedicated no space to internal management or procedures for issuing policies or compensation. As in any new company, the chief concerns were with paying up the much-advertised capital and limiting the shareholders' liability. Current financial law imposed no further requirements regarding publicity, accounting, or accountability upon the firm. It was with publicity and capital, rather than government requirements or questions of management, that the young insurance company was concerned.

Founding directors were expected to hold £1,000 in shares and to serve three-year terms. They were also expected—though there is reason to doubt this was enforced—not to hold positions with other companies. As in the London Stock Exchange, there was a nod, at least, toward avoiding conflicts of interest.[28] The directors' list included three men of note: Thomas Theophilius Metcalfe, Sir Richard Carr Glyn, and Isaac Goldsmid. Metcalfe had served the East India Company in India and would eventually become one of its directors as well as a member of Parliament. He was father to Charles Metcalfe and Thomas Metcalfe; Charles served as acting governor general in India and governor of Jamaica, and the younger Thomas foresaw Britain's imperial disasters in India. Glyn had served in Parliament and as lord mayor of London and was ultimately father to George Carr Glyn, a prominent banker who counted among his clients Globe Insurance. Goldsmid, similarly, was an established force in the City of London.

Globe's early business involved writing fire policies for the well-off around London, as well as for merchants and storekeepers. Some of the policies were very big, including one in the mid-1820s for Lord Harris of Belmont for £17,970, and another for £24,220 to insure Lord Belmont's stables, barns, and granary in Kent. The Marquess of Hertford insured his mansion on Piccadilly, while a pharmacist and druggist insured his laboratory as well as his musical instruments. Clergymen, coach makers, builders, and carpenters also took out policies in the mid-1820s, as did a surgeon, who insured the theater he used for anatomical lectures. A number of women are also represented in the Globe records—one entire page of the 1824 book is made up of policies held by women—some of them, as might be expected, widows living in London.[29]

As befitted its name, the firm almost immediately established a global presence. Globe provided insurance to East India Company agents in Calcutta beginning in 1820.[30] When agents of the company arrived in Calcutta in the 1830s, they could have visited Globe's agents, Mendieta, Uriarte and Company. If Lord Cochrane had returned to Chile in the 1820s, he could have found Globe's agents in Valparaiso. If MacGregor had visited the United States just two years after his 1818 visit, he could have taken out an insurance policy with Globe at their office on Wall Street.[31] Solari and Rapallo could have taken out accounts in either France or Italy.

By the late 1840s, and especially after the embarrassment of Watts's fraud, it had become clear that Globe needed to alter its modus operandi as far afield as India and as near as the first floor of its office on Cornhill. To counteract the openings for fraud produced by complex impersonal commercial relations conducted over long distances, Globe focused on three chief areas: internal management, rates and the issuance of policies, and the conduct of agents. In each realm, a similar pattern emerges. Knowledge built around reputation remained central, but the firm took an increasingly rigorous, aggressive, and organized approach to acquiring information. These changes were adaptations to the competitive landscape. As frauds in London and fake funerals on the continent demonstrated, the firm was failing to manage its agents and employees. To fix these problems, better routes to trust were needed, lest the company be forced to abandon agents altogether.

INTERNAL MANAGEMENT

In 1851, following Watts's fraud, the board unanimously instructed the chairs on business, including both domestic and foreign concerns, to form a committee, investigate current business and management practices, and institute reforms. Reform would begin with the management of the London office and its employees. Sixteen months later, the Special Committee on Business reported notable progress. In its report, presented on February 23, 1853, the committee looked to the high road regarding the firm's recent problems: "We disclaim most emphatically any intention, by comparison or otherwise, to reflect upon former management." In pointing out the recent changes to the company, however, that is exactly what it did. "Constant + unremitting attention," the committee continued, "has been directed to reorganizing the Establishment, + we may, we think flatter ourselves that a difference is striking between the recent want of order and discipline, and the system which now prevails. . . . The Globe is no longer considered an old-fashioned office that did not care about business, + with which it was not worth while to consult or attempt to co-operate: on the contrary, we are now on amiable + friendly terms of communication with all the leading offices." They had become, the chairs on business counseled, a model of modernity upon which others embarking upon internal reforms patterned themselves.[32]

By the end of 1854, the cost of running the main office was £1,451 less than what it cost in 1850, even though the business had grown by nearly 33 percent since then. Three years later, the committee on accounts could report confidently: "The Committee have great pleasure in reporting to the Board their high sense of the expedition and accuracy with which the Actuary and Accountant have completed the several extensive Valuations to the whole of the Business of last year. And in reporting their approval of the system and order which prevails in the arrangement and care of the Ledger and subsidiary Books." Efficient management, while it kept down London office expenses and ideally helped prevent future frauds, was only part of the challenge facing a global insurance company. It still had to modernize its method of measuring and distributing insurance.[33]

RATES AND ISSUANCE OF POLICIES

In 1852, Gilbert Currie, a Glaswegian, published *The Insurance Agent's Assistant: A Popular Essay on Life Assurance, Its Nature, Use and Advantages*, an impassioned defense of the insurance industry. He pointed to two features that made insurance an appealing and moral investment. First, it distributed risk: "The principle here discovered is none other than that embodied and enunciated in these three words, 'Union is Strength.'"[34] Second, insurance, unlike all other assets, paid off immediately. There was no maturation period. The minute one acquired a policy, its benefits could go into effect. Insurance was not gambling, Currie emphasized, but something closer to science: "Life Assurance is based apparently on the doctrine of chance, yet, strictly speaking, the laws of mortality are so well known and understood by those who have studied them, that they may be considered, will all proprietary, as fixed."[35] Of course, Currie was employing the established rhetoric of distancing responsible investment from speculation or gambling. Like other assets of firm reputation, such as the Consol, Currie suggested that insurance policies were low risk yet adequately rewarding. Indeed, at midcentury the major firms increasingly employed actuaries certified by such organizations as the Institute of Actuaries in London and the Faculty of Actuaries in Edinburgh. This rhetoric, particularly regarding the reliability of mortality tables, requires closer scrutiny.

Actuarial tables are symptomatic of the modern economy in that they represent efforts to grapple with the problem of complexity, size, and anonymity. The epistemological authority of statistical law, Jonathan Levy has written in his history of risk in America, *Freaks of Fortune*, "displaced communal rhetoric."[36] Yet even with constantly improving equations, actuaries needed data from which to work. To predict the future using numbers demanded that actuaries have access to accurate representations of both the past and the present. To accurately turn people into numbers, you have to find out who they really are or were—to know, for instance, their age, their gender, their occupation, their birthplace, their class.[37] The production of actuarial tables presented a paradox: greater accuracy demanded bigger numbers and more reliable detail. As these tables became more sophisticated from the late eighteenth century into the late nineteenth, the sample sizes consistently grew. The Northampton Table, constructed from mid-eighteenth-century burial registers taken by Richard Price at All Saints' Church, Northampton, was based on the records of just five thousand people. The Carlisle Table, constructed at the beginning of the nineteenth century by London insurance actuary Joshua Milne, drew on the information of nearly nine thousand people. The Government's Annuitant's Table of 1829 drew on the records of approximately forty-two thousand people, while the Old Experience Actuaries Table of 1843 drew on just over eighty-three thousand. The New Experience of Institute of Actuaries Table (1869) based its data on over 160,000 lives.[38] While the math grew more complicated and the sample sizes increased, a familiar problem arose: to retrieve accurate data on thousands of people around the country, one had to overcome the complex dynamic of distance and the reliability of strangers.

The long history of insurance tables speaks to how difficult this undertaking was. The Northampton Table was put together in the late

eighteenth century by Rev. Dr. Price from persons buried in the parish
of All Saints Northampton between 1735 and 1780. Though it was long
considered the standard, one prominent commentator noted that it was
"constructed in a manner which would not be tolerated now-a-days. . . .
It has been found that under it younger lives paid in more than was fair,
while older lives contributed too little," meaning that the table favored,
at least in financial terms, those that would pass sooner. The Equitable
Table, issued in 1825 by the London actuary Griffith Davies, using data
from the annual addresses to members of Equitable Life Assurance Society, also overly weighted older lives, failing to incorporate the life-
span expectations of the young. Even the great Carlisle Table gave too
much emphasis to women when men were more likely to be insured.[39]

The revisions of life tables spoke to how difficult it was to find sufficient records and to adapt the projections to the changing challenges
of urbanization and industrialization. In fact, the challenge for Globe
and other insurance companies was greater than simply devising accurate tables. The problem was not merely numbers but numbers and
fraud. Even if the tables had been more accurate, insurance companies
had to worry about deception by both clients and their own agents.
Globe was taking heavy losses abroad in both fire and life, which it
blamed not on tables but on the reliability of information from those
who bought and sold policies.

Having switched to the Carlisle Table on the continent in 1852—
or as the board called it, "a more solid principle of calculation"—Globe
recognized that the table was flawed when applied to other geographic
regions. The life insurance business was increasingly restricted to the
northern parts of Western Europe as the West offered better "durabil-
ity of human existence."[40] Even then, the tables presented a challenge.
What if men in Saxony and Sweden did not live as long as men in Carlisle? The firm surmised that in Saxony a man of forty-one would live
for 23.5 more years while those in Sweden would live for 24.[41] Nonetheless, the Carlisle Table proved acceptable, allowing the firm, according
to the chairs, to charge on average 10 percent more per policy on the
continent. Furthermore, through "more stringent detection of lives,"
no claims had been issued on new business life insurance (lives insured
under the new tables and regulations) in the past eighteen months. In

1852 and 1853, the company added five hundred new lives and lost but one claim.[42]

Nowhere was better risk management more necessary than in dealing with new opportunities and the associated potential for new fraud. "Our experience hitherto shows," wrote the committee on foreign business in September 1853, "that besides the common risks which the Premium charged was intended alone to cover, we have been cheated by insurers, duped by statements verified with every formality except the stamp of truth, and in one case even our Sub Agent was privy to, + a party interested in the fraud." The report cited numerous examples of risks poorly taken or mischievous or fraudulent by agents, or what the board called "non-natural or artificial risks": in Copenhagen, the firm lost £1,216 to "gross fraud" and another £640 on a man who was suspected of misrepresenting his health; in Hanover, a man bought a £1,500 life insurance policy in 1849 and died in 1850, much sooner than the tables or agent had predicted; in Stuttgart, an agent issued a £100 life policy to a seemingly healthy man, who died soon after—the agent, it turned out, had himself purchased a £500 policy on that same man; one man, Thomas Check, claimed life insurance and then "it is said, attended . . . his own funeral."[43]

The directors of Globe were under no illusions as to the reliability of reputation as an arbiter in their marketplace. In the end, turning the company around was a question not just of better math but of managing agents and customers. In the 1850s and 1860s, insurance remained a business where information and interests uncomfortably collided.

CONTROL OF AGENTS

Improvement in management and in application of actuarial tables would be worth little if the firm could not police its agents and clients. The risk distribution dilemma that had plagued principals, agents, and third-party lenders was in no way foreign to Globe. Its directors acknowledged early that "the business of the office will, in great measure, depend upon the due selection of proper persons as Country Agents."[44] Though the firm had at least 140 agents by 1804 and 158 by 1805, its records from the 1820s show Globe's foreign business to have been conducted largely by two agents. By midcentury, the number of foreign agents had grown to around four hundred.[45] They were normally merchants, clerks, solicitors, retailers, or other members of the middle class.

As the historian D. T. Jenkins points out, respectability did not necessarily make such moonlighting agents well equipped to manage policies or investigate claims. In fact, despite the claims Globe made about the agents' importance, they were in fact very poorly managed for the first half of the century.[46] Jenkins writes of the Sun Fire Office, whose management structure differed little from that of Globe: "In view of the importance of the agency system and the problem the major offices faced as a result of the failings of agents, it is surprising that large offices, like the Sun, paid so little attention to the appointment and supervision of agents. By the 1840s and 1850s safeguards were being established, but up to then the majority of agents of the London offices were unknown personally to their directors. . . . Little supervision and control was exercised and there was little check that instructions were obeyed."[47] Owing to the dual challenge of fraud and foreign courts, Globe acknowledged that reforms might not be able to turn the business around. The Chairs on Foreign Business, a committee within Globe, in particular held an increasingly skeptical view of their capacity to police agents. Nonetheless, firms survived or collapsed based, in part, on their ability to adapt their mechanisms of trust to the new dynamics of the marketplace. The principal-agent relationship, and the role of trust and interests within it, could not be abandoned and so had to be adapted.

One possible solution was to increase agents' incentives. It is clear that the company needed not only to add new agents but also to incentivize them differently. Those in high-growth areas like Manchester and Birmingham were encouraged with special agreements and allowances.[48] But adding agents and incentivizing them brought obvious problems. City lore held that the famed Equitable Insurance firm had never once appealed to law to settle a case. Globe had turned to the law, according to its own records, only once. But on the continent, it had been forced to pursue six cases in the eight years prior to the 1853 reports—and that was, it acknowledged, evidence only of the frauds managers thought they had discovered, not all frauds.[49]

By the end of 1853, it had become clear that Globe must either wind up its unstable offices or expand their capacity to investigate clients. Somewhat paradoxically, the company pursued both options, at once limiting its reliance on trust and expanding its agents' capacity to verify. In early 1855, the board voted unanimously to close the offices in Shanghai and Bombay. Since their founding in 1852, the offices had in fact been quite successful, taking on a good number of policies while suffering no losses. The problem was not the business but the agents. The chairs described the business as one "conducted at such distance + where a power of Attorney to take all risks + settle all claims must be given to the Agent so much depends on his judgment + integrity that it is a charge that should not lightly be delegated by a Company to an individual."[50] In the cases of Shanghai and Bombay, the chairs simply did not have the stomach for distributing such powers. The business in San Francisco was also wound up at a profit. At the end of 1854, having found no buyers, Globe also closed its offices in Bucharest, St. Petersburg, Gothenburg, and Stockholm.[51]

Even so, the number of agents increased, from 342 in 1852 to 429 at the end of 1854. Amazingly, those 429 agents served in 379 discrete locations. In 1854 alone, Globe added eighty-nine new agents in sixty-one new offices. "Great exertions have been made to increase the number of our agents + to obtain new agents in fresh places, + to improve the class of person who held the agency previously."[52] The firm had added not depth but breadth, attempting to both annihilate the effects of distance and drum up new business. This was, as we have seen, consistent with its domestic approach and was a pattern matched by other insurers. Firms were at once firing agents and hiring others, attempting to introduce a new level of reliability to their expanding networks.[53] The company records from 1853 on show aggressive attempts by the London office to manage and communicate better with its agents. Globe, again like Sun Fire, took a more active approach in the first five years following Watts's fraud, and the importance of agents was reiterated repeatedly in the firm's files. In 1853, the external correspondence with the secretary's office increased by one-third, while directors and four "special agents" made personal visits with agents, supposedly increasing the feeling of "sympathy" between agents and company.[54] In that year, sixty new agents were appointed in England alone.

At the end of 1853, the special committee also reported a shift in its approach to domestic insurance claims, particularly life insurance policies. Watts's lesson was in part about management but also about the firm's culture of trust. According to minutes from the meetings, Globe had dramatically increased its vigilance in domestic insurance cases. "Greater care," the committee reported, "has been given to the detection of Lives: the printed queries now put to the parties themselves, to their Referees + Medical attendants, are of a character so much more stringent + sifting that we are not so open to imposition as formerly."[55] Adapting to the challenges of a new marketplace of heightened competition and expanded risk, Globe had become more rigid and disciplined, and less easy with its trust.

Ultimately, in 1864, just a decade after the reforms were put in place, the directors of Globe sold to the Liverpool Insurance Company, which had been established in 1836 by local merchants who felt the rates charged by London insurers were exorbitant. At its founding, all twenty-one of its directors had to live within twenty miles of Liverpool town hall. They could insure, however, around the world. By 1853, they had boards offering insurance in Montreal, Melbourne, and Sydney and agents in San Francisco, Hamburg, Lisbon, Bombay, Calcutta, Rio de Janeiro, Canton, Hong Kong, Shanghai, and elsewhere. Archives show that the management of the Liverpool and London and Globe Insurance Company, as the new company was named, pursued various investments, including loans to railways and banks.[56] Between 1869 and 1884, they also issued just over seven hundred loans with life policies as collateral.[57] The approaches and the standards by which such policies would go forward were already clear in committee meetings of the early 1850s. Reputation mattered, as did networks, but other words appeared with increasing frequency: "detection," "special agents," "medical attendants," "stringent," "sifting." Such was the future of trust in the insurance industry, built around the body and its clues rather than the person and his or her character. In the meantime, Globe and ultimately

Liverpool and London and Globe did what so many other organizations did to address the problems of information and reliability over long distance: they sent more people to more places and corresponded with them more frequently. Agents were to remain irreplaceable tools of commerce, local and distant, but the manner in which one trusted and policed trust in them was continually revised by the demands of capitalism's new frontiers.

The commercial environment in which Globe operated at the time that Watts's fraud came to light was significantly more developed than that at its founding in 1803. Parliamentary legislation had opened the industry to new operators, expanding the insurance market and making it more competitive. New firms and old introduced new forms of insurance and sought to extend life and fire insurance throughout the commercial middle class. But new ways to manage risk opened new opportunities for fraud. The nature of business by the 1850s and 1860s—both within firms and between clients and companies—was increasingly impersonal and complex and thus prone to fraud, posing a distinct challenge both to the distribution and payment of insurance policies and to management of employees and agents.

In this commercial environment Globe sought to increase public confidence in the insurance industry, in general, and trust in itself, in particular, by publicly emphasizing its stability and history. Meanwhile, it sought to hedge against its own insurance risk through investment. Finally, given the problem of managing its employees and agents and insuring strangers, often at a distance, it began taking more active and aggressive approaches to information gathering. The business demanded that principal-agent relations continue, but the tenor and tone of those associates had to change. The networked trust of reputation was not abandoned, but it was to be bolstered by additional checks and inspections. This turn toward process and inspection eventually gave rise to an era in which verification, even more than reputation, became the foundation of commercial exchange.

Part III
Verification

The Observance of Trifles

Arthur Conan Doyle did not work for the Liverpool and London and Globe Insurance Company, but he could have. In addition to being a writer, Conan Doyle was a medical examiner and physician. As part of his professional training, he traveled to the coast of West Africa before settling down to his own practice in Plymouth, where one of his professional duties was evaluating the health and bodies of insurance applicants. Like his creation Sherlock Holmes, he was a detective of the body, one of an increasing number of such detectives who were employed by insurance firms like Globe.[1] When issuing life insurance policies, it had been the tradition of companies well into the nineteenth century to screen applications through a personal interview, a reference from a friend, and another from a medical attendant. The heightened competition in the 1850s required that such gatekeeping become more vigilant, and firms like Liverpool and Globe took care to evaluate and monitor their own agents.

The latter decades of the nineteenth century and first years of the twentieth saw a dramatic increase in the attention paid to minor details in order to overcome asymmetries of information and verify identity and veracity. The capitalist was to remain vigilant, even skeptical, but inspection and verification, often conducted by professionals with technological assistance, were now to be the crutch of trust. This was the culmination of the turn toward process and inspection begun by principals, investors, and governments in the 1850s and 1860s. The social exchange upon which trust was built became a process watched over by experts. Insurance firms hired medical examiners. Imperial agents and London police began fingerprinting. Clerks and managers were taught how to examine checks for fraud. Guidebooks for check cashing and "scientific investment" proliferated, as did financial newspapers promoting good investment and exposing fraudulent ones. In the United States, systematic descriptions of securities in journals would soon give way to modern rating agencies like Moody's.[2] People and paper were inspected and verified. The climax of nineteenth-century financial globalization was accompanied by a stark turn away from trust based on character or morality—instead, eager capitalists devised new systems to build the lubricant so necessary for commercial exchange, rooting trust in process and detailed inspection as much as in personal knowledge.

"A Thousand Minutiae of Character"

Sherlock Holmes was the great literary hero of the Age of Verification. In an urban and imperial world, Holmes looked objectively, used science, examined minutiae.[3] Guides to investment and check cashing offered their own versions of Holmes's fierce judgment of Watson: "You did not know where to look," he tells Watson, "and so you missed all that was important. I can never bring you to realize the importance of sleeves, the suggestiveness of thumb-nails, or the great issues that may hang from a bootlace."[4] The business of inspecting and processing, of verifying, increasingly became not that of individual judgment but of the technician, the trained clerk, the detective. Professionalization and training were more important than genius or character because process and procedure were more important; they became the centerpieces around which state institutions and commercial organizations promoted and automated trust.

Holmes of course finds nothing inscrutable. Conan Doyle gave him details, footsteps, bike tracks, bird calls, and photographs. He was the perfect detective for a world in which, as the cultural historian Carlo

Ginzburg has argued, bold assertions were replaced by hints, clues, details, and minutiae.[5] "You know my method," declares Holmes. "It is founded on the observance of trifles." These trifles come in the form of colonial money and postmarks, in the shapes of faces and in the fashions for clothes. Some of Conan Doyle's descriptions of the face and body could have come from midcentury physiognomy guides. So enters the King of Bohemia into Holmes's rooms: "From the lower part of his face he appeared to be a man of strong character, with a thick, hanging lip, and a long straight chin, suggestive of resolution pushed to the length of obstinacy." Holmes notices tattoos, the size of hands, the direction in which feet point. Details are everywhere, and rather than merely looking at the person, the character, or the class, he disassembles and then reasons.[6]

The inspection of the face, at least until the final decades of the nineteenth century, was thought to be an option for everyone. Physiognomy, the practice of judging people's internal character through external appearances, was pseudoscience for the masses. Though its origin is often associated with the Zurich-born Johan Caspar Lavater in the eighteenth century, its peak coincided with the expansion of the city and the stranger in the mid-nineteenth century.[7] In 1848, George Jabet, under the pseudonym of Eden Warwick, published *Nasology; or Hints Towards a Classification of the Nose*. True to the idea of "pocket physiognomy," Jabet argued that the revelation of character through the inspection of body parts was everyman's business: "Physiognomy, or the form which mind gives to features, is universally recognized. A pleasant mouth, a merry eye, a sour visage, a stern aspect are some of the common phrases by which we daily acknowledge ourselves to be physiognomists." Is it ludicrous to look for character in the nose, he asked, when "we all daily read each other's minds in the Nose's next door neighbours, the eyes and mouth?"[8] Noses, he advised, fell into six categories, including the Greek nose, well represented in history by a line of admirable Britons, painters, and Enlightenment thinkers: Petrarch, Milton (in youth), Spenser, Byron, Shelley, Boccaccio, Canova, Rubens, Murillo, Titian, Addison, and Voltaire. The list of illustrious "Hawk Noses" who had distinguished themselves in literature and history was kept to three: Vespasian, Correggio, and Adam Smith. The

Jewish nose, Jabet suggested, revealed an internal inclination toward commerce.[9]

The problem for Jabet and other advocates of physiognomy was that its democratic nature—it could be employed on the street, equally by everyone—came at the expense of the ability to systematize or archive its information. Even though he could point to famous noses of the past, nasology was too nuanced an affair for the portraitist: "A thousand minutiae of character may escape a biographer, which appear plainly in the man himself."[10] Such was the criticism of one English publication of physiognomy: "No order, no logic, no finish."[11] A system of storing and organizing information permits facts and data to become knowledge. If the portrait could not be counted upon, how could the face and its secrets be stored?

The last two decades of the nineteenth century saw a series of new systems for organizing and categorizing identity. These systems left less to streetwise flaneurs and more to organized entities, like the police, imperial agents, and insane asylum doctors. Photography allowed Francis Galton, a polymath whose talents extended to exploration, statistics, and the dark pseudoscience of eugenics, to create composite photographs that lumped together individuals into an image meant to capture their common characteristics. Under the influence of social Darwinism, such efforts produced a hierarchy of race, class, and ethnicity. Whereas in the early nineteenth century language and culture were often the distinguishing attributes used by British agents, by the end of the century race and ethnicity had come to the fore.[12]

It turns out that the most successful way to verify identity—for individuals, not groups—was being developed in Bengal. As Simon Cole shows in his history of fingerprinting, *Suspected Identities*, questions about how to properly identify criminals had plagued police and courts for much of the nineteenth century.[13] India and other imperial settings posed an acute version of the problem. In its vast population, not only criminals but, more frequently, pensioners who were owed money could not easily be identified. The fingerprint became a device for imperial bureaucratic control—in part to prevent fraud—before becoming the business of Europe's newly born police forces and its legion of criminologists. In addition to his work with photography and attrac-

tiveness, Francis Galton set to work in the 1890s on a system for categorizing fingerprints. Fingerprinting, he suggested, would solve "the great
difficulty in identifying coolies either by their photographs or measurements." It was not Galton, however, but the colonial police official
Edward Henry and especially his assistants Azizul Haque and Chandra
Bose who devised a system for categorizing the fingerprint. It went into
effect in Bengal in 1895, and in 1897 the governor-general of India had
implemented fingerprints as a way to verify identities stored in government cards. The first trial using fingerprints occurred in India a year
later. In 1904, an Indian court confidently declared that "finger impres-
sions . . . afford a surer criterion of identity than any other comparable
bodily feature."[14]

What started as an improvised means for British agents to police
and monitor the identity of Indian pensioners became a system to
monitor identities in India and potential criminals in London. In Britain in 1904, Scotland Yard processed and filed 350 fingerprint cards per
week.[15] Fingerprinting and other means of classification were of interest to specialists but were also accessible to, and increasingly became
the domain of, law enforcement officials. It became, as Cole points out,
something like clerical work. Like the inspection of a check, it required
technical skills, but these skills were not so specialized as to relegate
fingerprinting to the domain of experts. Science enabled bureaucracy,
as well as strengthening capacity for verification and control. Skilled
individual surveillance was increasingly replaced by controlled, ordered, and bureaucratized information. This was true in the realm not
only of crime but also of capitalism and the many spaces where crime
and capitalism met.

In 1854, the directors of Globe had increased their use of medical
referees, a change that would come to play a prominent role in the life
insurance industry. By the century's final decades, medical screening
was the preeminent approach to policy issuance. In 1856, William Brin-
ton published his first guide to such exams, which was later followed by
one by Edward Sievekling, an experienced medical adviser on life insurance policies. By 1884, due diligence on applicants had become so
cumbersome that some advocated a simplified approach. Geoffrey
Scott, a former fellow of the Institute of Actuaries, proposed changing

policies to diminish the extensive research. He explained one of the systems existing in London at the time: "The person whose life is proposed for Insurance has nineteen questions to answer. He is also required to give particulars as to his family, including his father, mother, brother, and sisters. He is further required to name the usual medical attendant, and lastly he has to impose on two of his intimate friends the duty of answering in a sort of clandestine way all that each of them knows about the past and present health and habits of the person whose life is offered for insurance."[16] These documents were then submitted to the medical authorities attached to each insurance office, who offered a report to the directors, who in turn had the power of final approval.

Charles Lyman Greene published his highly influential textbook *The Medical Examination for Life Insurance* in 1900 in the United States and in 1902 in London. The medical officer was, first and foremost, a professional, distinguishing him from a person qualified simply by personal knowledge or character: "Some of the most serious diseases do not for years affect unfavorably the applicant's outward appearance. If mere selection by a lay board were practiced, the most absurd errors would occur, many good risks would be rejected, bad ones accepted, and the sum total would be a sorry lot." Being a professional in that business meant meeting with the full range of humanity, especially the criminal element. The officer must be "prepared to meet occasionally with deceit, misrepresentation, cajolery, browbeating, and, hardest of all, misrepresentation and misunderstanding." The applicant was to be examined in detail: facial expression, contours of the body, attitude, gait, and movement. Of the tongue, he wrote, "a volume might be written."[17]

Such extensive inspection became commonplace. Issuing similar advice in February 1903, the noted doctor Joseph Bell, himself a medical examiner to the Glasgow Life Assurance Company, described the unreliability of recommendations from friends: "My own experience is that they are in 99 cases out of 100 absolutely useless and often misleading." Physical inspection was a must. He described the value of color: "The officer from India or Egypt may have a bronze colour which would suggest liver had he never been out of England, though the white forehead which the forage cap covered will help you. There is a fine high tint of the nose which is rarely present except in the victim of indigestion or alcohol. Purple cheeks generally indicate weak blood vessels, and a pallor, with a leaden tinge after a slight exertion, will guide you to a doubtful heart."[18] Commonplace though his advice may have been, one small fact did distinguish Bell from his colleagues. Arthur Conan Doyle had been his pupil, and he himself was the model for Sherlock Holmes.

The surviving records of Liverpool and Globe show that the company continued to issue a significant number of life insurance policies, approving the vast majority that were passed up to director level. In June 1895, the Finance and Life Committee considered forty-eight life proposals, approving thirty-nine at normal rates and eight at additional rates. It denied only one. The trend of nearly unanimous approval, which continued until the Great War,[19] suggests that Liverpool and Globe in its new form had taken on equally stringent inspection and verification procedures. Everything that passed the experts and specialists was approved by the directors.

This approach to knowing fingerprints and bodies was not limited to metropolitan police and medical examiners. Inspection, verification, attention to detail, and expertise were advanced as the foundations for trust in commercial affairs, ranging from clerical duties such as accounting to the consideration of investment opportunities. The social exchange through which trust was built was now a technical process taking place under the watchful eyes of bureaucrats and experts.

The Paper Trail

In 1884, the *Financial News*, one of the leading financial papers of the day and the subject of the next chapter, routinely listed the prices of more than eighty American railway shares on its front page. Railway shares, the financial concern of Anthony Trollope's famous confidence man Augustus Melmotte in *The Way We Live Now*, were one of the era's hottest commodities. Like exchequer bills, they were treated as negotiable, often traded as if legal ownership was changing. Technically, owners of the shares should have used their brokers to register their ownership with the railroad companies in America. This was a laborious process, and some bills were considered so reliable that traders took them on or traded them off without transfer of title.[20]

This common practice became a concern in the late 1880s and early 1890s when a series of frauds demonstrated the risk in not properly verifying and registering ownership. In the early 1880s, the executors of a trust deposited 1,210 shares of the New York Central Railroad with their stockbrokers. The brokers then obtained advances on the shares from the Colonial Bank and London Chartered Bank of Australia. When the brokers went bankrupt in 1884, the executors attempted to recover the shares from the banks, as the brokers had only been enlisted as agents, not as traders. The chief question, according to the *Economist*, became whether the banks "had taken proper steps to ascertain who was the *bonâ fide* holder of the shares."[21] The initial ruling went in favor of the bank but was later overturned by the Law Lords. The *Economist* applauded the ruling. Why? Because the bank had not properly verified ownership when taking on the shares: "It was held, and rightly so, that the character of the share certificate, should have put the banks upon inquiry, but that, as a matter of fact, they did nothing, and that this being the case, they must suffer the consequences." A decade later, another bank suffered for its failure to properly manage the details of its affairs. In November 1901, it became apparent that at least £170,000 had been pilfered from the Liverpool Bank. "What the public would like to know," wrote the *Economist*, "is whether there is in existence, and in working order, a system of precautions which renders such frauds most difficult to perpetrate, and, if perpetrated, most easy to detect?"[22]

For years, John Hutchinson had been attempting to answer just that question. In 1881, while an acting branch manager of Manchester and Liverpool District Bank, Hutchinson published the first volume of *The Practice of Banking*, which would become a multivolume, multiedition guide to the inner functioning of the banking system. Surely reputation and character still mattered. In the section on bills of exchange, Hutchinson wrote: "The manager should exercise very great care and discretion in the reception of bills, and none but those of the most unexceptionable character should be discounted by him. Two good names should be on every bill, and this rule should only be departed from in very exceptional circumstances." The rest of the section, which continues for 280 pages, is replete with concern for character, but it also demands a different approach from bank managers and clerks. Attention to detail, and through it the verification of documents, was at the center of his recommendations. "To the form of the bill, and its regularity and validity," he wrote before launching into an extensive list of checks, "the stricter attention should be paid."[23]

Process, standardization, verification: they do not make for gripping prose and are far afield from the earlier arbiters of trust such as status, character, reputation, and networks. But that is the point: we have entered the age of the accountant, the actuary, and the medical examiner. The check is like a face or fingerprint, with its own physiognomy, broken down into pieces, each detail addressed on its own merits. If impressionism serves as a good artistic match for the age of reputation, pointillism is the genre for the age of verification.

In the latter parts of *Practice of Banking*, Hutchinson described at great length how bankers might verify the documents that came through their hands. "To protect the banker [who is liable to changes] from alterations effected by the erasure or obliteration of the original writing, the use of paper coloured for the purpose and chemically porous is now pretty general, as any attempt to alter or erase the writing by chemical agency is at once detected from the effects upon the papers."[24] The importance of technology and science would only expand. The second volume of *Practice of Banking*, published in 1883, starts with a 210-page section titled "Inspection," including twenty-eight pages of inspection report examples. "Where the Bank is large and the Branches numerous," Hutchinson tells us on the first page, "the post of Chief Inspector or Inspector-General may be considered equal, and in some respects superior, to that of the Manager-General."[25]

In response to the 1901 Liverpool Bank fraud, the *Economist* had offered strikingly similar recommendations, focusing on processes of verification from an organizational perspective. The clerks who post checks should not be the same ones who pay out checks. Bookkeepers should periodically be shifted from one ledger to another to prevent long-term frauds, of which the Liverpool Bank fraud was one. The *Economist* advised that "every bank, without exception, has its ledger entries checked daily, and in all offices which have any claim to be well-regulated such checking is performed, not by the book-keepers themselves, but by independent officers. . . . Such verification, too, should not be done fitfully during the internals of other work, but at one time and away from the book-keeper."[26] This, like fingerprinting and insurance medical exams, is not a terribly complicated process, but it is a process, something achieved through management of an institution and beyond the capacity of individuals acting alone.

These systems had their successes. In September 1908, two men, having fraudulently acquired a checkbook, attempted to cash a check of £160 to the Standard Bank of South Africa but fled when the cashier began a thorough examination of the check. In that same month, two others succeeded in forging a transfer of £750 from one branch of the London and South-Western Bank to another. They were able to do so, the *Times* reported, only because "the form was of the usual character, and bore the code word of the bank, which is altered each day." With the help of Scotland Yard and the consul in Madrid, one of the perpetrators was arrested in Spain. The other, it turned out, was a cashier at the bank. In June 1910, a well-dressed man attempted to cash a check for £150 at Crompton and Evan's Bank at Buxton. Suspicious, the cashier called the police and eventually had the man arrested as he tried to board an express train to London.[27]

This market and its associated frauds were at once global and local. Legitimate commercial men and their fraudulent counterparts walked into banks in London to trade in assets and goods from around the world. At the end of May 1905, for instance, the *Financial News* ran a feature on the Investment Registry Ltd., of Waterloo Place, founded in 1880. The article extolled the virtues of expertise and observation. Many investors, it said, either bought stocks haphazardly when they saw an attractive prospectus or took "the advice of an 'authority'—usually the family solicitor and sometimes a 'friend in the City.'" But these days of impulse buying and reliance on reputation belonged to the past. "Safety of Capital and Income can be Obtained by a Judicious System of Observation," the article continued, in which "a number of experts daily search the financial press, scan the reports of public meetings, boil down balance-sheets, and generally keep au fait with what is happening in the financial world." The *Investment Registry* not only had experts but also had reliable clerks who attended to the details of each account. As in the insurance industry, a firm's ability to deliver for its clients was demonstrated, at least in part, by its internal well-being and management. "We can't afford to make mistakes, you know," jokes a manager at the article's end, "for we have to think of that quarterly review, when any mistake (if it were made) would come home to roost."[28] And the article did not quit there: it also noted that the problem of safe investment was one of complexity and global reach. A global world, the registry's approach to investment held, needed transparency and observation.

In *How to Protect Capital Invested in Stocks and Shares*, the Investment Registry's own 1905 publication, the firm acknowledged that investment options had become increasingly specialized and complicated. "It is owing to the bewildering nature of the movements of international finance that an investor will require some skilled aid in the reconstruction of his investment list."[29] "The multitude of Joint Stock Company investments is now so great," observed the registry in another publication, *Investment Risks and How to Avoid Them*, "and they are so diversified in character, that it daily becomes more necessary that investors should not rely upon their own unaided information." The answer to such complexity, the authors asserted again, was expertise and supervision: "Successful investment calls for a certain amount of specialization, and to achieve the best results it is necessary to have access to statistical data concerning a very large number of securities. . . . The supervision of investments is indeed a highly specialized profession. It is skilled knowledge and common sense in a particular manner, applied with special care."[30] A further answer, which anticipated later theories of portfolio management, was risk diversification and hedging on a global scale. "Trouble of any kind in any one or two countries is as likely as not to favorably affect some other parts of the globe," declared the guide. Therefore, the investor needed assets and investment schemes from all over the world, including steamships, telegraphs, and coal.[31] The firm did just this. At the registry's 1905 general meeting, Sir John Rolleston, a member of Parliament, pointed to the firm's positions in railway shares, capital issues and debentures, Japanese imperial loans,

Anglo-American telegraph stocks, Canadian railway bonds, the Antwerp waterworks, and the Cunard Steamship Company.[32] Of course, risk management through diversification posed its own challenges, not least those related to reliable information. In a classic pitch from the age of verification, they offered global investment overseen by experts who applied scientific methods to the business of making money.

The final decades of the nineteenth century are considered the heyday of gentlemanly capitalism, when the powers of the government and London's leading financial houses came together to fuel new imperial expansion while making overseas investment both safe and profitable. The globalization of trade and finance is indeed undeniable. In the Atlantic world, real wages and living standards converged dramatically over the final decades of the nineteenth century and first decade of the twentieth. Commodity prices converged as well.[33] Financial globalization also advanced, with the end of the nineteenth century witnessing unprecedented (and only recently surpassed) international capital flows. Between 1870 and 1913, the percentage of British wealth overseas increased from 17 percent to 33 percent. On the eve of the First World War, Britain was exporting 7 percent of its national income.[34] Meanwhile, real interest rates in the Atlantic economies converged, suggesting that capital was crossing borders more freely. Just as technology encouraged commodity price convergence, so too did it play a part in financial integration, as the telegraph linked markets across the Atlantic and allowed hedging through the use of futures markets.

This period of financial globalization and High Empire—Britain spread its reach vertically through Africa while also expanding into numerous territories in the Far East and Pacific—was also one of intense speculation. The increased attention to data, details, and opinion in no way meant that investment became coldly rational. The 1880s saw at least three mining bubbles, and at the end of the century there was even a small bubble in bicycle shares. In what one commentator called the *Fin de Cycle*, there was a boom of flotations between 1895 and 1897 in companies producing tires, tubing, and cycles.[35] As we shall see in the case of mining shares, promoters and investors no longer shied away from identifying their investments as speculation. The term no

longer implied reckless risk taking or unethical financial behavior. Instead, speculation meant (as it does today) buying or selling shares or
commodities simply to benefit from a change in price, rather than to
encourage economic development or earn long-term returns from dividends.[36] This activity became increasingly difficult to separate from investment. In the cotton market, for instance, futures were a form of
speculation on price changes but also a crucial hedge against market
volatility. Even bills of lading, which were held to represent real cotton,
were traded in a speculative fashion.[37] Just as new money flowed into
new assets in the merging space between investment and speculation,
so too did fraudsters and their offerings. Advertisements, court records, novels, and newspapers speak to the profound risk of fraud that
accompanied all sorts of financial capitalism.

The forces that at once enabled speculation and were further
unleashed by it—speed, vast numbers of assets, global financial
information—also served the efforts of those perpetrating frauds. New
mechanisms were needed to enable trust and the trade around which it
was built. As we shall see, investors in South African mining shares
and the cotton traders of Manchester, London, and Liverpool still valued reputation, but the role of sociability in shaping trustworthy behavior was now secondary. Technology was the new arena of social
exchange, and information the means. Investors in both instances
looked not only to the reputations of their trading partners but also to
new systems by which additional information could be obtained and
reputations verified. Forget morality: riches were still the aim, and trust
through verification had become the operating rule.

N • I • N • E

A Gorgeous Vulgarity

I n September 1871, Henry Morton Stanley, according to his own
report, uttered the most famous of imperial greetings: "Dr. Livingstone, I presume." Stanley had traveled thousands of miles and left
scores of dead behind him before he found the missionary and explorer
David Livingstone on the east coast of Lake Tanganyika in East Africa,
in what is now Tanzania. The two men would become good friends, but
they hardly shared the same high-minded ideals. Livingstone was a living icon of empire who had spent years in search of the source of the
Nile. He traveled, he famously observed, in service of the three C's that
were held to embody mid-Victorian England: civilization, commerce,
and Christianity. Stanley's guiding stars, meanwhile, were three A's: acclaim, adventure, and affluence.

Stanley, born John Rowland in Wales, understood from an early
age that the expanding British Empire was ripe terrain for a man on
the make who was willing to remake himself. He became a member of
the Confederate Army, which he deserted to join the U.S. Navy, which
he eventually left to become a journalist, changing his name and the
official details of his eye color and hair color with each move. At the
end of the Civil War, he became a traveling correspondent for James
Gordon Bennett Jr.'s *New York Herald*, traveling in the Ottoman Empire, Zanzibar, and East Africa. Over the next decade, Stanley lived a

famous life on the frontiers of European imperial and pecuniary ambitions.[1] He crossed the entirety of Africa between 1874 and 1877 and played an active part in Leopold II of Belgium's acquisition of the Congo. He was one of a new breed of informal imperial agents who understood, like their predecessors in India and even Latin America, that the expanding imperial frontier was the place to make a name and maybe a fortune. Before his second Africa expedition, Stanley returned to New York a famous and controversial journalist. If he had traveled to his old hunting grounds of New Orleans, he might have met a young man following in his footsteps.

Harry Marks was born in London in 1855, the son of the head of a Reform Jewish congregation. Briefly educated at the Athénée Royale in Brussels, he struck out in the world early, at the age of fifteen, moving to New Orleans, where his father had friends in a commercial house. Again like Stanley, Marks appears to have had a hardscrabble time, working his way by odd jobs up the Mississippi. Eventually, journalism launched him, too. He became, he later claimed, an editor at the *San Antonio Daily Express* during the presidential campaign of 1872 and then a traveling correspondent for the *Galveston Bulletin* before returning to Louisiana to join the staff of the *New Orleans Picayune*. In 1873 he moved to New York, where he obtained a position on the staff of the influential *New York World*. He relentlessly, desperately, pursued opportunities. He wrote columns for other New York papers, including the *Reformer and Jewish Times*, and founded a paper called the *Beer Glass*, which aimed at the temperance crowd by encouraging beer over liquor. He tried, failed, expanded connections, expended connections, and failed better. The *Beer Glass* gave way to the *Postal Card*, which in 1880 gave way to the *Daily Mining News*, which in 1881 became the *Weekly Mining News*. It was in America that Marks claimed to have mastered financial journalism and what he called the "Yankee bounce"—the capacity to gauge and make or break a business in a few dozen words. It was a form of journalism that fed off and fed into an expansionist and creative capitalism, purporting to solve asymmetries of information and limit risk in an increasingly complex market. It was just this sort of journalism that would make his largest success, the *Financial News*, for a time the most influential financial paper in London.

Both Stanley and Marks understood something implicitly about the changing capitalist world around them. Stanley crafted a career around supplying news and services that were increasingly in demand in the burgeoning period of High Empire. European expansion in Africa demanded information and agents on the ground, and he positioned himself to fill these needs. Marks also sensed that the period of global commerce and trade would demand global information. What is more, both men recognized the significant attraction that African resources—rubber, cotton, gold, diamonds—held for European industrialists and investors. Stanley eventually coupled himself with the worst of the coercive, extractive elements of imperial capitalism.[2] Marks, on the other hand, saw in changing financial capitalism a different opportunity. He understood that, as in Lord Thomas Cochrane's day, news still moved the market, but that more formal presentation and more information were needed to inspire confidence in a more complex, even overwhelming, marketplace. Investors wanted data, opinion, and expertise, and global capitalism required sources that conducted something akin to global verification. Marks also recognized that the nature of investment had changed. The country ideology's complaints about credit had long been laid to rest, and the pace and numbers with which new opportunities presented themselves had made the lay investor increasingly uncomfortable. Marks saw the New York and London markets in need of expertise and data and investors who, when given such information, would be free to speculate with their money.

In 1883 Marks returned to London permanently and, with £1,000 from an American investor, established the *Financial and Mining News*, renamed a year later the *Financial News*. He left African exploration to men like Stanley, opting instead for the financial jungle of London. Fin-de-siècle finance has been described as something of a closed world, open mainly to "gentlemanly capitalists" who shared social and educational backgrounds, as well as positions in the convergent power loci of Parliament, the Foreign Office, the Treasury, and the Bank of England. There is some truth to this depiction, but it is only part of the story. All sorts of capitalists, including the Scottish, are left out of this vision—as are the criminal capitalists and the speculators.[3] The final two decades of the century—despite the Panic of 1893 and other downturns—were good years for a man on the make in London. Capitalist ventures, and the trust needed to make them happen, continued despite an awareness of widespread fraud. Only the archetype of the man on the make had changed. As the century neared an end, a new animal hunted credulity: the stock promoter.

"Everything Was Swagger"

At their peak, stock promoters made Beaumont Smith's forgery look frugal and Walter Watts's embezzlement humble. Only now, in a financial world that increasingly welcomed speculation, the fraudsters often acted legally, if on the margins of the law. Men like Stanley and Marks were not so much self-made as self-invented. Their lives were outrageous public performances meant to inspire confidence and encourage greed. Henry Lawson, Ernest Terah Hooley, Horatio Bottomley, and Whitaker Wright were some of the more famous men who played this role. They used ad agencies, newspapers, jobbers, puffers, and men of all titles to sell shares in mines, minerals, bicycles, rubber tires, and electric trams. It was no longer news of Napoleon's death that moved the market but the likes of Hooley, the "Napoleon of finance," who at his peak owned two country estates and held political office in Cambridgeshire and the City. Such public positions and displays of wealth were keys to their success. "Everything was swagger," observed one publication of Whitaker Wright. "Swagger directors, swagger offices, swagger bankers, a swagger house at the West End, a swagger palace down at Surrey, a swagger yacht down at Cowes, swagger entertainments—all matched each other. The whole thing was a gorgeous vulgarity—a magnificent burlesque of business."[4]

The late Victorian and early Edwardian periods saw a dramatic and democratic expansion in their consumer culture, in everything from seaside holidays to department stores. It should come as no surprise that Thorstein Veblen, the American economist and sociologist, would coin his famous phrase "conspicuous consumption" in these years. Veblen recognized, like so many of his contemporaries, that the world was now made of strangers—what he called "transient observers"—and that consumption of goods, including clothes, was a way of communicating wealth and importance. It was just this system that the writers Edward Bulwer-Lytton and Anthony Trollope had described when they showed how blurred the line was between an epic fraudster and a man of wealth and standing. Veblen did not see it much differently: "The thief or swindler who has gained great wealth by his delinquency has a better chance than the small thief of escaping the rigorous penalty of the law and some good repute accrues to him from his increased wealth and from his spending the irregularly acquired possessions in a seemly manner."[5] Nor did Eustace Clare Grenville Murray, one of the period's most biting and controversial satirists, see it any differently. An understudy of Dickens and the bastard son of the Duke of Buckingham and Chandos, one of England's greatest landowners, Grenville Murray set out to depict not merely the pretense of power and society but the fakery behind it. He especially singled out "Adventurers," people of either sex who preyed on the credulous in all circles of London society. He saw, in short, Dickens's Veneerings everywhere:

> Let any man having a large number of acquaintances reflect a moment, and, if he be in the least observant, he will perceive that one or two of them are not precisely as they should be. There is something about them which makes them different from other people. They have interesting stories to tell about themselves, they are brilliant talkers, uncommonly amiable, full of plans or expectations. . . . And to sum up the whole matter, the worst rogues of all amongst Adventurers are generally those who succeed, and who come to no sort of harm. We find them in every walk of life, and lift our hats to them. They are very powerful.[6]

Consume with confidence, and make it conspicuous: that could have been Horatio Bottomley's motto. The son of a tailor's cutter in Bethnal Green in East London, he left Wright to do the yachting in Cowes, opting instead for women and horses. With surprising honesty, he would later write of himself: "I may observe that in the year 1890 I occupied a fairly respectable position in society. I had a West-end residence and a little country retreat, and enjoyed all the surroundings of unobtrusive prosperity. . . . I seldom, however, got intoxicated when entertaining my guests, and consequently little was known concerning my early career or exact position. In my presence I was spoken of as a great financier—in my absence, as a successful company promoter."[7] Bottomley held no illusions about his position in society. He understood that promoters and speculators were still subject to scorn by some, but also that the line between financier and speculator was flimsy and getting more so.

The mechanics by which Bottomley and others conducted their flotations were rather simple. They would buy up a private company with little working capital and then overcapitalize it by selling shares to the public. With far more capital than the business required, the promoters would issue themselves large dividends on shares they had purchased at much lower prices. They also commonly used working capital to buy land or pay sham vendors, who would then funnel the money back to the promoters. Meanwhile, the original business was largely neglected; once it failed, the firm would be "reconstructed." People who had purchased shares either lost them or were offered heavily diluted shares in a new concern that took over the liabilities of the old. The money to be made with this scheme was considerable. In the 1890s, Whitaker Wright raised the combined capital of a series of mining companies from £400,000 to upward of £5 million. Henry Lawson brought the working capital of Daimler Motor Company from £6,000 to £100,000 in a single year. Ernest Terah Hooley took on Bovril, a company with an original working capital of £400,000, and recapitalized it at £2.5 million.[8]

Such investment schemes could not work repeatedly on swagger alone. As George Robb points out in *White-Collar Crime*, their promoters also surrounded themselves with experts of many types. "Lured by the presence of distinguished directors, bankers, auditors, solicitors and brokers on a company's prospectus," writes Robb, "investors assumed that these experts had already examined the issue's *bona fides* and that they would not have lent their good name to anything questionable."[9] If capital was to stretch globally and the market was to show interest in new assets—some of which patently claimed to limit risk—new information was needed, and new types of experts were developed to match this need. Here is a crucial point: the credulity of investors was often the product not just of promoters but of the public trust in experts. Investors could not personally inspect a mine in South Africa or California, so they looked to experts for verification. It was in this milieu that the financial newspaper experienced a boom.

A number of promoters, recognizing the press's role in providing public expertise, bought or started financial pages. The *Statist*, the *Echo*, and the *Financial Gazette* were all owned at one point or another by promoters. At its founding, the chairman of the august *Financial Times* was none other than Horatio Bottomley. But no promoters enjoyed the level of success in the newspaper business that Harry Marks did. His *Financial News* became arguably the most important financial paper of the century's end. Marks was an enterprising, creative, and influential editor; he was also a shameless stock promoter. His paper, and specifically the legal problems he encountered in promoting a South African concern called the Rae Gold Mining Company, provide a good window into trust, crime, and capitalism in the age of verification.

The many holders of fraudulent exchequer bills who testified before parliamentary select committees in 1841 made it clear that reputation played a vital role in their trading habits, an approach made dangerous by the contagious effect a bad player could have in a network dependent upon reputation. Nearly fifty years later, when Harry Marks and other directors and shareholders in Rae Gold Mining were given the opportunity to explain in court why they promoted or held mining shares, the rules of trust had changed. Investors talked about it differently. They distributed it differently. Reputation remained important, but expertise and access to information were increasingly prized. Investors talked less about whom they knew and more about what they knew and where they had gotten the information. Witnesses, attempting to establish their responsible behavior, did not draw attention to the usual course of business as much as to their verification procedures. Even as it came to speculation, verification was now the rule, but its processes often left individuals both dependent on and vulnerable to sources of expertise. Harry Marks understood this. His journalistic ambitions and his financial investments suggest that he grasped early that morality mattered little in the market and that trust was now built and distributed through organizations with access to information and expertise.

The Victorian Internet

The newspaper market that Marks entered as a proprietor in 1883 had been revolutionized over the past three decades. As late as the 1850s, news from crucial places like the Cape Colony in southern Africa still traveled on ship in the form of letters or overseas papers, taking up to two months to arrive. Correspondents remained dependent upon settler colony newspapers.[10] Such networks of print created webs of transatlantic and imperial connections. In this imperial public sphere, sermons, commercial reports, magazines, and local newspapers circulated along commercial routes, often skipping the metropole and traveling from one imperial locale to another directly.[11]

By the 1870s, however, the speed of the telegraph had superseded the slow pace of shipborne communication. A story could travel to Bombay and back in a day. Tom Standage has even gone as far as to call this globalization of information the "Victorian Internet."[12] Thanks to the telegraph, information no longer had to travel physically: it could pass in electric code through cables. The world's first submarine telegraph cable was laid in India, across the Hooghly River in Calcutta in 1839. By 1864, India and what would later become Iraq were in instant communication.[13] In 1871, India, Saigon, and Hong Kong were connected by cable. In 1873, Europe was connected with Brazil and Argentina.

In 1869, the Agency Alliance Treaty effectively carved up the distribution of news by telegraph into spheres of influence: Reuters, the British agency, got the British Empire and the Far East; Havas, the French agency, would cover the French Empire, Italy, Spain, and Portugal; Wolff, of Germany, would cover a territory extending east from Germany into Russia.[14] The globalization of rapid communication had an undeniably international dimension, but it was a British-led phenomenon. Aided by deep capital markets, the unrivaled demand of

British traders, and the support of the government, British telegraph firms came to dominate global communication. John Pender's Eastern Telegraph Company, which in 1870 provided an uninterrupted link between England and India, soon had cables stretching to Australia, Asia, and Brazil. By 1890 it controlled 45 percent of the world's telegraph cables. Of the forty-one cable ships in the world in 1904, twenty-eight were British, with the French possessing just five.[15]

The rise of mass information, however, should not be confused with the democratization of communication. In 1851, messengers and porters in England and Wales, for instance, earned on average £88.88 per year. In 1860, meanwhile, the Associated Press could spend upward of $2,000 a day on these cables. In 1872, when Henry Morton Stanley telegraphed two letters of Livingstone's on to New York, the cost came to £1,600, more than the entire initial cost of his expedition. While the price of a transatlantic telegram dropped, on average, by 15 percent per year between 1865 and 1905, the cost was still too high for an individual to make frequent use of the telegraph—though that, too, would change.[16]

The effects of the telegraph were remarkable. In 1870 Western Europeans sent approximately forty million telegrams. By 1913, that number for Europeans had grown to 329 million telegrams.[17] Ships could now leave port without a determined destination. A steamer might head toward the Cape or Egypt or Argentina and let its final port of call be determined along the way by market conditions, passed on via the telegraph. "Futures" markets for agricultural commodities, pioneered in Chicago, developed extensively. In New York and Liverpool, for instance, the "spot" trades on cotton—which took place, as the term suggests, on the spot in real time—dropped noticeably after the development of the telegraph. Hedging over great distances became easier, as did arbitrage.[18] Tracking such information, along with the location of ships, became an industry in itself. Shipping information became the largest expenditure of Lloyd's after 1874, with most of the money spent on foreign telegrams. By the 1890s, Lloyd's had 40 telegraph stations in the United Kingdom and another 118 oversees.[19]

By the time Marks returned to London to establish his own paper, two revolutions in news were well established. The first, enabled by the telegraph, concerned the speed with which news was delivered. The second was readers' access to news. The repeal of stamp duties plus technological advances in the production of newspapers, such as steam presses and the linotype, meant that more people could afford newspapers than ever before.[20]

Marks, the man who struck out at fifteen to New Orleans and later wandered to Texas and took on New York, was not going to remove himself to the newsroom of the *Times*, editing provincial news for library readers. Instead, he put himself at the head of another major development in London's newspapers—the growth of the financial press. The Victorian financial article that might appear in the *Times* or *Morning Chronicle* had not changed dramatically since the *Times* reported the surge of activity in the Stock Exchange following Cochrane's fraud. Coverage of Beaumont Smith's fraud was extensive and opinionated, but the issue was treated more as a matter of government than of finance. On questions of politics, established newspapers had opinions and offered extensive comment, but on questions of commerce, particularly as it came to new concerns, they made no extensive practice of offering opinion or commentary. The *Financial News* would later say as much: "In our great morning papers politics and finance were and still are unequally yoked together. The practical interests of the country are subordinated: the City has to be content with the odd concerns that can be spared from Westminster, Old Bailey and the racecourse."[21] It was the advent of the *Financial News*, writes the historian Dilwyn Porter, that "challenged most decisively the staid conventions of the mid-Victorian money article."[22] In 1884, a guide to the press listed thirty-two finance and investment papers in Britain and Ireland. Ten years later there were fifty, and by 1904 the number had grown to at least ninety-two. On the eve of the First World War, at least 104 separate papers were publishing on financial issues.[23] For a market constantly reinventing itself, a new paradigm of information was well received if not needed. These papers offered explicit advice and criticism, as well as the opportunity for exposure and advertising. "A new development of British journalism is embodied in our columns," the *Financial News* declared.[24]

What did these new developments look like? More important, how did they go about earning the trust of their readers? Not unlike the

Financial Review of Reviews, which would later quote frequently from the *Financial News*, Marks's paper centered its pitch on a combination of information and expertise. The City was swarming with joint stock ventures and sovereign debt offerings. The *Financial News*, through a combination of global prices, City scuttlebutt, and financial specialists, could guide its readers through the complex waters of global finance and help them steer clear of the City's thousands of sham offerings.

Readers!! £13 Million in the Black

The *Financial News*'s columns might roughly be divided into two types, which, though seemingly at odds, in fact reinforced each other. On one hand, the paper offered objective numbers; on the other, it analyzed the potential behind the numbers and prospectuses that were meant to inspire potential investors. It was this combination of approaches that the liberal economist J. A. Hobson mocked with scare quotes when he wrote that the new financial journalism "imposes 'facts' and 'opinions' on the business classes."[25]

The late nineteenth century saw a boom in statistical knowledge, including, for the first time, retail indexes produced by the government.[26] The market, it seems, was ever more eager for numbers. Like the *Financial Review of Reviews*, the *Financial News* offered timely prices on hundreds of shares, debentures, and sovereign bonds. The tickers from the Stock Exchanges of New York and London came to meet in its pages. The front page normally carried a column on the London Stock Exchange, one on the New York Stock Exchange, and one on mining endeavors. Most of the rest was taken up with price listings. On July 1, 1884, the paper listed thirty-four American railway firms that were issuing interest payments on bonds on that day. It also contained prices of 68 shares from the New York Exchange and 160 from the London Exchange, as well as share prices of at least 91 mining companies, the majority being colonial or foreign. An additional column offered over 150 other stock and bond prices for, among other things, banks, American securities, and Canadian railways. That was page one. Page three covered the financials of at least eighty-one American railways—Ohio Central, Flint West, Oregon Southern, Texas and

San Francisco, and so on—over a two-year period and listed the capital stock and bonded debt for another fifty railways. An investor could also find traffic rates for a two-year period for foreign railways, from India to Sweden to Buenos Aires to Turkey, and bond and debt reports for nearly forty British railways. An investor in mines could find reports on thirty-six British mines, including shares issued and paid up, total dividends, date of last dividend issued, and total bonds and debentures issued. The same was provided for over forty foreign mines.[27] This was an onslaught of information to match the market's onslaught of opportunities, both good and bad.

In addition, there were reports on an array of the world's markets beyond the doings at the exchanges. An issue from July 1884 included separate reports on American produce markets, Indian salt taxes, French iron mines, Mexican mines, the American cotton market, Indian gold discoveries in Assam, the Bank of France, the status of the Antwerp and French ports, the West Coast of America Telegraph Company, the Rio de Janeiro Gas Company, the salt tax in India, the growth of property values in New York, the financial status of Norway, and the state of the Canadian Pacific Railway.[28]

The *Financial News* also offered expert opinion, delivered with confidence and bite. It not only provided numbers and inspected the potential behind the numbers but also set about making or destroying companies. Not unlike the period's playwrights, novelists, and satirists, the editors of the *Financial News* saw fraudulent schemes and shady players everywhere. A lead story in February 1886 announced, "The American Markets: An Unsuccessful Attempt to Advance Prices"; the article noted that "the upward movement was attributed to manipulation and to the speculative buying of the Morgan party." An article in the next column announced details of "An Impecunious Stock and Share Broker." The next column offered share prices.[29]

The most dangerous predators in the City, Marks and his writers asserted, were stock promoters. A lengthy piece in summer 1886 explored the "species" of promoter. "Every lane in the City swarms with them. . . . Like the strolling player of the last century, he may be a welcome guest at night and be hunted out of the village next morning by the beadle. The promoter is a species of animal in financial zoology whose position has not been clearly defined. And the City does not quite know what to make of him. It fears him, distrusts him, looks down on him and runs after him, all in a breath."[30] The prospectus remained these promoters' chief instrument. A certain skepticism of such documents was commonplace, and the *Financial News* was hardly unique in drawing attention to the tempting danger they presented. The same year that Marks established his paper, Thomas Rickard published *The Gold Fields of the Transvaal*. It was a guidebook, not unlike the one written by Gregor MacGregor's Thomas Strangeways, that was meant to instruct investors on the ins and outs of mining and the potential risks and rewards in opening and managing a mine. Rickard sought to warn off eager investors: "We feel compelled to say that the prospectuses of certain companies formed to operate in the Transvaal, are by no means exempt from the vice so common with this class of manifestoes." He continued: "They hold out hopes which, if not absolute impossibilities, are on their very face gigantic improbabilities."[31] The *Economist*, meanwhile, faulted prospectuses not only for what they promised but also for what they failed to divulge. "Much of the fraud and deceit at present practiced," wrote the publication near century's end, "would be checked if it were made incumbent upon promoters and others concerned in the flotation of a company to disclose fully in the prospectus all those matters which it is essential for an intending investor to know in order to enable him to judge the merits of the undertaking."[32] In 1886, however, reform of director liability laws was decades away.

Yet amid such skepticism, the market continued to advance fraudulent schemes, and the prospectus remained a central instrument for assessing new offerings. Nobody suggested that they should be done away with but, rather, that they should be more transparent and subject to greater scrutiny. Not surprisingly, the *Financial News* pitched itself as an expert resource for vetting new offerings. Two years into its existence, the editors proudly declared: "We publish a newspaper to print the news, and we print all that is obtainable, no matter whom it helps or whom it hurts."[33] Around its second anniversary, the paper began trumpeting its record, pointing to advice it had given regarding gold mines in South Africa. "The conditions of successful mining speculation have been made as clear to outsiders as to the experts, and the game has become more equal," declared the editors, adding: "In these columns people have been reading for months back about the wonderful new goldfields in South Africa which our cautious and careful contemporaries are now discovering. The subject has not been treated by us as a passing marvel, but in a practical and useful spirit. Every week its progress has been recorded, and the inevitable sequel of a mining boom has been confidently foretold."[34]

Such was the *Financial News* vision of itself: reliable source to the outside investor, informed expert on the mines of South Africa, reliable provider of information for speculation but with a vision for long-term trends. Like other financial papers and reviews, it claimed to offer analysis and expertise that the individual investor could not access alone. It vetted offerings and did so in the name of the lay investor, the "outsider."

Marks would eventually quantify just what this advice had been worth. The *Financial News*, he observed in 1890,

> has warned the public against going into companies which were withdrawn or have since failed, their aggregate capital being thirteen millions; it has given timely warning of every important decline in securities, and in most cases of impending crises; it has warned the public against inflation of Nitrate snares; it predicted the panic in Argentine securities, and advised holders of stock to sell; the advice has been sound, the information invariably accurate, and those who have acted upon it have saved money where they have sold, and made money where they have bought.[35]

Thirteen million pounds over seven years—that was the bottom line, in black, that the paper claimed for its readers. But Marks did not make the claim in an editorial or in one of the paper's self-congratulatory self-histories. He offered it while in the witness box of London's Central Criminal Court, where in December 1890, amid the ruckus of free market capitalism, he was suing a Californian called George Washington Butterfield for libel.

Such suits had grown increasingly common. Between 1815 and 1913, the Old Bailey, the Central Criminal Court in London, conducted 653 trials for libel. These numbers may not be representative of all of England or Britain, or even London. They do not include trials for seditious libel brought by the government instead of individuals, but these were nowhere near as numerous.[36] As the records of the Old Bailey show, the bringing of libel charges by individuals against other individuals is largely a phenomenon of the second half of the century. Only 45 of the 653 cases were brought before 1850. In the subsequent decade there were twenty-six cases, or just under 4 percent of the total. Fifty-two cases were tried in the 1860s, and 101 in the 1870s. The number grew to 163 in the 1880s and fell to 112 in the 1890s. The Old Bailey hosted 154 in the final thirteen years before the outbreak of the First World War. All of which is to say that more than 80 percent of the libel cases brought over a roughly one-hundred-year period occurred from 1870 onward.[37]

Butterfield, the defendant, and Marks, the plaintiff, were no strangers. The year before, in June 1889, Butterfield had sued Marks for libel following a negative report issued in the *Financial News* about a California gold mining company Butterfield was floating in London. Such cases were commonplace. Over the previous two years, from 1888 to early 1890, Marks and the *Financial News* had been connected with two other libel cases, both of which reflected poorly on Marks's and his paper's names. In 1888, the paper called the promoter of a bottle company a liar for having claimed the *Financial News* sought payment for positive coverage. The promoter won his case. In early 1890, a separate case was brought against Marks's brother for attempting to blackmail a gold mining company with poor press coverage. As the Old Bailey statistics showed, reputation had become an increasingly litigious affair. The first round of *Butterfield v. Marks* went against the Californian. Butterfield was obligated to pay £940 of legal costs for Marks, who claimed that his actual costs were £3,000 to £4,000.

The growth in such libel cases represented, in part, a search for an official vindication of character. Members of Parliament, solicitors, and newspaper proprietors had long disagreed on how publications should officially rectify potentially erroneous character defamation.

John Hollams, a solicitor in the City and a veteran of thirty-four years' worth of libel trials, did not feel the scene of the crime was the right space for atonement: "It never seems to me that explanations or apologies are quite satisfactory; they do not remove the evil which the injured man has sustained. It may sometimes be the only mode of redress, but it cannot be considered as curing the evil. It is a great misfortune to a private individual to have his name dragged before the public; and it is poor consolation a day or two afterwards to see a paragraph saying that the previous statement was not true."[38] But something else was also going on in many of these trials. Butterfield, for one, paid none of his debt, opting instead to declare bankruptcy. This, too, had become a familiar practice. In testimony before a parliamentary committee on libel a decade earlier, Francis Larken Soames had been asked about the reliability of legal costs as a deterrent to libel suits. Soames, a solicitor at Lincoln's Inn Fields and for ten years the solicitor to the *Times*, estimated that eight of ten actions for libel were brought purely as speculation. Frequently, these cases were "brought by persons who have no real grievance and no means of paying costs if they lose, simply in the hope of extorting a compromise." Isaac Latimer, the proprietor of the *West Daily Mercury*, a paper of more than thirty years, gave similar testimony. "You have felt the pressure of speculative actions being brought against you by men of straw?" "Yes, I have," he responded.[39]

Though bankrupt, Butterfield scraped together funds to print pamphlets and placards attacking Marks. "Placards were posted to my house," Marks would later testify, "and to all my friends; every friend and associate I had; I had them myself, they were posted to my house addressed to me, and in a female handwriting to my wife." Butterfield's pamphlet attacked Marks on two seemingly disconnected fronts.[40] They accused him of having swindled his American mistress, Annie Koppel, and having left her and their child in New York, absconding to London under a fake name. As would turn out to be more important, the pamphlet also charged Marks with using his paper to puff stocks of which he himself was a promoter. Readers in the City and West End learned that in 1886 and 1887 Marks had been a promoter and prominent shareholder in a venture called Rae Gold Mining. Rather than serving the outsider, the pamphlet suggested, the *Financial News* had served Marks, talking up the venture as he sold off shares. The first charge was meant to impugn Marks's character; the second, the integrity of his newspaper.

Marks responded by going after Butterfield with an aggressive public display. He had the placards announcing the warrant for Butterfield's arrest posted around the City and even on the walls outside Butterfield's house. Late one evening, Butterfield was seen entering his house, but two detective sergeants from the City were denied entrance. In the morning, they followed him through the streets of London and, showing him the warrant, escorted him to the City for trial.

The trial spanned ten days, the courtroom filled with friends and enemies of both sides who reacted to testimony with applause and boos. The court record—composed only of answers, not the lawyers' questions—runs to nearly one hundred pages and often reads, as the *Saturday Review* commented, as endless and unintelligible.[41] The trial serves as an undeniable reminder that the question of character remained prominent in the late nineteenth century. More important, the testimony of numerous directors and shareholders of Rae Gold Mining, as well as employees of the *Financial News*, showed just how these new financial papers went about inspiring confidence and how they were read and received by investors. Indeed, the case of Rae Gold Mining and the *Financial News*, as played out in the courtroom of the Old Bailey, shows how commonplace speculation had become and how crucial the information provided by experts had become in speculative endeavors.

When Harry Met Annie

Once the trial began, in December 1890, revenge showed itself to be a double-edged sword. As Oscar Wilde discovered in his 1895 libel case against the Marquess of Queensberry ("I am the prosecutor," Wilde would famously proclaim, when put on the defensive), the plaintiff in a libel suit was liable to have much of his or her life exposed. Opening the trial in the witness box in Marks's suit was Annie Koppel, née Doyle, Marks's New York paramour. A good portion of her testimony, as well as that of Marks and other witnesses, concerned the courtship, the cou-

ple's love affair, and the baby that might have come of it. Koppel's and
Butterfield's lawyers, aware of the accusations to come, took care to depict her as a woman of character and good standing before her encounter with Marks. "There is no truth whatever in the suggestion that
during my husband's lifetime I worked in a shop, or was in any employment, or that I had sought for means to live," she declared. "In my husband's lifetime we lived in a fairly good position."[42] The picture of
bourgeois respectability, she had been the mother of two, possessed
jewelry and furniture, and was wife to a deceased husband who owned
a relevant newspaper.

Marks, according to Koppel, had conducted himself with anything but respectability. They had never met before her husband's passing, but on the evening after their first encounter, he showed up at her
door. "I thought at the time it was a very audacious thing to do, for a
young man I had never seen till that afternoon, to call," she said, clari-
fying, "I gave him nothing to eat, drink, or smoke. . . . We talked about
business, strictly business; there was no love-making, no approach to
anything of the kind."[43] Maybe not on the first night, but the lovemaking commenced without much delay, based, she claimed repeatedly,
upon the promise of marriage. According to Koppel, her landlords on
29th Street and then on St. Marks in the East Village were both under
the impression that she either was or would soon be Marks's wife. Soon,
however, Marks's behavior changed. He rakishly bragged of other women
and at one time went to England for vacation under a pseudonym. To
end the romance, she claimed, Marks had her arrested and briefly imprisoned for insanity after her supposed destruction of his rooms.

Was there any proof, Marks's lawyers asked, that he had promised
marriage? "I have no paper in which I have ever suggested he promised
to marry me," she responded. "I do not know why I did not call on him
as a man of honour, who had seduced me under promise of marriage,
to fulfill his promise." There was no paper, suggested Marks, whose testimony came five days later, because there was no promise. "I became
criminally intimate with Mrs. Koppel," though, he added, "that inti-
macy was never procured by any promise of marriage on my part. . . .
There is not one syllable of pretence for the suggestion that there was
any talk of marriage then or at any other time." Marks depicted Koppel

as mentally unstable. "I was constantly watched," he testified. "I had my footsteps dogged, and on going home at night I found a servant on the doorstep. . . . This went on for six or seven weeks." She wrecked his rooms and even went to a lawyer and made libelous claims that Marks had stolen her jewelry and her husband's watch. When he confronted her, Marks testified, she apologized and said only that "she had been mad with me because I had not been to see her." Annie's Harry was a smooth-talking swindler who took advantage of a naïve innocent; Harry's Annie was a jealous, delusional liar who stalked him around the streets of New York. At the end of all this, Koppel claimed to have been left with Marks's daughter. He protested: "I had no doubt that she was *enceinte*," he stated. "I had a doubt as to being the father of her child." When asked why he had such doubts, Marks feigned taking the high road. "I had reasons," he stated. "I would rather not state what they were, unless you rule, my Lord, that I must; I had a doubt as to my being the father."

Love affairs that result in libel suits seldom have happy endings. Although much of the trial's first days concerned Marks's behavior toward a recently widowed woman, the question of paternity did not dominate the trial, nor did issues of lovemaking or courtship. Amorous affairs were secondary to financial ones. The attorneys on both sides seemed to be as interested in Marks's treatment of Koppel's jewels and money as they were in her newborn daughter. Character here was about love but more about money.

"I became very much attached to him," Koppel stated. "I would have signed anything he asked me." "I had no want of confidence in him then," she replied to a follow-up question. Her testimony was that of a mother, a naïve lover worthy of empathy, and it sold. Her amorous credulity came first at the price of her deceased husband's paper, the *Reformer*, which Marks took over on the promise of improving its returns. Soon the newspaper was gone, sold, and Marks took checks Koppel received from her late husband's insurance societies, including $1,000 from the Forrester's Lodge. "My statement," she said in court, "is that Marks possessed himself of all my husband left, and never gave me a halfpenny except 10 dollars." Such behavior would have resonated with a London judge and jury. Female stock- and bondholders, often widows, were common in the nineteenth century. At midcentury, women made up nearly half of the investors in the Bank of England (though they held just 30 percent of the shares).[44] Though all male, the jury members would have known women who had come into wealth at the passing of their husbands.

Marks began selling jewelry and other household goods, Koppel claimed, forcing her to sign the receipts over to him. He was, by her account, captivating, amorous, duplicitous, and greedy, a man after means by any means. "I do not know that I knew I was signing receipts; they never let me know what I was signing," she claimed. "Probably I was drunk, as Mr. Marks has often made me drunk."[45] She was left largely destitute, unable to pay for a case against Marks, pawning jewelry and furniture to pay rent on her apartment on St. Marks.

These could not have been an easy two days for Koppel, recounting the death of her husband, the birth of a daughter without a father willing to claim her, and a love affair that ended in destitution and brief imprisonment. Nonetheless, she had crossed the Atlantic to testify, knowing, as she must have, that those two days might be even worse for Marks. He was married, the owner of an important newspaper with capital raised up to £100,000, and a connected man in the City.[46] A maker and destroyer of concerns, he had recently acquired a country-seat at Callis Court near Broadfield, had appeared in *Vanity Fair*, and, representing Marylebone on the London County Council, had evident parliamentary aspirations. Such accounts of lewdness, he knew, were ripe material for society journalists and potentially injurious of his character. But treatment of Marks's relationship with Koppel was not dominated by Victorian prudishness. At question was an alleged pattern of behavior. Was it indeed Marks's modus operandi to use a position of power, authority, and trust to serve his own ends? He had done so not only as a lover, Butterfield's attorneys suggested, but also as an editor.

He Said, They Bought

Nearly four years before the trial, in 1887, the *Financial News* had run the prospectus of a firm called the Rae Gold Mining Company. According to the prospectus, the directors of Rae Gold Mining sought to raise £75,000 capital, with £25,000 in shares reserved for allotment to the holder of the South African land where the mine was located. Most of the prospectus was filled with expert testimony on the mine's location and the company's capacity to navigate local challenges. "The Property has been favorably reported upon by the following eminent authorities, in whom the Directors have perfect confidence," declared the prospectus. The reports of expert engineers and miners—W. H. Peaning, late of Her Majesty's Geological Survey of England, and J. E. Gunister, late of the gold commission of the Lydenburg Goldfields—could be inspected at the company's offices.[47] The company assured investors of the mines' abundant resources and of its own solid management and local know-how: "Several Transvaal properties owned in England have so far failed to realize the expectations entertained of them, partly by reason of inefficient management and partly because they have been overweighed with excessive capital and expenditure. . . . It is intended in the management of this Company to follow closely upon the lines adopted by the local Companies." Rae Gold Mining promised to merge global finance and local knowledge, offering a route to success predicated on its ability to overcome problems of distance and knowledge.

The Rae prospectus took a familiar rhetorical stance, distancing itself from failures and pointing to successes. There were, on both points, many cases to point to. Both Henry Morton Stanley and Marks may have been apprenticed in the United States, but their mature ambition was directed toward Africa and Britain's swelling imperial domains there. Cecil Rhodes, for one, had ambitions of extending a British railway and thus British commerce from Cairo to Cape Town. The British had occupied Egypt in 1882 and fought the Mehdi's Army at the Omdurman in the Sudan, with Churchill witnessing the slaughter of upward of ten thousand Ansar, or dervishes, at the hands of British and Egyptian forces. To the south, at the Shangani River in 1893, Rhodes and his British South African Company solidified their mining frontiers in a battle that claimed at least fifteen hundred Matabele. It was of this expanding empire that the British historian J. R. Seeley famously observed in 1884, "We seem, as it were, to have conquered and peopled half the world in a fit of absence of mind."[48]

For men with mining interests like Cecil Rhodes and Harry Marks, the Transvaal was the most tempting of these new locations. In the mid-1880s, following early discoveries in 1870, large reefs of gold were found in Moodie's Mountains, Heidelberg, and Witwatersrand (the Rand). The Transvaal—whose southern boundary began some seven hundred miles north of Cape Town, extending four hundred miles farther north to the Limpopo River and west to the Kalahari Desert—was an independent Boer republic, but British capital and miners flooded in. At century's end, British capital was invested in gold mines in India, West Australia, Queensland, New Zealand, British Columbia, Rhodesia, and the Transvaal. The mines in South Africa were the most important of these, attracting nearly three times as much capital as all mining activities in Canada or Australia.[49]

The press would play an especially crucial part in encouraging the era's mining booms. On the ground, men like Rhodes expanded the minable territories through sheer will, coercion, and violence. To do so, they needed capital from investors, who were urged on by the presses in London. J. A. Hobson was one of the fiercest and most celebrated critics of the financial and economic dimensions of empire. As he saw it, the flight of British capital abroad led to stagnating job creation and wages for the working class in Britain itself. His targets included not only the creators of the imperial channels by which money traveled, but also the press. In his most famous work, *Imperialism*, published in 1900, the section on the press was titled "Economic Parasites of Imperialism." "Apart from the financial press, and financial ownership of the general press," Hobson wrote, "the City has notoriously exercised a subtle and abiding influence upon leading London newspapers."[50] Whether the City influenced the press or the press fed share fever in the City, the opportunities for investment coupled with detailed reports on those opportunities produced a knowledge conducive to trust and financial exchange in what were otherwise very risky plays.

Though Hobson wrote this work at the turn of the century, the *Financial News* of the 1880s would have been an obvious target for his ire. Marks's paper was consistently bullish throughout the 1886 gold boom. In August of that year it reported: "Goldfields have the providential quality of turning up when they are badly wanted." The paper compared the effects of South African gold to those of South American silver in the seventeenth century and California gold in the mid-nineteenth, adding: "Where the big strike is to be is not yet apparent, but the premonitory symptoms of it are strong. There is an electric feeling in the air which portends the important event."[51] By the next month, the paper was running reports from South African newspapers that focused not on potential but on present riches. The *Financial News* ran a report from the *Grahamstown Journal*: "The development of gold mining in South Africa—for it can no longer be limited to the Transvaal Republic—is one of such rapidity that the figures of today's accounts are to-morrow the facts of primitive history."[52] The *Financial News* heaped praise on its own coverage of South African gold mines in its special October 1886 supplement. "In these columns people have been reading for months back about the wonderful new goldfields in South Africa which our cautious and careful contemporaries are now discovering. The subject has not been treated by us as a passing marvel, but in a practical and useful spirit. Every week its progress has been recorded, and the inevitable sequel of a mining boom has been confidently foretold."[53] Share prices of the Transvaal Gold Exploration and Land Company, the chief Transvaal mining venture listed in the *Financial News*, moved dramatically, from a low of under £8 in July to almost £16 near mid-October, before dropping back to settle around £7 near Christmas.

In the wake of unpredictable price movement and unequivocally positive coverage of the Transvaal, Rae Gold Mining published its prospectus in the *Financial News* on January 15, 1887. On that same day, the paper offered on its second page an initial assessment of the new company: "The Rae (Transvaal) Gold Mining Company, the prospectus of which is issued today, comes into existence under very favourable auspices," began the report.

> Its promoters have evidently profited from the experience of previous English mining in the Transvaal, and they have been careful to avoid the errors by which they have suffered. The property has been favourably reported upon by authorities of undoubted responsibility, including one member of the board of directors, who has personally visited and examined it. . . . Under such conditions the Rae has every

element of success, and we believe that its shares will prove a very safe and remunerative investment. Judging by the demand for shares which existed yesterday afternoon already, they are likely to prove a good speculation as well.[54]

The following day, the *Financial News* published the report of a correspondent from the *Kimberley Independent* who described "improving prospects in the Transvaal." On the 17th, the paper again ran the Rae Gold Mining prospectus.

This was no slow rollout but something closer to a media blitz. Such dispatches and official advertisements were not the only way the paper encouraged readers to invest. As an institution to which potential investors could turn for information they could otherwise not get, the newspaper was a source for answers to very specific investment questions. Its second page frequently contained a section called "Answers to Correspondents," in which readers who wrote in to the *Financial News* could have their questions answered in print. But because the *Financial News* did not print the question, readers could feel safe that they would be the only ones able to act upon the advice. The section was an anonymous investment advice column, the average reader knowing neither who answered the query nor what shares were under discussion. On January 16, the paper advised a reader who had written in under the name "Suburban": "Suburban—The fellow is a swindler who trades under a half dozen aliases, and has victimized hundreds of people. You will gain nothing by suing him. Your best course would be to hand him over to the police." Another reader, "Plutus," had two questions, one of which was answered: "We think very well of the Rae (Transvaal) Gold Mines." Two days later, the paper offered more advice:

Seacombe—Fair.

Lynn—(1) Yes (2) Yes.

Nemo—We think well of the concern.

Dollard—We should advise you to hold.

Constant Reader—The committee has had a fit of morals

The next reader had four questions, which were answered: "F.D.—(1) Fair. (2 and 3) No. (4) The Rae (Transvaal) Gold Mining Company is a good mining investment." In the forty-six answers offered on that day, Rae Gold Mining was the only company named explicitly. The company was mentioned again on the 27th and the 31st and on February 1. In total, Rae was named nine times in the paper's "Answers to Correspondents" section.

According to witnesses in Marks's libel trial, this advice worked. James White, a clerk in Hammersmith, testified to the paper's power. "I then wrote to the editor of the *Financial News* for a cheap mining investment," he stated, and then read aloud the response, which declared that Rae had "energetic management" and that the editors "had no reason to doubt [the company] would prove a very profitable investment." He promptly bought thirty shares. The clerk added: "I had no knowledge that Marks was a promoter." Other investors also testified to having followed the potential of the goldfields in South Africa in the financial press. Charles Dawson Philpott was a bank manager of more than three decades' experience who had established and managed the South Kensington branch of the London and Provincial Bank. He was also Marks's brother-in-law. "I saw," he testified, "these favourable reports published in the *Financial News* as they came home, and in the *Standard* and *Times*, and every other paper." From the answers recorded by the court reporter, it is difficult to tell exactly what Marks himself thought the *Financial News*'s role was in promoting the stock, but it is clear what he wanted it to be. "I was desirous that the public should contribute to the mine," he stated, adding, presumably of the featured article on the venture, "I think such a leaderette as this was calculated to influence the public mind."[55]

Such influence was far different from that of, say, the *Times* reports on the state of the wars in France leading up to 1815. Those reports provided news upon which investors acted. Papers like the *Financial News* provided explicit financial advice based on the pretense of expertise that could overcome the challenges of asymmetric information associated with distance and complexity. Investors were not simply attempting to gauge the effects of international events (though they certainly still did that). Many were explicitly engaging with sources that purported to offer specialized knowledge and investigative capacity. And the financial papers, combined with prospectuses, accomplished just what Marks envisioned, influencing the public and helping to drive numerous bubbles in South African mining shares.

Public investors like James White were not the sole shareholders in the Rae mining venture. The shareholders also included directors and mining engineers who had more intricate knowledge of the venture itself. These men had access to the actual mines. They could inspect company books. Men like Marks's brother-in-law Charles Dawson Philpott are a crucial component of the Rae mining story. The way these men, including Stephen Henry Fry, a cement manufacturer, and William Bevitt, an engineer and one of the two directors to visit the fields, came to have confidence in Rae's prospects was notably different from that of the public investors. Fry and Bevitt testified not just as directors and investors with access to information but also as losers in the investment scheme. Explaining their losses required a different rhetorical stance, in which they drew attention to their own ignorance to show how crucial inside information was to any financial exchange. In their claims of ignorance as to the mine's speculative elements, the men spoke to just how difficult it had become for even the best-connected people to see through the clouded webs of international investment.

The Usual Course of Business: Speculation

Was the mine legitimate or another Poyais? The *Financial News* suggested the former, describing it as safe, remunerative, possessing every ingredient of success. A good number of shareholders and directors testified to their earnest belief in its potential. This is no small point. Respectable investors with successful careers put money in Rae, and not all of them did so recklessly. Some invested on the advice of friends or family, old networks of reputation at work. On the stand, all took care to identify the many different pieces of evidence they looked at to verify the mine's potential.

Disentangling what these directors and shareholders knew from what they claimed to know is a difficult feat. It seems nonetheless apparent that a number of directors legitimately invested in the mines as a productive and not merely speculative enterprise. Philpott, Marks's brother-in-law, was a director of Rae and seems to have had intimate knowledge of its expense books. "You will see by the minute-book," he stated, "when the men went out they took out a mill, machinery, picks and amalgamators; the amount spent upon it will appear in the cash-book every meeting." Judged by its expenses, Philpott suggested, the company seemed a bona fide concern. Initial reports from William Henry Penning, the first inspector at the mines, were encouraging, and not opposed by the other mining expert, Bevitt. "Mr. Bevitt could only listen to what Mr. Penning said, he had not been out to the property at the time," remembered Philpott, "we honestly believed we were working on a substantial concern."

Bevitt, an engineer, shareholder, and director, was eventually the second of two directors to visit the fields, leaving England in November 1887 and arriving at the property in February 1888. It had the appearance of potential: "If I had gone on the property in the first instance I should have formed a favourable opinion, judging from the outcrop." But, he added, the initial reports and investment had perhaps been premature, something he must have realized when he arrived at the Rae mines and found twenty to thirty mine shafts, one up to thirty feet, but little potential for gold. At that point, the enterprise consisted of one three-stamp mill, picks, shovels, bars, a manager, and nine to ten Africans. Most of the labor had been dismissed. Bevitt testified that he would never take a property before it was worked, but as an investor he had done just that. He had inspected all reports and the prospectus, which bore his name. He even encouraged his friends to apply for shares.

Stephen Henry Fry, previously a cement manufacturer, was the second-largest named shareholder in the company. He appears to have been introduced to the firm by Penning, whom he knew from previous business and whom he described as "a leading expert in mining matters." Fry said he took the shares on Penning's recommendation. "In the standard work on the Goldfields he is referred to as one of the first, if not the first, to whom the discovery of the Transvaal Goldfields is due," Fry testified. "He induced me in the first instance to take shares, and I took all my 1,050 shares on his inducement."

Almost exactly fifty years earlier, the select committees of the exchequer bills fraud had listened as dozens of witnesses attempted to prove that they had conducted their investments responsibly. Those witnesses repeatedly drew attention to reputation, familiarity, and the usual course of business. They may not have taken appropriate care, or perhaps any, when applying such criteria, but trust was nonetheless couched in terms of reputation. By 1890, the terms had changed. It can be fairly debated whether the Rae directors did all they could to verify the claims to which they put their names and in which they invested their money, but now trust was spoken of in terms of facts, experts, and verification.

Such explanations, however, went only so far. Intimate though he was with the firm's financial affairs, even Philpott, brother-in-law and bookkeeper of sorts, was blind to intricate dealings by the firm's promoters. He had to admit that some of it did not make sense to him. "I do not know the explanation of the entry of Florence Isabel Skeats, Fanny Chamberlain, Benjamin, and Barnard," he stated of the book of shareholders. There was much that was absent from his books:

> "I do not know who Florence Skeats was, I never heard of her in my life, I cannot tell you whether there was any cheque for her £850."
> "I made no inquiry of the secretary who she was."
> "I made no inquiry about 'Fanny Chamberlain, £1,000.'"
> "I do not know what Benjamin had to do with it, or Barnard; I never saw him."

The most important piece of information that Philpott and others seemed to be lacking concerned Frederick John Smith. Smith was seven years a clerk at Lloyd's before becoming clerk to Frank Barnard, a stock broker. In January 1887, Barnard sent Smith to Marks's office at the *Financial News*. Smith had never met Marks, but the editor offered the clerk £200—80 in sterling, 120 in shares—to become the vendor or nominee of Rae Farms, the site of the Rae Transvaal gold mines. This meant, in essence, that Smith was a figurehead who technically possessed the capacity to sell the land to the company's shareholders. He did not know the prices of the properties. He simply did what he was told, signed what he was told, and left without any receipt or documents. Such testimony makes a mockery of the position, but the paper and the checks from investors kept coming his way. He estimated that £20,000 in cheques passed through his hands. There was nothing illegal about Smith's role as a nominee. He was properly registered as the vendor of the farms. It is not even clear that this arrangement was unusual. "Whether the practice be commendable or not," Smith testified, "it is usual for property such as this to be sold through a nominee." Ernest Smith, a solicitor who had worked frequently with the *Financial News*, also stated: "There was no concealment of the fact that Smith was acting as nominee . . . that is the usual practice."[56]

Marks was just as blunt about the usual course of business (fig. 3). *Caveat emptor,* he testified, was the rule, and speculation was the game. When he took the witness stand, he must have recognized how much the trial had turned against his interests. Like Oscar Wilde, he ended up on trial in a case in which he was nominally the prosecution. Having shared with the packed courtroom details of his personal conduct as a young man, he was allowed on December 15 to talk about another seemingly contentious relationship: that between mining and financial speculation. Asked about a nominee shareholder whose name he used to hide his own stake, Marks replied in a series of answers:

> "I don't suppose he even knew he held the shares till he was told of it; he was simply a nominee."

> "It takes place every day."

> "He was told, 'I used your name for the transfer of shares.'"[57]

With regard to advice meted out in his correspondence section, Marks was equally forward: "To some of my correspondents throughout January, February, March and April, 1887, I did from time to time recommend the mine as a speculation. . . . The term 'mining invest-ment' may have been used, but I think the term contradicts itself, as any money put into a mine is not an investment but a speculation, the nature of the venture is itself so essentially speculative." The unabashed

VANITY FAIR

June 8 1889

Vincent Brooks, Day & Son Lith.

"Financial News"

Marks: Trusted Editor; Speculator. *Harry Marks, "Financial News"* by
Arthur H. Marks, *Vanity Fair*, 1889. *(Reprinted with permission of the
Archives and Special Collections Division, City College of New York, CUNY)*

use of the word "speculation" from the era's pioneering financial journalist is not to be easily dismissed, nor is the implied point that most holders of Rae shares were themselves speculators. Marks was not shown to know there was no gold, but he himself admitted that gold was secondary to the quick movement of share prices. He understood two things: people turned to his paper for data and expertise, and they used that information to speculate.[58] Both the form of knowledge and the nature of the trades themselves, not to mention the complexity of the market, had changed.

How many shares did Marks hold? During the trial, some shareholders guessed that he owned upward of a thousand shares. He later provided his own estimate: "Of the 52,290 I had only 23,000 or 24,000." Could the purchasing public or even the directors have known about his extensive stake in the company? "I don't know in what names I had my shares," he testified; "I had some in the name of Head. . . . I see no objection to placing shares in the names of nominees." The cavalier nature of this practice is clear, but it was not beyond the norm. Marks described it as commonplace. When he sold the shares, the legal transfer of ownership never took place: "If it were done it would be done in the way of jobbing, and they would not appear in a transfer or anything of that sort; they would simply be a transfer in the market."[59]

What are we to make of this opaque, cavalier financial capitalism? It might be easy to dismiss Marks as unscrupulous and Rae Farms as an outlier, if not for the fact that the story was a familiar one and speculation the concern of so many at the time. When J. H. Curle of the *Economist* published his extensive and authoritative *The Gold Mines of the World* (1899), he too saw speculation as an unavoidable aspect of mining investment, recognizing that as much as three-fourths of all transactions in mining shares came under the heading of "gambling, pure and simple."[60] Undoubtedly, mine shares followed the path established by Latin American bonds and railway shares in their appeal to eager investors hoping for significant returns above those of the stable Consol. But the prevalence of speculation speaks to an investment milieu similar to that described by Trollope and feared by Adam Smith.

Consider the advice offered to potential investors by Curle, who drew his report from a decade's worth of knowledge and visits to eighty-eight mines in the Transvaal. The City, he noted, was teeming with "ornamental directors" who gave an offering the appearance of standing. Such directors tended to have titles in front of their names and initials after them, being commonly lords or members of Parliament. They were to a prospectus what reputable friends and a new home with a sitting room were to the Veneerings: symbols meant to inspire confidence. For a fee, such directors could lend legitimacy to a board while taking on little personal risk. Should a company dissolve and the prospectus prove bogus, the directors would plead ignorance. Sham vendors like Smith were also commonplace. Curle provided his readers a list of dos and don'ts:

> *Don't* get taken by "decoy ducks," or ornamental directors; do not invest in bad prospectuses; do not "believe in newspaper paragraphs"; do not trust ticker tape prices or listed share prices; do not invest in discount share prices; do not trust experts blindly.
>
> *Do* invest in mines offered at a premium; verify the opinions of experts against those of friends experienced in mining; scrutinize the directors list; invest in firms with high working capital; scrutinize the vendor's interest; allow that mines may take many months to prove a success, so do not trust negative reports in papers.[61]

Curle's is a classic investment guide from the age of verification, nodding to reputation but insisting that the investor inspect every possible detail of information. He also described an investment environment that was teeming with deception, risk, and fraud and yet often bullish. It was a fully matured version of the capitalism that people like William Cobbett and his fellow advocates of the "country ideology" and even Adam Smith had feared, operating with reckless disregard for the long-forgotten value of virtue. It possessed none of the attributes of David Hume's virtuous luxury and all those of vicious luxury. Marks was a classic figure of criminal capitalism, blurring the lines between trust building and fraud and between legitimate exchange and the

abuse of position and speculation. Perhaps nothing is more revealing of
Marks's approach than the fate of the *Financial News* even after the doings in South Africa came to light.

"The *Financial News* Lives"

Butterfield was found not guilty of libel, his statements being found
true and presented for the "public benefit." Marks was ordered to assume Butterfield's legal costs, and Marks's reputation took a beating in
the press. The *Saturday Review* appeared to care little about Marks's
personal character: "To show that eleven or twelve years ago Mr. Marks,
then a very young man, seduced and swindled a German widow in
New York, cannot, with all due deference to the jury, do the slightest
good to any rational human being." But when it came to his standing as
a trustworthy editor, the *Saturday Review* joined the angry chorus: "But
was there not mud thrown at Mr. Marks for equivocal conduct on connection with a gold mine in which there was no gold? It is within our
recollection that the mud in question was thrown and that some of it
adhered." The public, the *Saturday Review* admitted, was fascinated by
Marks's escape and his love life in New York. But perhaps the jury
had looked at the more substantial matter: "The whole story of the Rae
Mine, with its nominal vendor, its sham gold, and the unscrupulous
'bearing' of the shares in the *Financial News* was most discreditable to
Mr. Marks, and must have strongly influenced the jury."[62] Marks eventually won a seat in Parliament representing St. George's-in-the-East,
which he held from 1895 to 1900, and Thanet, a district in Kent, which
he represented from 1904 to 1910. But that was no proof of good reputation. After all, it was during this period that the famed chameleon
Ignaz Trebitsch Lincoln—Jew, Christian missionary, Buddhist monk,
Balkan oil magnate, German spy, British spy, outlaw—also became a
member of Parliament.[63] Even then, people went on dragging Marks's
name through the mud. In Thanet he was accused of buying votes
through society memberships, free banquets and smokes, and gifts of
milk, coal, and food.[64] The satirist G. K. Chesterton featured him as an
example in dialogue: "Go and persuade the orators of the Tariff Reform

League not to appeal to mobs. Go and persuade the editor of the *Daily Telegraph* that the press is a pest and a tyranny. Go and persuade Harry Marks that moral considerations are primary."[65] To Chesterton, Marks was the paradigmatic example of the triumph of Mammon over morality. The historian of the *Financial Times*, David Kynaston, notes that Marks's reputation never fully recovered, but this can lead to the wrong conclusion. Marks's name took the occasional beating, but what damage had the trial and the accompanying revelations done the paper itself and to his position as editor?

Though his morality may have been found lacking, readers apparently were not shocked by the revelations of rampant speculation—even that promoted by the paper itself. Horatio Bottomley, the legendary share promoter and one of the *Financial Times*'s founders, would later recall a less successful endeavor, the *Daily Recorder of Commerce*: "This journal aimed at being to the commercial world what the *Financial News* was to the financial. I soon, however, discovered a fundamental distinction between them; for whilst every person is more or less interested in stocks and shares, the *clientele* of a purely commercial concern is practically limited to those engaged in the markets with which it deals."[66] In 1890, *Sells Dictionary of the World Press* observed that the *Financial News* had become "the recognized authority upon financial affairs, domestic and foreign."[67] Like other financial papers, the *Financial News* lost advertising revenue through the financial downturn of 1893 but was bailed out by another mining boom the following year. It survived, as did, apparently, its appeal and usefulness. In 1898, the paper successfully reconstructed itself, increasing its capital to £200,000, held in £1 shares.[68] "The *Financial News* lives," Marks declared with his chest puffed, near the end of his career; "the schemes it attacked are dead."[69] Its twentieth anniversary was celebrated with a forty-page special edition covering all the commercial affairs of the British Empire and beyond. In a section titled "Company Promotion," the paper estimated that during its existence, no fewer than 62,300 companies had registered in London, with at least £3,843,000,000 in aggregate nominal share capitalization. The edition, distributed for free, included a poem in the *Financial News*'s honor, which ended:

Whate'er thy Fate. Great Realm, indeed,

Our humble part we claim to bear,
Strong in the faith of Honour's creed
Prudent to keep, yet bold to dare![70]

The *Morning Post* described the special edition as "the most remarkable pennyworth ever published." Sir Arthur Conan Doyle attended a banquet in celebration.[71] The *Financial News* was, for the time being, alive and well.

At the general meeting in London of Investment Registry Ltd. the following year, 1905, Sir John Rolleston announced a new monthly publication by the firm. The *Financial Review of Reviews*, which first appeared in November 1905, was to be a guide to those who wished to operate with objective data and reliable reporting, without the whims and risks of the Exchange and its alleys. It promised original scientific overviews of market performance, including "The Dangers of Argentine Railway Investments," "The British Colonies as an Investment Area," and "Prosperity of South and Central America." The second issue, in December, included "Investment an Exact Science (with Charts and Diagrams)," as well as dividend results for over thirty-five hundred investments quoted on British Stock Exchanges, amounting to 132 pages of statistical records.[72]

The *Review of Reviews* also offered a selection of the best financial reporting, chosen by its experts. The *Financial News* appeared frequently in its pages. Pointing to a world of compromised financial data, the *Review of Reviews* promised reliable data; it would watch the watcher. In the complicated, anxious investment world the Investment Registry described, it was the prospectus and the burgeoning financial press that held the most sway. "How the British Public Invests," an article in the fourth edition of the *Review of Reviews*, squeezed in before the expanded four thousand securities' prices, observed: "Strange to say the very man who would regard a change of bootmakers as a step towards revolution is the most prone to fall a victim to the insidious wiles of a well-concocted prospectus—the man who venerates the old-fashioned bootmaker as a god, turns lightly aside from the contemplation of an old-fashioned security to offer incense to some idol with feet of clay in the shape of a brand new company. . . . This folly the British investor continues to repeat throughout his life."[73] The answer to this folly, as offered by the *Review of Reviews*, was expertise, supervised data, and the ability to identify the best of financial reporting.

At its beginning in 1905, the *Review of Reviews* placed its own article-cum-advertisement in the *Financial News*. The Investment Registry promised risk diversification through a scientific process, and the editing and keen eye of professionals. As an example of the dangerous financial terrain, the authors presented the unregulated, unsupervised operation of the ticker tape installed in the Stock Exchange in the 1890s. It might provide updated prices, but who would be answerable for the tape's contents? Not the directors of the Exchange, the *Review of Reviews* answered, but a private company that operates largely on its own. The authors employed a familiar technique, questioning the reliability of financial information and then offering their own services as a solution.[74] How, they asked, did they come to know that the ticker tape company and its information might be suspect?

The *Financial News* had pointed it out.

The Verification Bureau

Long before Harry Marks cut a swath through the world of financial information, he had tried his hand in the cotton business in the American South. It was in New Orleans and New York that he had learned financial reporting. And it was in the American South, New York, and Britain that one of the largest frauds of the young twentieth century hit.

In April 1910, brokers and bankers in Liverpool, London, Le Havre, Bremen, and New York realized over a two-day span that they had purchased and resold upward of $5 million worth of forged bills of lading from the Alabama firm Knight, Yancey, and Company. The perpetrators appeared to be John W. Knight and W. J. Yancey, two well-connected good-time boys from the American South who for years had been in the business of trading cotton and other goods on future markets and through bills of exchange and lading—which is to say, they were in the business of trading representations of cotton rather than the real thing. The losers, bankers and insurers all around the Atlantic, were out the equivalent of more than $2 billion in today's terms, and news of the fraud rippled across the Atlantic.[1] Anglo-American relationships were decidedly important at century's end. The United States was a testy, difficult, upstart ally, but by the late nineteenth century the former colonies had become Britain's biggest economic partner. If Asia and Africa accounted for around 30 percent of British overseas investment, white settler colonies such as Australia and the United States attracted around 45 percent.[2]

Evidence of this special economic relationship abounds in British and American fiction. Caspar Goodwood, one of Isabel Archer's spurned suitors in Henry James's *The Portrait of a Lady*, is an heir to a New England cotton mill. Though Archer suggests there was nothing "cottony" about him, he did have American manners despite his Harvard training. American ways—straightforward, honest, fair-dealing but controlling—also appear in Wilde's *The Picture of Dorian Gray*: "The Americans are an extremely interesting people," one character observes. "They are absolutely reasonable. I think that is their distinguishing characteristic." Liverpool and London cotton merchants and bankers knew better, as did the Americans themselves. One of the most famous American stories of deception is Herman Melville's *The Confidence-Man: His Masquerade*. Written shortly before the outbreak of the Civil War, Melville's novel takes place on a steamship traveling south on the Mississippi River toward New Orleans. As one might expect from the title, little is as it seems, as a shape-shifting stowaway moves among the steamer's passengers, playing with their trust. "He looks honest, don't he?" asks one character, only to be quickly reminded, "Looks are one thing, and facts are another."[3] It is a steamer of strangers. An inscription on a pasteboard sign hangs from a nail near the boat's barbershop: "NO TRUST."

For the cotton merchants of Liverpool and bankers in London, as for the passengers on Melville's steamer, trust had to be gained between equal partners with unequal information.[4] Reputational mechanisms had their limitations, and by the early twentieth century cotton financiers, merchants, and insurers were seeking more proactive, organized ways to manage trust and discourage fraud. Although governments had recently shown themselves capable of dealing with certain challenges in global trade, the liabilities that came with verifying and regulating the cotton trade were not something either the British or American government wanted to take on. Rather, true to the long-standing spirit of free trade, responsibility for encouraging confidence and policing the market fell to private actors within the market itself.

The process of reorganizing the cotton trade and its bills of lading, so central to Anglo-American commerce, began almost immediately after news of the Knight, Yancey, and Company fraud broke. The efforts built on a framework developed by those in various aspects of the trade who long feared just such an extensive fraud. Money from New York and cotton from the South would pass through brokers from all over England and Europe via a standardized process of verification overseen by a transatlantic body of interests. The routes to building trust in this arrangement went far beyond reliance on status and sociability. They depended instead on self-regulation, inspection, and standardized process.

Globalized Trade, Localized Self-Regulation

England's cotton trade had long taken place in the public sphere, informally and without any official rules or regulations.[5] The Cotton Brokers Association, formed in Liverpool in April 1841, and its traders passed its initial years without extensive codification of rules (fig. 4). In this it was not unique: earlier in the century, the London Stock Exchange charted a similar course. But unlike the London exchange, the Liverpool Cotton Brokers' Association and its American analogs came to self-regulate more because of geopolitics and technological change than out of concerns with conflicts of interests and shareholder structure. The complete interruption of American cotton exports to Britain during the American Civil War was a potentially catastrophic event for the textile mills of Britain—and for the bankers and exporters who relied upon those mills. The war may have been American, but its economic impact was global, affecting cotton markets and labor practices as far afield as India and South America and spurring a new wave of imperialism.[6] Cotton production boomed in Egypt, Brazil, and India in particular. In the three decades following the beginning of the Civil War, for instance, European consumption of Indian cotton increased sixty-two times over.[7] In all three cotton-producing regions, the upsurge in demand brought a major shift in labor patterns, as labor moved from manufacturing to raw cotton production. As would prove true in the American South once the war ended, cotton production was frequently accompanied by a system of credit and indebtedness that kept a great deal of labor tied to the land. The difficulties caused by the absence of American cotton also contributed to a new, more aggressive imperialism aimed at procuring raw materials for domestic industries. Cotton would eventually emerge as Uganda's dominant cash crop, partly as a result of efforts to reduce dependency on American cotton.

Nonetheless, the American market was not easily replaced. By 1877, the United States had reestablished its antebellum market share in Britain; by 1891, the American producers were turning out twice as much cotton as they had in 1861—providing 66 percent of French raw cotton and 61 percent of German.[8] In 1903 and 1904, the American South was still exporting over 60 percent of the world's cotton.[9] The

Cotton traders of the Liverpool exchange self-regulating through a snowball fight reminiscent of the gentlemanly skirmishes in Hogarth's *South Sea Scheme. Exchange Buildings—1854*, by John R. Isaac, 1854. *(Liverpool Record Office, Liverpool Libraries)*

British market in 1891 obtained more than 80 percent of its cotton from the United States.

It was as the American producers were reasserting their dominance that the Liverpool Cotton Brokers' Association began to take a more serious approach to regulating and codifying the cotton trade. The disruption and speculation that had accompanied the conflict were a significant impetus, as was the dramatic effect of the telegraph upon cotton trading: Time trades had long been an option for speculators and, indeed, played a role in the Lord Thomas Cochrane hoax, but the ability to invest on future prices changed dramatically with the faster movement of information. The association's official history summarized this neatly: "The laying down of the cable brought America and Liverpool within a few hours of each other, while the establishment of the system of selling 'futures' led to a complete change in the method of moving the cotton crop from America to Europe."[10] Auguste Bruckert, a chronicler of the Liverpool cotton market, described the advent of the cotton futures market as a moment of sudden financial creativity. "It was in 1868," he wrote, "that a Liverpool broker found, that with the help of the Atlantic Cable, which was just then finished, it had become possible to the Liverpool broker to get to know quickly at what price one could actually buy Cotton in the South, and the approximate date at which it would arrive in Great Britain."[11] This trader, and the hundreds who soon followed, could sell cotton (set to arrive in two to three months) today, based on the current price and the price he estimated in the future—all at one time.

Futures trading, as Jonathan Levy has argued, finally and completely detached financial assets from the commodities they represented. For some, they were a form of risk management, an insurance against price movement. According to this line of argument, advanced most commonly by the exchanges, the planter could sell future cotton when his current staple was underpriced or turning out poorly. Spinners could protect themselves against market fluctuations. Weavers and manufacturers could purchase futures to guard against merchants and importers holding stocks to drive up prices. Those importers and merchants could sell futures to cover themselves, at least partially, against a sudden drop in cotton prices. Others, however, particularly agrarians and some farmers, viewed futures as a way for financial markets and exchanges to strip the farmer of control over his product.[12] Nonetheless, exchanges for futures trading proliferated in major cities—as well as in bucket shops where nonmembers of exchanges, including farmers themselves, could trade. These shops, spread across America's small cities and towns, depended on the telegraph's ability to deliver instantaneous prices. Futures markets developed in horses, mules, tallow, grease, coffee, flax, and more. By 1890, futures trading had become, by volume, the dominant mode of commodity exchange in the United States.[13]

When the New York Cotton Exchange was finally incorporated, in 1871, three decades after Liverpool's, it had two ambitions: to introduce standard contracts and rules for trading, and to regulate this newly born futures market.[14] What regulation existed in the futures trading market was thus organized separately through each exchange, with Liverpool free to develop rules different from those of the newly established New York exchange.[15]

Speculation in futures may have been commonplace, but there was still real cotton to be traded. In addition to regulating the futures market, the New York Cotton Exchange also provided cotton inspection for members when "actual cotton" arrived. The services of the inspector, who was supported by the Committee on Classification and the Cotton Exchange Inspection Fund, were available at a small fee to all members of the exchange, including those located outside New York.[16] Ultimately, distance made verification in this system very difficult, a problem of which the exchange was well aware. Raw cotton required compression to be shipped efficiently. This process was prone to frauds of all sort and made inspection even more challenging. Worse, the cotton might never pass through New York—it might go immediately across the Atlantic from New Orleans. As late as 1908, nearly forty years after its founding, the New York Cotton Exchange was still grappling with this problem. The Special Committee on Certifying Cotton issued a circular to Exchange members: "We must get at the bales *as near the plantation as possible*, so as to sample and examine them *before* they are compressed. In this condition our inspectors can examine every bale so thoroughly that false packs, mix packs, sand, dirt, country damage, gin-tag, etc., cannot escape detection (as they too often do in compressed tables).”[17] Even in the age of railroad and telegraph, verification over distance was a challenge. The Board of Managers, the committee reminded members, retained the right to dispatch New York inspectors (traveling or resident) to any warehouse.

More frequently, though, cotton was represented by bills of lading, which in their simplest form were merely paper representations of cotton received or in transit. Even the trade in "actual" cotton had come to be a trade in paper. The men of the cotton exchange were much more likely to hold and inspect bills of lading and cotton futures than actual cotton from Texas or Alabama. A cotton purchase could take place without New York, Liverpool, or London ever seeing the real cotton. If a bank in New York decided to sell a thousand bales of cotton to a merchant in Liverpool, it would acquire a bill of lading for that cotton from a broker or agent in the South. The bill was meant to represent that the cotton had been received at a warehouse, by a railway company, or by a shipping company. Furthermore, New York often took on cotton for consignment at a discount before the cotton was needed. This, too, would often come in the form of a bill of lading rather than as real cotton. When he decided to sell on to London, the New York trader would draw a draft or bill of exchange on a merchant's bank in London or Liverpool using these bills of lading. Once this was done, the bank would call in the merchant or the merchant's agents to verify the two bills. If they met with approval, the merchant would approve acceptance of the bill, and the bank would pay New York. The bill of lading, long a fixture of long-distance trade, was not just a receipt but also a document of title to goods. It could be bought and sold as if it were actual cotton—or cotton in the future.[18]

The value of goods thus traded was enormous. In 1912, Guaranty Trust Company of New York handled, on its own, $236 million in foreign bills of exchange. A prewar estimate placed the total business conducted in bills of lading at $25 billion a year, with $5 billion being handled by the New York banks.[19] The futures market, as the official historians of the Liverpool Cotton Brokers' Association noted, had remade the market, allowing for a different approach to risk taking. Players in the market argued that futures were a useful hedge against risk.

Fraud, however, was a risk separate and apart from that of price move-ment, weather events, or grain yields. As the Knight, Yancey, and Com-pany fraud would soon show, complex new dynamics, meant to protect against risk, did not provide any similar protection against fraud.

Reputation and Regulation

Few failed to see the magnitude of the problem. In 1907 and 1910, two conferences convened on the question of bills of lading: the first made up of private actors; the second, of government representatives. The 1907 conference took place in Liverpool. In attendance were repre-sentatives from the Liverpool Cotton Brokers' Association, the Bre-men Cotton Exchange, and Syndicat du Commerce des Cotons and Ancien Courtiers en Cotons, both from Le Havre. Like many inter-national agreements both before and after the First World War, the Liverpool conference agreement—which sought to limit the types of bills of lading acceptable for exchange—had a fundamental weakness: compliance was by choice, and there was no authority with power of enforcement.[20]

This power had long resided in national and imperial capitals. In numerous instances throughout the nineteenth century, for example, the British government had intervened to protect British commercial and financial instruments. Michael D. Bordo and Hugh Rockoff have argued that adherence to the gold standard allowed for cheaper bor-rowing as it was thought to protect lenders against political risk. Niall Ferguson and Moritz Schularick have also shown how the instruments of power of Britain's empire—including not just its law but its navy—helped to make lenders more confident in their debtors.[21] A military threat, however, was not an option in the cotton trade with the United States.

Following on the 1907 conference, it fell to a group of state actors to attempt to provide security in the trade of bills of lading and ex-change. The Conference on Bills of Exchange was held in The Hague in the summer of 1910. More than thirty-one countries, including the United Kingdom, the United States, Argentina, Brazil, Peru, Panama, Mexico, Russia, Germany, and Austria-Hungary, sent representatives.

Early on, Sir Edward Grey, the British foreign minister, had written the
Dutch representative (Baron Grenicke d'Herwijen) that while the British would participate, their laws on such matters were already well
established—and any change would be highly unlikely.[22] Grey's directions on the eve of the conference to the British representative, Sir
George Buchanan, were even more direct: "As a general rule the British
Delegate will not hold out any hope that English rules of law are likely
to be substantially modified and brought into conformity with continental rules, particularly in cases where the English rule prevails, not
only in the United Kingdom, but also throughout the English-speaking
world."[23] At its conclusion, the conference drafted a uniform law regarding bills of lading that was approved by all delegates, except those
from Britain and the United States, who stood aside. Buchanan may
not have voted, but he made his government's opinion heard: "It is no
question of national pride or obstinacy which has given rise to this attitude, but the necessity of safeguarding the interests of our mercantile
community. A law which governs more than 120,000,000 people—
including the United Kingdom, the British colonies, and most of the
States of the United States of America—without counting the vast population of the Indian Empire—cannot be modified without disturbing
long-settled commercial relations, and without creating divergences in
legislation among the members of the Anglo-Saxon family."[24]

　　The governments of the United States and Great Britain were not
going to alter their legal codes or establish further international regulation to encourage confidence in the exchange of bills of lading. As the
historian Frank Trentmann has neatly put it, "British Free Trade was
commercially internationalist but politically isolationist."[25] Certainly
liability issues loomed large, but Buchanan's response was also rooted
in the idea of the free market.

　　That same year, the Liverpool Cotton Brokers' Association—and
in particular a man named Hans Kern—turned to market forces in the
hope of inhibiting systemic fraud. Kern, of German birth, headed
the Liverpool Cotton Bills of Lading Committee and emerged from the
conference emboldened for the fight. Soon after the 1907 conference,
he had pleaded with association members: "We must not allow any
breathing time, but must follow up our successes and not rest contented

until we have defined the day." By "defining the day" he meant defining the rules of the bill of lading.[26] He feared a destructive shock to Liverpool and London banks based on fake American bills of lading.

For at least three years after the conference, the task of defining these rules fell to Kern, who possessed no punitive powers. In January, he dispatched a circular to dozens of banks, exchanges, and insurers, including Lloyd's of London and the Bremer branch of Deutsch Bank. "We now want London and Continental Bankers to follow suit," he wrote of the agreement, but then admitted, "My Committee is not in a position to put pressure on them, but you, the different bodies represented at or invited to the Conference, can do so through your members."[27]

How did Kern, with no enforcement power, hope to cajole relevant parties to abide by the agreement? He looked to reputational mechanisms that had been commonplace in the century prior.[28] First, he proposed that insurance companies might be of help. Insurers might be encouraged to increase general rates by a small amount and then offer a corresponding reduction to ship owners and agents who signed on to the terms of the agreement.[29] Kern admitted that he had no ability to compel or entice insurance companies to do this; he could only encourage those familiar with the companies. He embarked on a program of publicity that sought to improve the business prospects of those acting in accordance with the agreement, which would thus encourage others to join.

Almost as soon as the terms of the agreement were declared, Kern began circulating a list of those who had signed it. Over the years the list was frequently altered, and those who had violated the agreement had their removal from the list publicly circulated through the Liverpool association dispatches. In January 1908, Kern dispatched a circular that described the list as his committee's most important mechanism for making the reforms effective. The committee is charged, he wrote, with "keeping the list *a jour*, i.e., to make it complete and keep it so."[30] His lists often ran on for pages, including scores of shippers, agents, buyers, and growers from around the world: the American Line of Liverpool and Philadelphia; the Atlantic Transport Company of London, Baltimore, New York, and Philadelphia; the Austro-Americana and

Fratelli Cosulich, Trieste and New Orleans; and firms from Norfolk, Pensacola, Belfast, Bremen, Antwerp, Glasgow, Houston, Naples, Barcelona, Bristol, Christiana, and Newcastle-on-Tyne.

"*All Shipowners and Agents who are so far not on the list are therefore requested to send in their consent immediately,*" Kern urged in a dispatch at the end of January 1908.[31] Soon he began publishing a list of shipowners and agents from whom he had received no response, attempting to shame them into joining the agreement. Both lists kept growing, as Kern added consenting shipowners and discovered and exposed more whose responses were lacking. When members of the list veered from the terms of the agreement, they were to be informed upon by other members. "All cases where this condition has not been fulfilled," Kern wrote of cotton being in port when a bill was signed, "should at once be reported to me with full particulars."[32] For those who were caught, ignominy was supposed to arrive in the form of a prominent place in the Liverpool association's circular. On the first page of an October 1908 dispatch, Kern chastised the wayward:

> In spite of this Circular, and in spite of remonstrances made by other Ship Agents in Savannah, the Ocean Steamship Co. of Savannah, and the Merchants' and Miners' Transportation Co., of Savannah, have seen fit to deliberately break their agreement, and have made a practice of issuing Bills of Lading by Steamer which were not in port. My Committee has consequently by a unanimous vote resolved to-day:—
> "That the names of the of the *Ocean Steamship Co. of Savannah*, and of the *Merchants' and Miners' Transportation Co.* be and are hereby struck off the list of consenting Shipowners and Agents."[33]

Such was the public process by which shame was meant to affect reputation and, the hope was, business. At the cotton exchange in New York, the names of bankrupts and defaulters were posted on the bulletin board.[34] The Liverpool Cotton Brokers' Association attempted to force honest behavior on international merchants, insurers, financiers, and shippers in much the same way. Kern envisioned market forces, channeled through reputation that was bolstered or harmed by public information, as encouraging good behavior and confidence.

Kern's lists featured agents and shipowners from Galveston, Houston, Wilmington, Brunswick, Savannah, Charleston, and Port Arthur, but none from the bustling Alabama city Decatur. Yet it was a firm from Decatur, which never appeared in any of Kern's circulars, that would show the weakness of the 1907 agreement.

"Cotton Circles Agog"

John W. Knight was the sort of good-time boy whom Kern, the dedicated but unappreciated and unempowered sheriff of international bills of lading, would have looked upon with distrust. Born in Selma, Alabama, Knight was the oldest of four brothers, his father having worked as a freight agent for the East Tennessee, Rome, and Dalton Railway. The movement of goods was the Knight family business. The son failed in real estate and then insurance, and then moved to Decatur, where he opened his cotton firm around 1895. He made a success of himself and was known for enjoying his cars, his drives, his boats, his fishing. He was familiar in Alabama society.[35] Knight's partner, W. J. Yancey, worked from Memphis, but his most prominent associate in the cotton trade was W. D. Nesbit of Mobile, Alabama's State Railroad Commission and, according to the *Montgomery Advertiser*, "one of the best known businessmen of the South."[36] Nesbit was also chairman of Alabama's State Democratic Committee. Knight and his colleagues were not unknown confidence men newly arrived in the South's cotton hub, nor were they Dickens's Veneerings, suddenly invented by clothes and furniture. Knight was well-to-do, from a known Southern family, and Nesbit was a community pillar, involved in public administration and state politics.

Exactly when and why Knight, Yancey, and Company began forging faked bills has never been clear. As early as 1905, according to Knight, the firm took major losses in the cotton futures market.[37] Most likely, at some point soon after, the firm changed its modus operandi—and like Beaumont Smith, Walter Watts, and so many others, the men of Knight, Yancey, and Company were transformed from honest

brokers to fraudsters. The firm continued to sell bills for cotton it had
not yet purchased, but now its employees began forging the signatures
of the railway and port agents. Knight, or someone in the firm, would
draw up a bill of lading for cotton delivery and then apply a copy of a
receiving agent's signature to the bill. This was simply a matter of pa-
perwork and the facsimile of a signature. It did not have to involve any
cotton at all. Knight could sit in the company's office in Decatur, invent-
ing cotton and, with it, request payment.

Bills of lading must be tied to real cotton, Kern had insisted, inspected by agents and captains who had endorsed his list. Knight, Yancey,
and Company understood that bills were negotiable instruments, traded
like shares upon the presumption that somewhere, perhaps thousands
of miles away, the cotton that they represented actually existed. But
even false bills of lading, as long as the money was there, could eventually be delivered upon. "When the cotton arrived in Europe," wrote the
New York Times later, "it seems to have been delivered by the steamers
without any suspicion that some of the bills of lading were irregular
until recently."[38] This structure resembled what would become known
as a Ponzi scheme, yet as long as all purchasers did not immediately
demand their cotton, or the company did not sell too many false bills,
the scheme could continue indefinitely. For years, this is exactly what
Knight did, forging signatures on contracts and receiving payments
earlier than they normally would have been received. His fraudulent
business functioned for years much like his legitimate one, from one
fraudulent set of bills to the next.

But in mid-April 1910, steamship companies became suspicious of
some bills and refused to carry the company's cotton, a move to which
importers were quickly alerted. In Liverpool and on the continent, importers discovered a series of questionable signatures and, more important, that cotton was still promised against a good many of them.
Liverpool, and presumably New York, demanded that the forms be
explained and the missing cotton supplied immediately. Such a rush to
deliver all expected cotton, without access to capital from current bills of
lading, left Knight, Yancey, and Company unable to meet its obligations.

On April 21, 1910, the fraud became public, unfolding almost simultaneously across the South, in New York, Great Britain, and conti-

nental Europe, revealing a fraud that progressed along the exact lines
Kern had been fighting against.[39] Numbers flew wildly. In New York,
the president of the cotton exchange noted that the fraud was limited
to a single company and that the failure amounted to relatively little
money, perhaps $20,000.[40] London suggested the English exposure
would be much higher. The *New York Times* dispatch from Liverpool
estimated that twenty-six English firms were exposed in the failure to a
combined amount upward of $2 million, or twenty-five thousand bales
of cotton.[41] Another fourteen thousand bales were said to have been
purchased by importers on the continent, bringing the total cotton
supposedly shipped from New Orleans, and already paid for by purchasers, to more than $3.5 million. Eventually, the trustee of the firm's
creditors testified that Knight, Yancey, and Company had $1,120,316 in
assets, with outstanding liabilities of over $5 million.[42]

The end for Knight, Yancey, and Company was only the beginning for the importers and brokers. In the press, the process of guessing the exact size of losses reflected regional and national rivalries. The
Charlotte (NC) Observer commented, "The local cotton men are inclined to rejoice at the news that Liverpool cotton brokers are heavy
losers."[43] A news agency reported from Bremen: "The matter was much
discussed today on the Bourse, where shares of the Deutsche National
Bank of Bremen were sharply depressed because it was assumed that
the house had sustained severe losses through the forged bills of lading."[44] The European responses were coupled with action. The day the
story broke, foreign cotton houses dispatched dozens of cotton agents
to Atlanta to try to claim remaining assets.[45] These agents found that
they were already behind the local actors, public and private. On April
24, only four days after the company declared bankruptcy, U.S. marshals began seizing Knight, Yancey, and Company cotton on orders
from the federal courts. In Mobile, Alabama, a deputy U.S. marshal,
acting on an injunction from the District Court of the Southern District of Alabama, seized forty-two hundred bales of cotton aboard the
British steamship *Meltonian*, bound for Le Havre, France. The *Meltonian* was set to sail in only two days, and the injunction had been issued in response to a request from attorneys representing the receivers
of the company. The reason for the urgency is clear: the court cases and

recovery might take years, and it was better to keep the cotton in the United States.

Meanwhile, the lawyers set to work. The court battles started almost immediately but lasted for another nine years, during which time appeals abounded and a pair of U.S. district court judges showed themselves almost completely unable to grapple with the convoluted standing of documents that functioned as receipts, contracts, and commercial paper. The creditors of Knight, Yancey, and Company, whether American, French, or British, had two routes through which to try and reclaim their assets: they could pursue the bankruptcy trustee, the law firm of W. S. Lovell, for a share of the remaining assets; or they could pursue the New York banks and Southern brokers who had passed on to them the forged bills of lading. But the first case brought, *Lovell v. H. Hentz and Co. et al.*, in September 1910, featured a twist, with Lovell attempting to reclaim assets kept by a firm to which Knight, Yancey, and Company had consigned cotton. In an Alabama district court, Lovell and the trustees were represented by a prominent Alabama law firm, including Walker Percy, father of the famous writer of the same name. Lovell claimed that though the brokers had consigned cotton with the defendants, and though the defendants had a forged bill of lading to Knight, Yancey, and Company cotton, they did not have a right to that specific cotton. Instead, they had a claim upon the general holding of bankrupt assets—just like every other creditor. The judge seemed to agree, but he issued a long, convoluted charge to the jury, rife with hypotheticals, jargon, and general confusion: "The character of the transaction," he told them, was "to be governed by the intention of Knight, Yancey & Co., as evidenced by their acts; that is, their executed intention, shown by their acts—not what Mr. Knight might have had in his mind, not disclosed by his outward acts, but his intention as gathered from the transaction."[46] Whether or not they understood the advice, the jury agreed with the judge and found that the particular bill held by the defendants was representative of cotton, but no specific cotton. Judges and juries elsewhere were coming to different decisions. In January 1912, the U.S. Court of Appeals for the Fifth Circuit overturned the Alabama district court decision, remanding it for a new trial, in part based upon a separate case it had heard involving Knight, Yancey, and Company.

On May 23, 1911, a district court for the Southern District of New York had ruled on the first case brought by foreign buyers against a bank in an attempt to recover from the fraud. Brought by Anthony S. Hannay, from Liverpool, against Guaranty and Trust Company of New York, the case involved a claim of only $7,320 but was a test for other importers. The implications were clear and significant: at this point, the total loss by English firms was estimated at $2.5 million, with another $1.5 million claimed by French firms and others on the continent.

The case differed from the Alabama trial in a crucial way. In Alabama, Lovell essentially represented Knight, Yancey, and Company in trying to claim the company's assets. In the trial in Manhattan, *Hannay v. Guaranty Trust Co. of New York*, the links to the con men were much less clear. Judge Walter Chadwick Noyes of the Southern District Court of New York made this abundantly clear in its opinion: "There is no contention that the defendant in presenting the draft had knowledge of the spurious nature of the bill of lading, and the question presented is: Upon which of two innocent parties . . . should the loss fall?"[47] This is not an uncommon legal issue, nor is it wildly different from some of the issues involved in the discussions of the exchequer bills fraud or the Factors Acts: how to distribute risk and thus loss when both parties have made "a mutual mistake of fact."[48] Mutual innocence did not make this district court judge's job any easier—or his opinion any clearer. In the end, based on precedent, he decided that the draft drawn by the British bankers was conditional, as was its approval, on the delivery of cotton. It was money for cotton, but no cotton had been provided. In other words, until the cotton arrived in Liverpool, the New York banks bore the responsibility and the risk.

But this ruling was not to be long-lived. On the day of the ruling, the *New York Times* noted: "If Judge Noyes's decision is upheld, little if any of the loss will actually fall upon the New York banks as most of them have practically the same claim upon railroads which certified the false bills of lading."[49] The railroads were no doubt prepared for a battle, but as the *Times* hinted, the ruling would soon be reversed. The Court of Appeals for the Second Circuit reversed the decision of the district court, applying English law. "All the transactions took place in England," Judge Henry Wade Rogers observed in the circuit court's opinion. "There is no doubt but that the law of England, as a place where acceptance was made and was to be performed, must govern and determine the right and liabilities of the prospective parties."[50] The observation shows how far removed from actual cotton the trade had become. The banks in the commercial and capital cities were dealing in bills, and the location of the underlying cotton was irrelevant to the exchange. Reception of the bills was the same as the reception of cotton. In fact, the Second Circuit Court observed, the case might better have been brought in England, where the law held the Liverpool side (the payers), not the New York side (the payees), responsible.[51]

Guaranty Trust had called an expert in English law, a barrister of forty years and a King's counsel, to make this point to the judge. The English side did not call any experts to rebut the testimony. "They have introduced," wrote the judge, "no evidence to show that under English law A. can recover back from B. money which has been paid under mutual mistake, where the mistake made related to a fact which, as between A. and B., the law made it the duty of A. to know."[52] It is a fascinating moment in international law. The judge criticized one party for not preparing testimony on the laws of a foreign country, while noting that U.S. laws did not apply to the case at hand. The risk, the U.S. court asserted in this backward way, was borne by the buyer.

Had the English merchants and banks been forum shopping? Did they, knowing that pursuit in English courts would be futile, opt instead to pursue the action in New York? It is hard to say. Nonetheless, by early 1911, no fewer than thirty-seven cases had been brought by foreign companies against American banks and railroads.[53] And in 1913 the Second Circuit Court decided that the cases, at least the English ones, should not be decided under U.S. law. Recovery of assets was surely the plaintiffs' intention, but something larger was also at stake. Across the United States, judges were, at best, disagreeing about where the risk inherent in a bill of lading should fall. At worst, they were simply refusing to claim jurisdiction.

"One of the most important questions of international banking which has arisen from many years," declared the *Economist* in September 1911, partly in reaction to the fraud, is "the question of who is to bear the risk of fraudulent bills of lading and how the frauds themselves can be prevented."[54] For years, governments on both sides of the Atlantic had wrestled with how to make the bill of lading more dependable without negating its usefulness. The problem, as the fraud would ultimately bear out, was not a national one to be addressed in congresses and parliaments, but one requiring international action. The *Economist* surveyed the scene: "None of the parties concerned have shown any willingness to take the risk, while all are anxious to shift the burden of responsibility on to other shoulders." Absent the creation of new assets to protect against the risk of fraud in the trade, some form of coordinated action was needed. Instead, everyone was trying to pass on risk. Representatives of the British and American governments attended a conference at which, even before their arrival, they had committed to not participating in any uniform international policing of bills of lading.

Past losses were one thing, but such uncertainty about the form and standing of the bill of lading was a threat to present and future trade. How could Liverpool merchants and banks sign a draft to a bill of lading with any confidence, when they bore all the risk and little capacity to verify cotton that, even if real, might reside on consignment in a warehouse in Alabama? How could they do it with any confidence to the tune of millions of pounds of cotton, in thousands and thousands of bales?

Self-Regulation, International Style

Hans Kern thought he had a solution to the problem, and it did not involve governments. In mid-1910 he had a vision for an international center, privately funded, that would address problems of risk and verification in order to safeguard legitimate profits in the cotton trade. International organizations had never been the domain of states. On the contrary, over the final years before the First World War, nongovernmental organizations far outnumbered those organized between states. Numbering at most five before 1850, these organizations, associations, and institutions flourished at century's end, with around ten being established every year in the 1890s. By the outbreak of war there were at least three hundred.[55] These organizations presented themselves as pursuing global awareness and reform, not imperial power or profit.[56] Whereas groups such as the Salvation Army, YMCA, and YWCA legitimately had no profit motive, Kern's bureau was to service the cotton trade exclusively, in the name of safeguarding trade and profit.

In August 1910, railroad officials and American bankers met in White Sulphur Springs, West Virginia, a summer resort for wealthy Southerners, to try to salvage confidence in the cotton trade. No new organization was established, and the distribution of risk in the trade was not altered. Rather, the railroads east of the Mississippi and the bankers agreed to add a new check to the trade: agents would attach a certificate of authenticity to bills, thereby denying actors like Knight the opportunity to forge certification by signature. "The certificates will be issued to the agents in the same manner as passage tickets and the same check be made of these documents in agents' hands as of passage tickets," observed the *New York Times*.[57] This system of stricter checks at the point where railroad agents assumed control of the bills was an improvement but in no way went far enough for the English. In September, the *New York Times* Liverpool correspondent telegraphed "that it is generally understood that English and continental banks will limit their cotton trading until they get a guarantee from the American buyer that the document attached was valid before they accepted it."[58] The merchants and bankers of England and Europe did not want an additional check at some railroad depot in the United States; they wanted centralized inspection and a shift in liability, and they were willing to use their market leverage to bring it about.

Negotiations for such a system began in December and continued for months in both Liverpool and New York. In attendance were representatives from the American Banking Association, prominent railroad companies, and of course, the Liverpool Bill of Lading Conference Committee, led by Kern. The conference finally concluded with one crucial idea: the establishment in New York City of a central bureau for the verification of bills of lading.[59] A copy of all bills, the conference proposed, could be sent to the central bureau, where attention to details would form the basis of inspection.

By August 1911, Kern was reporting to his members that "the machinery for protection against forgery is now in working order" and had been agreed to by the American bankers and at least fifty railroad companies.[60] The Liverpool committee proudly distributed a guide to its system: "The Bill of Lading and Signature Certificate are most carefully scrutinized as to the proper filling out and stamping of the latter, as to the cross references to the Bill of Lading number in the Certificate and *vice versa* and as to all other details. . . . The clerk who is checking the Bill of Lading initials it and then passes it to another clerk who goes through independently and compares notes afterwards, thus preventing mistakes and oversights in the checking." The bill would then be checked for both signatures and numbers against all other bills received from that station, which were kept in the "Steel Box Filing Cabinet." Finally, the bill was filed so that it might be easily checked against any bill or receipt submitted by a ship's agent or master. A bill might be inspected by the bureau twice: once on submission of the railroad agent and once at the behest of the steamship master or agent. As he had with his list, Kern now wrote to European bankers and merchants, urging them to treat unchecked bills as irregular.

In September, just one month later, a disappointed Kern had to dispatch a circular informing readers that the system had hit two substantial roadblocks. The first problem came from the American South, where newspapers reacted to the bureau plan with indignation. "Southern Cotton Men Thoroughly Angered: Bills of Lading Validation Clearing House in New York Is Reflection Upon and Insult to the South," read the headline in the *Biloxi Daily Herald* of Mississippi.[61] "The plan is drawn entirely in the interest of the foreign cotton buyer and banker and the New York exchange buyer," observed the article, which treated the idea with xenophobic suspicion. "A letter was being printed in 17 different languages to be issued to cotton importers and foreign banking interests all over the world, requesting said cotton buyers to comply with the plan and to request American exchange buyers to have all their documents approved as to their genuineness through the central office in New York." Kern found this resistance "curiously contradictory," especially the claim that the bureau was an "insult to Southern commercial integrity."[62] More substantially, buyers and bankers in New Orleans and beyond feared that the bureau would further increase the prominence of New York and thus reduce their standing. This challenge was overcome by making New York's approval not a prerequisite but relevant only in cases of fraud. New York would telegraph the South only if bills were found fraudulent.[63] Efficiency and order were to be the bureau's hallmarks. "There is *no delay* involved in the system," reported the Liverpool committee. "Documents will *not* be held up in New York and the Exchange buyer will only be notified by the Bureau after the Auditor of the railroad has declared a Bill of Lading to be irregular or fraudulent."[64] The process of preventing fraud, the committee understood, could not come at the price of preventing trade, or even slowing it.

The second challenge came from the bankers of New York, who had previously agreed to the bureau but now worried that in submitting bills for verification they would implicitly be taking on more responsibility and thus more risk. New York interests insisted that Liverpool cotton merchants, as represented by the Cotton Brokers' Association, could not get both verification and liability protection from risk. To get the system up and running, Kern had to assure the New York banks and traders that they had taken on no new risk. In essence, to gain verification, Liverpool merchants and European financiers agreed to take liability off the bargaining table.[65] The weight of trust, gained here through verification, was to rest on the same shoulders as those who bore the risk.

Upward of ninety railroad companies signed on, as did a dozen New York Cotton Exchange buyers and the American Bankers Association. The Bank of New York and American Express agreed to the plan.[66] In November, the report from the Annual Convention of American Bankers, held that month in New Orleans, appeared in the *New York Times*: "The actual working of the Central Bureau has proved conclusively that it is possible to check up bills of lading with certainty."[67] Guaranty Trust Company sent notice to customers that it would handle only bills of exchange accompanied by bills of lading verified at the bureau.[68] In July 1912, the Liverpool Cotton Brokers' Association, Bremen Baumwollbörse, and Syndicat du Commerce des Cotons in Le Havre issued a "Declaration by European Importers" that reaffirmed their allegiance to the bureau. Kern went back to list making, providing a list of shippers from eleven countries who supported use of the bureau.[69] In its early controversial days of September and October 1911, the bureau inspected fifty-three hundred bills representing 467,000 bales of cotton. Over the same period in 1912, the bureau inspected sixty-nine hundred bills representing at least 570,000 bales.[70]

Players in the cotton trade obviously thought the central bureau useful. But was it worth the bother? In summer 1913, Charles E. Mather, the president of Transportation Mutual Insurance Company, which specialized in tracing and insuring cotton, wrote to the Liverpool Cotton Brokers' Association. He had been running the central bureau at his company's expense and out of their offices near Wall Street but now informed the association that he could not continue without significant financial contribution. For this he turned not to the Americans but to the European merchants and banks. In London on July 22, the interests on the Cotton Bill of Ladings Committee for the European Banker's Conference agreed among themselves to fund the central bureau. Liverpool would pay £500, the Bremen exchange £300, and the Syndicat du Commerce £100 to keep the office running for the upcoming cotton season.[71] The committee did so with a caveat: the European Bankers' Conference had some additional requests and issues for the Liverpool association, which they passed in the form of a resolution. They wanted European cotton importers to require U.S. shippers to use the bureau, and they wanted all American exchange buyers "in remitting Bills of Lading to Europe, [to] indicate in the case of each Bill of Lading whether the Bureau has been notified or not."[72] The bankers had reaffirmed the bureau and sought to extend its reach. Where reputation had once stood, they put their money behind verification.

On September 23, 1911, John W. Knight was arrested by U.S. marshals and taken to Huntsville, Alabama, to stand trial for "fraudulent use of mails." For months, post office inspectors had been investigating whether Knight had passed spurious bills of lading through the U.S. mail. The trial began in federal district court on December 6 in front of Judge Grubb. Railway agents, bank tellers, and associates were called as witnesses in courtroom sessions that ran up to nine hours. On December 12, after a parade of railway agents testified to having not signed bills attributed to them, Knight took the stand for seven hours. He claimed the authority to sign the agents' names and assured the court that, had bankruptcy not intervened, he would have delivered all the cotton he had sold. The *Dallas Morning News* concluded its coverage of the day's events: "Defendant was taken off the stand at the conclusion of his direct examination, to permit examination of character witnesses, all of whom said Knight's reputation is excellent."[73]

It was with some of these character witnesses that Knight presumably passed the nearly eight hours awaiting the jury's decision. He was cool and calm, reported one paper, relaxed, chatting with his friends in the court's hallway when he was called into the courtroom to hear that he had been found not guilty. The issue in this trial was not forged signatures, which he admitted producing, but the use of the U.S. mail. Having defrauded banks and merchants of nearly $5 million, Knight walked out of the Huntsville courthouse a free man. On the same day in New York, and on the day after and the day after that, indeed for months and years to come, clerks in New York checked and double-checked the signatures and numbers on hundreds of bills of lading. Reputation was not enough for trust; verification was also essential.

On June 18, 1914, the Archduke Franz Ferdinand was assassinated in Sarajevo. Slightly less than a month later, the Austrians issued an ultimatum to Serbia, demanding the perpetrators of the crime. Within the week, Austria had declared war on Serbia, setting off a chain of declarations by European powers that would bring the whole continent and much of the world into war. It is hard to imagine Kern working through the summer of 1913—drumming up money for the central bureau, defending its successes, arguing with intransient Americans—for an operation he assumed would within a year be overwhelmed by a global war.[74] Historians continue to debate the perceived inevitability of the conflict, but for the French, German, and American companies that contributed to the bureau in July 1913, it can hardly have seemed inevitable.

One year and four days after Hans Kern wrote proudly to members of the Liverpool Cotton Brokers' Association about the agreed-upon international funding for the central bureau in New York, Britain declared war on Germany. The next day, Parliament passed the Alien Registration Act, soon followed by a series of Defense of the Realm bills. Aliens were required to register with local officials, and enemy aliens could not engage in banking except with the written permission of the secretary of state.[75] Kern was probably naturalized in Liverpool, but even so, he was likely subject to suspicion. By the end of summer, aliens were registering themselves with officials in England. The following year, in 1915, the King's Council took advantage of power given it by Parliament to issue order 14B, which allowed people considered of "hostile origin or association" to be interned. Kern's working life had been spent on questions of authenticity and honesty in commerce, ends he hoped to serve through internationalized efforts at verification. Barely had his most organized and impressive effort gotten off the ground when the long and unprecedented period of financial globalization, built up over decades and to a degree centuries, unraveled in a matter of weeks.[76]

CONCLUSION

"Money, Money, Money, and What Money Can Make of Life!"

I n 1942, safe in his perch in Cambridge, Massachusetts, Joseph A. Schumpeter completed what would be one of the most influential books on capitalism ever written, *Capitalism, Socialism and Democracy*. Schumpeter, a professor at Harvard University, had seen his share of adventure, both in the world and in the market, rising to become finance minister in his native Austria and later losing his fortune in the tumult of 1920s German and Austrian finance. He knew that capitalism was constantly evolving and possessed the capacity to undermine its own success, to sow the seeds of its own end. It was Schumpeter who coined the phrase "creative destruction." The world, as he saw it, was made and defined by commerce: "Unlike the class of feudal lords, the commercial and industrial bourgeoisie rose by business success. Bourgeois society has been cast in a purely economic mold: its foundations, beams and beacons are all made of economic material. The building faces toward the economic side of life. Prizes and penalties are measured in pecuniary terms. Going up and going down means making and losing money."[1] He also saw capitalism as a force of improvement in the world that had enhanced not just material well-being but liberty itself. Capitalism, in Schumpeter's view, had improved the qualities men and women valued and rewarded in commercial society. Metaphysics, mysticism, and romanticism had been sidelined in favor of rational behavior. "The stock exchange," he admitted in another memorable phrase, "is a poor substitute for the Holy Grail." But this was very much for the good. Heroism had been replaced by care for efficiency, service, and responsible behavior.[2]

Schumpeter was undeniably right that it was a commercial world; it had been so for some time. "The whole life I place before myself is money, money, money, and what money can make of life!" observes Bella in Dickens's *Our Mutual Friend*.[3] Bella would not have felt alone in Victorian London. The cause of liberty pulled Britons to the Latin American wars of independence, and the extension of Christianity and civilization may have driven Livingstone on his African journeys, but it was money that the holders of Latin American bonds were after, and it was money that the investors in South African diamond and gold mines sought.

But what of Schumpeter's other claim: had capitalism really made its participants better and more rational people? Adam Smith may have been the prophet of self-interest, but he was also the preacher of responsible commercial behavior. He noted the importance of skill, prudence, frugality, and responsibility, and he decried extravagance, overtrading, and speculation. But the commercial world that followed upon Smith's century little resembled the arena of probity and sociability that he encouraged. As his student John Millar predicted, sociability faded in a world of greater complexity, distance, speed, and quantity than ever before. The criminal capitalism of the nineteenth century stretched from the hawkers of tainted candy on the streets of London to the forgers of bills in the American South. Beer was adulterated, bonds faked and traded. Financial and commercial markets created remarkable innovations, bequeathing to the twentieth century new forms of sovereign debt, new types of insurance, and opportunities for trade and investment all over the world. New assets and riches were forged, in both senses of the word. Speculation only grew more prevalent, while misinformation flooded the City and its journals and papers. Fraud and forgery were everywhere in Britain's newspapers, novels, and courtrooms. From all over the world, strangers came singing of riches to be had in the mines of Latin America, the railways of North America, the mines of South Africa. This was the work of Gregor MacGregor, Benjamin Disraeli, Beaumont Smith, and Harry Marks.

In 1890, the *Economist*, a staunch defender of capitalism, expressed significant concern over stock puffing through the publication of fraudulent prospectuses. In an article titled "Company Promoting Frauds," the publication affirmed that investors bore ultimate responsibility for their actions. Nonetheless, it advocated certain "safeguards." "There is one suggestion of so much importance," they urged, "that we venture once more to urge it upon the Government: it is that every new company applying to the public for the subscription of capitals should at first have only a probationary existence of two or three months." At the end of the decade, the magazine was still forcefully making the same point, in language that Schumpeter would have found familiar: "There is nothing heroic in asking for full disclosures in prospectuses, and in demanding that the director who deems ignorance his best protection and consequently shuts his eyes to frauds, upon those whose interests he is supposed to safeguard, should not be permitted to do so without impunity."[4]

The cotton traders of the Atlantic did not seek government regulation, but they, too, recognized the need for enhanced oversight of their interdependent financial network. By the end of the nineteenth century, those participating in commerce and those endorsing commerce had come to recognize the need for enhanced policing of the criminal aspects of capitalism. "Money," Dickens's Bella also observed, "might make a much worse change in me." Not just for Bella but for all commercial relations, this was a distinct problem.

Here is a fundamental point about free market capitalism and trust within it: without social exclusion or extensive processes of verification, trust is very hard to come by. Whereas other risks could be hedged or managed through new assets or new types of insurance, the risk of fraud became more prevalent only as the market expanded. Simply put, trust was sometimes a market inadequacy but always a market necessity. A range of solutions were sought, all pointing to the fact that faith in the mere morality of another offered little comfort. Some sought to forge relations and build confidence through marriage and social networks. Others used networks of political and financial institutions to harness power and align the interests of people from similar backgrounds. As the pursuit of self-interest became more acceptable, people looked not only to character and status but also to reputation of commercial conduct. As reliance upon reputation became riskier, verification of information and assets assumed heightened importance. Just as the market kept evolving, so too did the manner in which trust was distributed, often through processes ever more elaborate and suspicious. This evolution of trust—responsive to a shifting marketplace and consciously vigilant against the most human of risks—was crucial to capitalism's survival and expansion. By century's end, the distribution of life insurance, the cashing of checks, and the transfer of shares were all meant to share similar processes. Bodies were inspected, agents reviewed, checks verified and reverified, shares properly registered and checked for valid ownership. This was a world of process and specialization, where the excesses and risks of self-interest were meant to be held at bay by, in part, objective evaluation. The sociability in which Adam Smith had placed his hopes for harnessing self-interest was not a sufficient safeguard in the sometimes criminal capitalism of the ruthless free market. Instead, trust was built through a series of deliberative approaches created or enhanced over a century.

In its twentieth anniversary edition, Harry Marks's *Financial News* bragged of the millions of pounds that had been invested in speculation during its existence. It was forced to acknowledge, however, that investment in shares, especially mining shares, had taken a precipitous drop following the passage of the Companies Act of 1900. That act, and that which followed it in 1908, extended limited liability for directors, but it also increased directors' risk with regard to misinformation and demanded increased transparency regarding prospectuses. And while nineteenth-century legislation had generally increased the amount of information available to the public, the early twentieth century, beginning with the Companies Act, would see an increased role for government in regulating financial information. Prospectuses now had to show how many shares each director held and what fees promoters had been paid. Additionally, all companies, for the first time since 1856, had to submit annual audits. The first audits may have been unreliable, but here was a direct state intervention in policing information and managing the risks associated with asymmetric information.

Over the next hundred years, such attempts to shape and police the marketplace would come in many forms, both private and public.

Corporations, not unlike Globe Insurance Company, sought to manage efficiency and encourage sociability and communication while also entrenching systems of verification and inspection. Firms began to take more active and systematized approaches to managing employees. For some, this meant aggressive inspection of employees' work,[5] while for others it meant systematizing management.[6] In the twentieth century it would become clear that large firms benefited from encouraging trust and discouraging authoritarian hierarchy. Firms became institutions in which trust was to be built through shared culture and values.[7] They became, and remain, sites of manufactured sociability and trust.

Modern trust relies on a series of overlapping institutions, not all of which are the sole province of the private sector. In Britain, the early decades of the twentieth century saw stronger laws regarding fraud, accounting, and the presentation of financial information, both in company reports and in prospectuses. The state—its power and ability expanding—played an increasingly important role not only in regulating information but also in verifying individual identity, through mechanisms like the passport.[8] On both sides of the Atlantic, the excesses of capitalism, as represented by monopolists and robber barons and as practiced in margin trading, would become targets of government regulators. The Great Depression would not only necessitate state intervention in social welfare but also would further demonstrate to liberals and progressives that the market could not be left alone. The two world wars greatly increased the role of the state in the private sector, but much of the justification for state involvement could be found in the abuses and excesses of self-interest.

Adam Smith had described a system that would bring violence and crises, that would not cure economic inequality, but that would bring greater material well-being and perhaps more freedom and opportunity than ever before. In *The Wealth of Nations* he memorably wrote: "It is not from the benevolence of the butcher, the brewer, or the baker, that we expect our dinner, but from regard to their own interest."[9] As for the butcher and brewer, so too for the banker and broker, the merchant and insurance agent: pursue self-interest but harness it with virtues that limit excess.

One hundred and sixty-eight years later, in 1944 Friedrich Hayek published *The Road to Serfdom*. He addressed another central concern of Smith's, the role of the state—in this case centralized planning rather than mercantilism. Writing in London, he, like Schumpeter, saw a world at war but also a longer history of remarkable development. "By the beginning of the twentieth century the working-man in the Western world had reached a degree of material comfort, security, and personal independence which a hundred years before had seemed scarcely possible."[10] But just as *The Wealth of Nations* was buttressed by Smith's earlier *Theory of Moral Sentiments* (1759), so too did Hayek's most famous work have a buttressing text. In 1960, ensconced in Chicago, Hayek published *The Constitution of Liberty*, a radical and profound defense of individual choice and freedom. "A free society probably demands more than any other that people be guided in their action by a sense of responsibility which extends beyond the duties exacted by law and that the general opinion approve of the individuals' being held responsible for both the success and the failure of their endeavors."[11]

The greatest intellectual salesmen of free market capitalism all supposed the market would be buttressed by morality. You could not responsibly unleash the power of one without the support of the other. Hayek, for his part, advocated spontaneity over central planning, liberalism over socialism, and market distribution over state distribution. In this world we would get richer, and indeed we have. Of course, such a world had existed before, and if the stories and actions of its players are to be trusted, their persistence and creativity helped make them richer, while their morality let them down—not for the last time.

Notes

INTRODUCTION A Definition; An Argument

1. Francis Fukuyama, *Trust* (New York: Free Press, 1995), 26. For a similar definition, see also Steven Shapin, *A Social History of Truth* (Chicago: Chicago University Press, 1994).

2. Fukuyama, *Trust*, 33–41.

3. Fukuyama, *Trust*, 30; Oliver Goodenough and Monika Gruter Cheney, "Is Free Enterprise Values in Action?," in *Morals and Markets: The Critical Role of Values in the Economy*, edited by Paul J. Zak (Princeton, NJ: Princeton University Press, 2008), xxiv. See also Rafael La Porta, Florencio Lopez-de-Silanes, Andrei Shleifer, and Robert W. Vishny, "Trust in Large Organizations," *American Economic Review*, vol. 87, no. 2 (May 1997): 333–338. In their study, La Porta et al. found the effects of trust on performance to be "statistically significant and quantitatively large." See also Stephen Knack and Paul Zack, "Trust and Growth," *Economic Journal*, vol. 111 (April 2001): 470. Luigi Guiso, Paola Sapienza, and Luigi Zingales, in "The Role of Social Capital in Financial Development" (*American Economic Review*, vol. 94, no. 3 [June 2004]: 316), conclude that "trust itself is positively and significantly related to growth in every case when it is included in growth regressions with a measure of formal institutions or of social distance." It is important to note that there is also such a thing as trusting too much. Following upon the collapse of the housing market, the fall of Lehman Brothers, and the 2008–2009 recession, three economists analyzed the relationship between the trust levels of particular individuals and their economic well-being. Highly trusting people, they found, are more likely to be cheated by banks or in commercial exchanges. According to their study, highly trusting people are three times more likely to be cheated than people who have the "right amount of trust." The history presented in this volume will bear this point out repeatedly. Highly distrustful people also paid

a pecuniary penalty, though due to loss of opportunity rather than swindling. See Jeffrey Butler, Paola Giuliano, and Luigi Guiso, "The Right Amount of Trust," NBER Working Paper Series 15344 (Cambridge, MA: National Bureau of Economic Research, 2009).

4. Robert L. Trivers, "The Evolution of Reciprocal Altruism," *Quarterly Review of Biology*, vol. 46, no. 1 (March 1971): 35–47.

5. For historical perspective on this, see Nathan Nunn and Leonard Wantchekon, "The Trans-Atlantic Slave Trade and the Evolution of Mistrust in Africa: An Empirical Investigation," Working Paper no. 100 (Afrobarometer, June 2008).

6. World Values Survey, 1995–2009 (www.jdsurvey.net/jds/ShowMap.jsp ?Idioma=I&MAPA=FCMap_WorldwithCountries&ID=2, accessed December 11, 2011). The World Values Survey is conducted via questionnaire and interviews in the selected countries and is a product of the World Values Survey Association, an independent collection of leading social scientists. The standard survey question on trust is: "Generally speaking, would you say that most people can be trusted or that you can't be too careful in dealing with people?" For debate on the accuracy of the survey and its trust question, see Paola Sapienza, Anna Toldra, and Luigi Zingales, "Understanding Trust," NBER Working Paper 13387 (Cambridge, MA: National Bureau of Economic Research, 2007); and Noel D. Johnson and Alexandra Mislin, "How Much Should We Trust the World Values Survey Trust Question?" (GMU Working Paper in Economics no. 11-44), *Economics Letters*, vol. 116, no. 2 (2012): 210–212.

7. See World Values Survey.

8. To begin with, see Peter Bernstein, *Against the Gods: The Remarkable Story of Risk* (New York: Wiley, 1996); see also Edward Chancellor, *Devil Take the Hindmost: A History of Financial Speculation* (New York: Farrar, Straus, Giroux, 1999); David A. Moss, *When All Else Fails* (Cambridge, MA: Harvard University Press, 2002); and, more recently, Jonathan Levy, *Freaks of Fortune* (Cambridge, MA: Harvard University Press, 2012).

9. Levy, *Freaks of Fortune*, 37.

10. "Report of Chairs on Foreign Business," 22 September 1853, No. 2 Reports, GH: Ms 11662/1, pp. 35–45.

11. Karl Marx, *The Communist Manifesto* (New York: W.W. Norton, 2013; originally published 1848); Joseph A. Schumpeter, *Capitalism, Socialism and Democracy* (New York: Harper Perennial, 2008; originally published 1942).

ONE   "All Trades and Places Knew Some Cheat"

1. Adam Smith, *The Wealth of Nations* (New York: Modern Library, 1994; originally published 1776), book 4, chapter 2, 485. For an extended conversation on the "invisible hand," see Emma Rothschild, *Economic Sentiments* (Cambridge, MA: Harvard University Press, 2001), chapter 6.

2. Adam Smith, The *Theory of Moral Sentiments*, 2 volumes, 7th edition (London, 1792), vol. 2, 51.

3. Smith, *Theory of Moral Sentiments*, 132, vol. 2.

4. Smith, *Theory of Moral Sentiments*, 187, vol. 2.

5. J. G. A. Pocock, *The Machiavellian Moment* (Princeton, NJ: Princeton University Press, 1975), 470.

6. As Emma Rothschild has pointed out, there were three main concerns around which the critiques of political economy turned. The first regarded the denial by those advocating free trade of the role government had already played and was playing in protecting economic exchange, particularly at great distance. The second concerned the confidence in individuals, particularly those with connection to political power, not to abuse their power in a corrupt fashion. Smith shared this concern, as did he the third, which focused on the risk implicit in open exchange, as it required, or at least they thought, civility and virtue. See Rothschild, *The Inner Life of Empires* (Princeton, NJ: Princeton University Press, 2011), 152.

7. David Hume, "On Commerce," in *Essays Moral, Political, and Literary*, vol. 1 (London: Longmans, Green, and Co., 1875), 196.

8. David Hume, "Of Refinement in the Arts," in *Essays Moral, Political, and Literary*, 301–302.

9. Albert O. Hirschmann, *The Passions and the Interests* (Princeton, NJ: Princeton University Press, 1977), 70–81. See also Rothschild, *Economic Sentiments*, for an extended conversation of Nicolas de Condorcet's later role in the development of such ideas.

10. Hirschmann points out that for Montesquieu, as well as for James Steuart, this was largely a "deterrence model," which did not draw the executive into encouraging commerce but did keep the executive from arbitrary interference. Hirschmann, *Passions and the Interests*, 8.

11. Rothschild, *Economic Sentiments*, 25–37; see also Pocock, *Machiavellian Moment*, 470.

12. John Millar, *Historical View of the English Government*, volume 4 (London: 1803), 202.

13. A library has been spent parsing the concepts of morality as opposed to ethics. For this work, I have chosen to follow the lead of Deirdre N. McCloskey in *The Bourgeois Virtues: Ethics for an Age of Commerce* (Chicago: University of Chicago Press, 2006) and not belabor the differentiation.

14. Smith, *Theory of Moral Sentiments*, vol. 2, 85.

15. Rothschild, *Inner Life of Empires*, 3, 183. The British owed much of this conception of a unified, naturalized economy, linking a nation of agents to a single economic sphere, to their French counterparts, including, as Bernard E. Harcourt indicates, François Quesnay. Harcourt, *The Illusion of Free Markets* (Cambridge, MA: Harvard University Press, 2011).

16. Bernard Mandeville, *The Fable of the Bees: or, Private Vices, Publick Benefits*, 3rd edition (London, 1724), 3.

17. Mandeville, *Fable of the Bees*, 3.

18. Mandeville, *Fable of the Bees*, 9.

19. In a single year, shares jumped from just over £100 to over £1000. In August 1720, the bubble popped, having taken in some of the day's great minds, including Alexander Pope and Sir Isaac Newton. French investors were taken by a similar scheme, rushing into shares of the Mississippi Company, the undertaking of John Law, an exiled Scotsman. Both were classic investment bubbles in which investors crowded into exciting new opportunities with more regard for the share price than the prospects of the company itself. The results, however, were dramatically different. In France, the Mississippi Company collapsed, carrying down with it any semblance of financial stability and leaving behind a mistrust in financial innovation and institutions for the remainder of the century. In England, shareholders were given the option to convert their shares into perpetual annuities, anticipating the Bank of England annuities that would ultimately become at mid-century the trademark British financial asset, the Consol. In the face of a gigantic scandal, confidence in banks, securities, and debt was largely saved in England. For more on the South Sea bubble and Mississippi Company bubbles, see Larry Neal, *The Rise of Financial Capitalism* (New York: Cambridge University Press, 1990), chapter 4; also see Niall Ferguson, *The Ascent of Money* (New York: Penguin Press, 2008), chapter 3. Neal argues that the bubble has less to do with irrationality than with effects stemming from financial innovation, particularly international financial flows. Thomas Levenson points out that Newton's loss was the equivalent of roughly forty years of his salary at the time. Levenson, *Newton and the Counterfeiters* (London: Faber and Faber, 2009), 244.

20. Millar, *Historical View*, 187.

21. Millar, *Historical View*, 247.

22. Pocock, *Machiavellian Moment*, 502.

23. Millar, *Historical View*, 236, 249–250.

24. Hume, "Of Refinement in the Arts," 309.

25. Data from William McNeill, *The Great Frontier* (Princeton, NJ: Princeton University Press, 1983), 34; Angus Maddison, *The World Economy: Historical Statistics* (Paris, France: Development Centre of the Organization for Economic Co-operation and Development, 2003), 410–415, table 1a.

26. This phenomenon was not limited to England. The population of India increased by one hundred million, or nearly fifty percent, from 1820 to 1913, while that of China grew from 381 million to 437 million. This is a question not just of numbers but of location. North America, sub-Saharan Africa, and the Pacific region saw rapid rises in their urban population. C. A. Bayly, the chronicler of global historical trends, estimates that between 1870 and 1900 the percentage of the world population living in urban centers expanded from 12 to 20 percent, particularly in cities like Melbourne, San Francisco, and Kimberley, which experienced either trading or mineral booms. See Maddison, *World Economy*, table 5-1, p. 530, and table 5a, p. 538; C. A. Bayly, *The Birth of the Modern World: 1780–1914* (New York: Wiley-Blackwell, 2003).

27. Joel Mokyr, *The Enlightened Economy: An Economic History of Britain, 1700–1850* (New York: Yale University Press, 2010), 302.

28. Richard Sennett has drawn a distinction between two types of strangers, the first being outsiders, but who can at least be recognized as outsiders, and the second being a person that is unknown, who cannot be placed in station or background. The latter type of stranger was the stranger of London in the nineteenth century, common as they are in periods of social and economic transition. See Sennett, *The Fall of Public Man* (New York: Knopf, 1974), 17–49. See also J. A. Banks, "Population Change and the Victorian City," *Victorian Studies*, vol. 11 (1968): 277–289.

29. Sennett, *Fall of Public Man*, 133; Mokyr, *Enlightened Economy*, 222.

30. Henry Mayhew, *London Characters: Illustrations of the Humour, Pathos and Peculiarities of London* (London, 1881), 20. On Dickens's young life in London, see Michael Slater, *Charles Dickens* (New Haven, CT: Yale University Press, 2009), 19.

31. Boyd Hilton, *The Age of Atonement: The Influence of Evangelicalism on Social and Economic Thought, 1795–1865* (Oxford: Clarendon Press; New York: Oxford University Press, 1988), 67–70.

32. Linda Colley, *Captives: Britain, Empire and the World, 1600–1850* (London: Jonathan Cape, 2002), 4; Niall Ferguson, *Empire* (New York: Basic Books, 2003), 202. Ferguson estimates that the European empires ruled over nearly 60 percent of the world's area and population just prior to the First World War.

33. Robert Vaughan, *The Age of Great Cities* (London, 1843), 115.

34. Tony Ballantyne and Antoinette Burton, "Empires and the Reach of the Global," in *A World Connecting*, edited by Emily S. Rosenberg (Cambridge, MA: Belknap Press, 2013), 354. Admittedly, this interconnectedness Vaughan described had multiple poles as Germany and France extended their reaches in Africa, not to mention China, Indochina, and the South Sea, while Russia stretched its power farther into Central Asia and beyond. And not all the world's trade and information had to flow through the European imperial capitals of London, Paris, Berlin, and Moscow. India, the jewel of the British Empire by the end of the nineteenth century, had commercial networks that skipped London altogether. Prior to the Napoleonic Wars, Indian trade with Europe had consisted largely of textile exports swapped for bullion import. Over the second half of the century this pattern shifted, as Indian exports focused around raw goods such as opium, cotton, food grains, and jute. By the turn of the century, Bombay cotton was the chief provider to the burgeoning Japanese textile market. Roy Tirthankar, *The Economic History of India, 1857–1947* (Oxford: Oxford University Press, 2000).

35. Walter Bagehot, *Lombard Street* (London, 1873), 6, 43; Ranald Michie, *Guilty Money: The City of London in Victorian and Edwardian Culture, 1815–1914* (London: Pickering and Chatto, 2009), 4–5; A. J. Christopher, "Patterns of British Overseas Investment in Land, 1885–1913," *Transactions of the Institute of British Geographers*, new series, vol. 10, no. 4 (1985): 455.

36. In *Free Trade Nation* (Oxford: Oxford University Press, 2007), Frank Trentmann divides the idea of free trade and its application into four different eras: the late seventeenth- and early eighteenth-century critique of mercantilism; 1815–1870, a period of advancing trade liberalization; the end of the nineteenth and early twentieth century, during which time, while much of the world went protectionist, Britain expanded free trade, employing no tariffs and allowing the intellectual foundations of free trade to extend into popular and democratic culture; the final period, which brings us into the present, he suggests, is defined by post–Bretton Woods multilateralism. Of course, the notion of a "free market" is itself something of a construct, and an especially controversial one at that. In *The Illusion of Free Markets*, Harcourt shows just how much regulation, often self-regulation, underpins markets that we think relatively free today; meanwhile, some of the most famous mercantilist markets, he argues, operated with greater freedom than previously thought.

37. George Smeeton, *Doings in London: Or, Day and Night Scenes of the Frauds, Frolics, Manners, and Depravities of the Metropolis* (London, 1828), 10.

38. *Old Bailey Proceedings Online* (www.oldbaileyonline.org, version 6.0, April 17, 2011): tabulating year against offense category where offense category is forgery and verdict category is guilty; tabulating year against offense category where offense category is fraud and verdict category is guilty.

39. Rob Sindall, "Middle-Class Crime in Nineteenth-Century England," *Criminal Justice History*, no. 4 (1983): 29; Barrett as quoted in Sindall, "Middle-Class Crime," 31.

40. Edward Bulwer-Lytton, *Money* (London, 1853; originally published 1840), 2.

41. Bulwer-Lytton, *Money*, 45.

42. Mayhew, *London Characters*, 13, 40.

43. Shirley Robin Letwin, *The Gentleman in Trollope* (Cambridge, MA: Harvard University Press, 1982).

44. Anthony Trollope, *The Way We Live Now* (New York: Modern Library, 1996; originally published 1875), 503.

45. Eustace Clare Grenville Murray, *Under the Lens: Social Photographs*, volume 1, 2nd edition (London, 1886), 157.

46. John Maynard Keynes, "The Works of Bagehot," *Economic Journal*, vol. 25, no. 99 (Sept. 1915): 371.

47. Bagehot, *Lombard Street*, 10, 69.

48. Bagehot, *Lombard Street*, 158.

49. P. G. Cain and A. G. Hopkins, *British Imperialism, 1688–2000* (London: Longman, 1993), 114–127; Youssef Cassis, *City Bankers, 1890–1914*, translated by Margaret Rocques (Cambridge: Cambridge University Press, 1994). Cassis centers his study upon those families and figures who held "key" positions in the City, guessing that his figures represent those that made up 45–50 percent of the City and 15–20

percent of the banking community, not including executives and employees below the general manager level.

50. Cain and Hopkins, *British Imperialism*, 126.

TWO Unreliable Virtue

1. See Maya Jasanoff, *Liberty's Exiles* (New York: Knopf, 2011), for the ways in which Loyalists reconstructed their lives after leaving America while also altering the shape of the nineteenth-century British Empire.

2. William Brodey Gurney, *The Trial of Charles Random de Berenger, Sir Thomas Cochran* (London, 1814), 120. The account was taken in shorthand by W. B. Gurney, who was shorthand writer to both houses of Parliament. All quotations from the trial come from the court reporter's published copy of the trial. As was true for speeches in Parliament, it was commonplace at the time for a judge to have the opportunity to review and edit his comments before publication. This tradition, which the presiding judge, Edward Law, 1st Baron Ellenborough, made use of in this case, makes his summary suspect, and it is treated as such. As it turns out, however, it strengthens the remainder of the account as a source. In the extended public letter written to Ellenborough in 1815, Thomas Cochrane suggested the judge altered the final record of the trial's proceedings. Though Cochrane himself acknowledged that it was common practice for a judge to view the record of proceedings before publication, he argued in his letter that the changes to his charge to the jury were especially extreme and were used to hide the bias with which he addressed the jury members. The charge, then, has to be taken as unreliable. Cochrane stated that Richard Butt, his co-accused and broker, had employed a separate shorthand notetaker and that his representation of the charge was quite different, presumably without edit. This copy is not known to exist. Nor, I would argue, with the exception of the charge, do we need it. Cochrane argued that the published version was edited, but only the charge. He meticulously went through the proceedings of the trial without suggesting they were altered. In fact, he used Gurney's shorthand to argue his own points. Cochrane, who had access to the other copy of shorthand, found this version reliable and consistent and used it for his argument.

3. Gurney, *Trial of Charles Random de Berenger*, 120.

4. Lord Thomas Cochrane, *The Autobiography of a Seaman* (Canada: Lyon's Press, 2000; originally published 1860).

5. Ron Chernow, *Alexander Hamilton* (New York: Penguin Books, 2005), 31.

6. Cochrane, *Autobiography of a Seaman*, 47; see also the biography by David Cordingly, *Cochrane* (London: Bloomsbury, 2007), 57. Cordingly's thorough and readable biography is the best place to go for the reader seeking a full-length treatment of Cochrane's life. He dedicates a chapter to the hoax and is especially good with the treatment of his naval career. Cordingly points out that Cochrane's surgeon later corrected details of this description, but deception was very much the game and tactic. Another extended treatment of the hoax is provided by Richard Dale in *"Napoleon is*

Dead": Lord Cochrane and the Great Stock Exchange Scandal (Stroud: Sutton, 2006). During early periods of research, I also found Paul Johnson's online article "Civilising Mammon" very helpful. Johnson grapples not only with Cochrane but also with Harry Marks. Johnson, "Civilising Mammon: Fraud and Profit in Nineteenth-Century London," fathom.lse.ac.uk/Features/121984/, retrieved April 18, 2011.

7. In the seventeenth century, the Crown reserved the right to a sizable portion of seized goods, with Elizabeth I, for example, claiming 50 percent. This changed with the Convoy and Cruizers Act of 1708, and until 1808, when the relevant act was revised, the captain of a ship could claim up to three-eighths the value of seized goods deemed by the Admiralty to be prizes of war. The remainder would be divided among the rest of the ship's crew on a descending scale.

8. Richard Hill, *The Prizes of War: The Naval Prize System in the Napoleonic Wars, 1793–1815* (Stroud, UK: Royal Naval Museum Publications, 1998), chapter 1. All prize hearings were held at Admiralty Court, in a place called Doctors' Commons. The prize-taking system was carefully regulated by the Admiralty to keep the system from growing out of control—in essence, as Hill points out, the question was always whether or not the goods could be categorized as a lawful prize.

9. British National Archives: CRES 2/791. In 1829, he purchased Hanover Lodge, a villa in Regent Park.

10. Cochrane, *Autobiography of a Seaman*, 230.

11. Cochrane, *Autobiography of a Seaman*, 224. For more on the Basque Roads, see W. B. Gurney, *Minutes on a Court Martial* (London, 1809), where Cochrane's version is presented as transcribed from Lord Gambier's Courts Martial.

12. Gurney, *Minutes on a Court Martial*, 46–48.

13. For an extended discussion of the relationship between war and financial institutions during this period, see John Brewer, *Sinews of Power: War, Money, and the English State, 1688–1783* (New York: Knopf, 1988), and Niall Ferguson, *The Cash Nexus* (New York: Basic Books, 2001), chapter 1. Between 1685 and 1813, Ferguson points out, British military spending consumed between 55 and 90 percent of central government expenditure.

14. "How seldom," John Millar would later ask rhetorically when discussing 1688, "are kings prevented from going to war with each other because they happen to be relations?" Millar, *An Historical View of the English Government*, vol. 3 (London, 1803), 486.

15. John Millar, *An Historical View of the English Government*, vol. 3, 4.

16. Douglass C. North and Barry Weingast, "Constitution and Commitment: The Evolution of Institutional Governing Public Choice in Seventeenth-Century England," *Journal of Economic History*, vol. 49, no. 4 (1989): 803–832. See also Millar, *Historical View*, 496: "The consequence of this new deposition was to place the new king in circumstances which prevented him ever after from calling in question those powers of parliament which he had solemnly recognized."

17. "By all I have yet read of the history of our own country, it appears to me, that the national debts, secured upon parliamentary funds, were things unknown in

England before the last revolution under the Prince of *Orange*," would write a caustic Jonathan Swift in *The History of the Last Four Years of the Queen* (London, 1753), 156.

18. Brewer, *Sinews of Power.*

19. James Macdonald, *A Free Nation Deep in Debt* (New York: Farrar, Straus and Giroux, 2003), 252–254; Ferguson, *Cash Nexus*, 112–117.

20. Larry Neal, *The Rise of Financial Capitalism* (Cambridge: Cambridge University Press, 1990), 90.

21. Swift, *History of the Last Four Years of the Queen*, 170.

22. See Craig Muldrew, *The Economy of Obligation: The Culture of Credit and Social Obligations in Early Modern England* (New York: St. Martin's Press, 1998); Muldrew, "'Hard Food for Midas': Cash and Its Social Value in Early Modern England," *Past and Present*, no. 170 (February 2001): 78–120; and Carl Wennerlind, *Casualties of Credit* (Cambridge, MA: Harvard University Press, 2011). Money, Muldrew estimates, formed less than one-fifteenth of the value of exchanges in the merchant world.

23. Daniel Defoe, *A Tour through the Whole Island of Great Britain* (London, 1724), iv–vi.

24. Ferguson, *Cash Nexus*, 124; Neal, *Rise of Financial Capitalism*, 225, 277.

25. Charles Kindleberger, *A Financial History of Western Europe* (New York: Oxford University Press, 1993), 160–162.

26. Kindleberger, *Financial History*, 78.

27. David Kynaston, *The City of London: A World of Its Own, 1815–1890*, volume 1 (London: Chatto and Windus, 1994–2001); Kindleberger, *Financial History*, 84.

28. Anti-City sentiment was nothing new and would reoccur in waves over the nineteenth century. Rather predictably, it tended to follow financial crises and the collapse of investment bubbles. There are a number of insightful texts on the commercial culture and life in the City of London in the nineteenth century. Ferguson's Rothschilds biography is especially helpful on the financial dimension. See Niall Ferguson, *The House of Rothschild*, volume 1 (New York: Viking, 1998). I have found the work of Kynaston—and in particular his history of the City—and of Michie to be especially helpful. See David Kynaston, *The City of London: A World of Its Own, 1815–1890*, volume 1 (London: Chatto & Windus, 1994; Ranald Michie, *Guilty Money: The City of London in Victorian and Edwardian Culture, 1815–1914* (London: Pickering and Chatto, 2009), 13–26. See also Youssef Cassis on the dynamics of European capitals in the late nineteenth century and Lance Davis and Larry Neal on the logistics of institutions and international finance. See Youssef Cassis, *Capitals of Capital: A History of International Financial Centers*. Trans. Jacqueline Collier (Cambridge: Cambridge University Press, 2006); Davis and Neal, "Micro Rules and Macro Outcomes: The Impact of Micro-structure on the Efficiency of Security Exchanges, London, New York, and Paris, 1800–1914," *American Economic Review*, vol. 88, no. 2 (1998): 40–45 and the standard works of P. J. Cain and A. G. Hopkins, in particular *British Imperialism: Innovation and Expansion, 1688–1914* (New York: Longman, 1993).

29. William Cobbett, *Rural Rides* (London, 1830), 45, 69, 7.

30. Practical Jobber, *The System of Stock-Jobbing Explained Exposing the Ground of the Art . . .* (London, 1816), iv, 12.

31. Cobbett, *Rural Rides*, 11.

32. J. G. A. Pocock, *The Machiavellian Moment* (Princeton, NJ: Princeton University Press, 1975), 407–408.

33. William Thackeray, *Vanity Fair* (London, first published 1848), 30, 35.

34. Davis and Neal, "Micro Rules and Macro Outcomes"; Larry Neal and Lance Davis, "The Evolution of the Structure and Performance of the London Stock Exchange in the First Global Financial Market, 1812–1914," *European Review of Economic History*, vol. 10 (2006): 279–300. Davis and Neal, two leading historians of the Exchange, have demonstrated that the structure assumed by the Exchange at its inception and immediately thereafter guided its shape and form for nearly two centuries. Micro-structure, as they put it, had macro-effects.

35. Neal and Davis, "Evolution of the Structure and Performance," 282.

36. Davis and Neal, "Micro Rules and Macro Outcomes," 43. It is useful to be reminded of Patrick Joyce's description of the particular form of British freedom that was born in the early nineteenth century: "In liberalism rule is ceded to a self that must constantly monitor the very civil society and political power that are at once the guarantee of freedom and its threat." Patrick Joyce, *The Rule of Freedom: Liberalism and the Modern City* (New York: Verso, 2003), 4.

37. *Rules and Regulations Adopted by the Committee for the General Purposes of the Stock Exchange* (London, 1812), 38.

38. Meaning the government could buy back the debt with sterling at its discretion if the price of the security rose above its face value.

39. Adam Smith, *The Wealth of Nations* (New York: Modern Library, 1994; originally published 1776), book 4, 131.

40. David Ricardo to Sir John Sinclair, October 31, 1814, in David Ricardo, *The Letters of David Ricardo to Hutches Trower and Others, 1811–1823*, edited by James Bonar and J. H. Hollander (Oxford: Clarendon Press, 1899), 7.

41. Emma Rothschild, *The Inner Life of Empires* (Princeton, NJ: Princeton University Press, 2011), 173.

42. Gurney, *Trial of Charles Random de Berenger*, 164.

43. Ferguson, *The House of Rothschild*, 94; Lord Victor Rothschild, *The Shadow of a Great Man* (London, 1982), 2, 9.

44. Consol prices from the *Times* and James VanSommer, *Tables Exhibiting the Various Fluctuations in Three Per Cent Consols* (London, 1834). East India Company and Bank of England prices from Neal, *Rise of Financial Capitalism*, 252–253. Prices reported in many sources, including the *Times*, were often taken from the list issued by the Stock Exchange around midday. Prices were collected at various hours throughout the day, which explains, in part, why prices appear slightly different depending upon the publication.

45. Gurney, *Trial of Charles Random de Berenger*, 82–84.

46. Vary T. Coates, Bernard Finn, et al., *A Retrospective Technology Assessment: Submarine Telegraphy: The Transatlantic Cable of 1866* (San Francisco, CA: San Francisco Press, 1979), 1; Tom Standage, *The Victorian Internet* (New York: Walker, 1999), 2–21. As with subsequent revolutions in communication, commerce, security, and power were intertwined with the telegraph from its very beginning. In 1808, Cochrane and the *Imperieuse* briefly sailed France's Languedoc shore destroying French semaphores.

47. *Times*, January 15, 1814, and February 22, 1814.

48. Ranald Michie, "The London and New York Stock Exchanges, 1850–1914," *Journal of Economic History*, vol. 46, no. 1 (March 1986): 171–187.

49. These are the numbers his traders presented in the trial, that the exchange offered as evidence against him, and that he himself offered in his affidavit.

50. Nathan Rothschild received the news of Napoleon's defeat at Waterloo nearly forty-eight hours before Wellington's official dispatch reached his government. It has long been part of the Rothschild story that early information on Wellington's victory allowed Nathan to preempt the market and secure a huge profit. Turning information into profit, however, is not always an easy or straightforward exercise. As Ferguson has shown, the period following Waterloo was in fact an especially tenuous one for the brothers. The Rothschilds' triumph came not because a Rothschild was present at Waterloo, but simply because Nathan correctly timed a longer bet on the 3 percent Consol and the Omnium. He had gone heavily into the two in late 1815 and got out five months before the market's peak in December 1817, turning a profit of £250,000. That is not to say that Nathan had not acted upon the early information received after Waterloo. The London papers reported that he made great purchases. It is not clear whether this was indeed the case, and it is doubtful that the purchases would have proved of exceptional profit because the extent of the purchases he could have legally made was limited to 20,000 per agent, which would have left a profit of 7,080.

51. Ferguson, *House of Rothschild*, 94–100.

52. Bernard E. Harcourt, *The Illusion of the Free Markets* (Cambridge, MA: Harvard University Press, 2011), 39–41.

THREE Vice on Trial

1. William Brodey Gurney, *The Trial of Charles Random de Berenger, Sir Thomas Cochran* (London, 1814), 130, 142.

2. Pretrial publicity was commonplace in nineteenth-century England, despite being punishable by the charge of contempt. Newspapers often covered famous cases before the trial commenced, often with a bias toward the prosecution. See David Bentley, *English Criminal Justice in the Nineteenth Century* (London: Hambledon Press, 1998), 44–46.

3. Hastings was ultimately acquitted, and Ellenborough emerged more than three thousand pounds richer and looking toward a bright future. See Nicholas B. Dirks, *The Scandal of Empire* (Cambridge, MA: Harvard University Press, 2006).

4. Edmund Burke, *On Empire, Liberty, and Reform: Speeches and Letters*, edited by David Bromwich (New Haven, CT: Yale University Press, 2000), 383.

5. Gurney, *Trial of Charles Random de Berenger*, 16.

6. Gurney, *Trial of Charles Random de Berenger*, 70.

7. Cochrane would not have been allowed to testify in his own defense, a statute that was in place in fact to keep defendants from having to implicate themselves.

8. Gurney, *Trial of Charles Random de Berenger*, 269.

9. Gurney, *Trial of Charles Random de Berenger*, 34.

10. Gurney, *Trial of Charles Random de Berenger*, 479.

11. Gurney, *Trial of Charles Random de Berenger*, 276.

12. Cochrane's affidavit appears in Gurney, *Trial of Charles Random de Berenger*, 38.

13. Gurney, *Trial of Charles Random de Berenger*, 169.

14. Gurney, *Trial of Charles Random de Berenger*, 298.

15. Gurney, *Trial of Charles Random de Berenger*, 28, 440.

16. Jury members had to be men between the ages of twenty-one and sixty who met certain property-holding requirements. Traditionally, jury members were selected by ballot from a list kept by the local sheriff or magistrate. In particular cases, however, the prosecution could seek a special jury. These juries were often used in political trials, but in Cochrane's case, it was the financial elements of the crime that justified the special jury. A list of potential jurors would be selected from a list of freeholders, and the solicitor and defense counsel would each strike undesirable jurors until the list was halved, from which it was chosen at random. Cochrane's special jury was composed entirely of merchants from the City. David Bentley, *English Criminal Justice in the Nineteenth Century* (London: Hambledon Press, 1998), 89–97.

17. *Kents Original London Directory, 1814* (London, 1814).

18. George Smeeton, *Doings in London: Or, Day and Night Scenes of the Frauds, Frolics, Manners, and Depravities of the Metropolis* (London, 1828), 289.

19. "The Apprehension of Lord Cochrane," *Times*, March 22, 1815.

20. Richard Gude, *The Practice of the Crown Side of the Court of the King's Bench . . .* , vol. 1 (London, 1828), 404–406.

21. Gude, *The Practice of the Crown Side of the Court of the King's Bench*, 404–406.

22. In January 1815, Ellenborough urged a fellow lord on the Privy Council to attend the next sitting of the council: "In this age of misrepresentation false and unfounded reasons would be suggested for your absence on the 2nd day after attending on the first." Ellenborough to Thompson, January 25, 1815, British National Archives: 30/12/17/6, no. 28.

23. Lord Thomas Cochrane, *A Letter to Lord Ellenborough from Lord Cochrane* (London, 1815), 124.

24. Lord Thomas Cochrane, *The Autobiography of a Seaman* (Canada: Lyon's Press, 2000; originally published 1860), 341, 352. See also, for more detail, Cochrane, *Letter to Lord Ellenborough*. The fraud, which would follow Cochrane and Ellenborough for the rest of their lives, continued to shadow them even after death. In 1897, Ellenbor-

ough's family published the first of two defenses of the trial and its result, the latter of which, *The Guilt of Lord Cochrane in 1814*, was published in 1914 by the judge's grandson.

25. Thomas Metcalfe, *New Cambridge History of India*, volume 3, part 4 (Cambridge: Cambridge University Press, 2008), 29.

26. Burke, *On Empire, Liberty, and Reform*, 398.

27. Thomas Babington Macaulay, "Minute on Indian Education," in *Selected Writings*, edited by John Clive and Thomas Pinney (Chicago: University of Chicago Press), 249.

28. D. C. M. Platt, *Latin America and British Trade, 1806–1914* (London: A. and C. Black, 1972), 31.

29. W. D. Weatherhead, *An Account of the Late Expedition against the Isthmus of Darien, under the Command of Sir Gregor McGregor, London, Longman, Hurst, Reese . . .* (London, 1821), 126.

30. "Greece," *Times*, August 24, 1825. The article acknowledges that other causes may have contributed, but the effect of Cochrane's reputation cannot be avoided.

FOUR An Empire of Optimism

1. William Alexander Mackinnon, *On the Rise, Progress, and Present State of Public Opinion, in Great Britain, and Other Parts of the World* (London, 1828), 1–12, 22.

2. The concept of the public sphere was developed by Jurgen Habermas to describe, in short, the process by which public, supposedly rational, discourse became more prevalent in the century prior to the French Revolution. He used Britain as a paradigmatic example. The idea is a controversial one and has come under frequent attack from historians. As David Waldstreicher points out, much of this criticism has been rooted in Habermas's supposed Whiggish view of history, or its associated counterpart, modernization theory. Other criticisms, like those of Brian Cowan and Phil Withington, focus on the component parts and dating of "public sphere." Cowan has challenged the idea of coffee houses—crucial loci for the public sphere—and their supposed "discourse-oriented" space as truly being separate from the state. Withington, meanwhile, has argued that corporate "bodies" such as guilds and companies provided a framework and structure for public activity. The social composition of this public activity, he argues, was more diverse than the public sphere of the seventeenth and eighteenth centuries that is often associated with the expansion of the press and towns. In many ways, the public sphere is more useful as a concept than as a specific, temporal historical description. See Habermas, *The Structural Transformation of the Public Sphere: An Inquiry into a Category of Bourgeois Society* (Cambridge, MA: MIT Press, 1989); Waldstreicher, "Two Cheers for the 'Public Sphere' . . . and One for Historians' Skepticism," *William and Mary Quarterly*, third series, vol. 62, no. 1 (January 2005): 107–112; Cowan, "The Rise of the Coffeehouse Reconsidered," *Historical Journal*, vol. 47, no. 1 (March 2004): 21–46; Withington, "Public Discourse, Corporate Citizenship, and State Formation in Early Modern England," *American Historical Review*, vol. 112, no. 4 (October 2007): 1016–1038.

3. In 1792, according to Habermas, the idea of "public opinion" entered the House of Commons, replacing terms such as *common opinion* and *sense of the people*. Habermas, *Structural Transformation of the Public Sphere*, 6.

4. See Patrick Joyce, *The Rule of Freedom*, (London and New York: Verso, 2003), on map making and cities as public spheres.

5. Linda Colley, *Britons* (New Haven, CT: Yale University Press, 1992), 322; see also David Bell, *The First Total War* (Boston: Houghton Mifflin, 2007); Boyd Hilton, *Corn, Cash and Commerce: The Economic Policies of the Tory Governments, 1815–30* (Oxford: Oxford University Press, 1977).

6. Alexander von Humboldt, *Political Essay on the Kingdom of New Spain* (New York, 1811), ii–xiv.

7. Calvin P. Jones, "The Spanish-American Works of Alexander von Humboldt as Viewed by Leading British Periodicals," *Americans*, vol. 29, no. 4 (April 1973): 442–448.

8. John Lynch, "The Origins of Spanish American Independence," in *The Cambridge History of Latin America*, vol. 3, edited by Leslie Bethell (Cambridge: Cambridge University Press, 1985), 24; D. C. M. Platt, *Latin America and British Trade, 1806–1914* (London: A. and C. Black, 1972), 29.

9. There is less evidence of this portion of his life than many others. David Sinclair has pieced together much of it, and the hazy montage runs something like this: MacGregor visits Washington, DC, and pitches the young U.S. government on invading Amelia island, a territory of the Spanish; he sells property rights to the island to residents in South Carolina, Georgia, and New York; sailing from Charleston, he drives the few Spanish forces from the island and quickly sets up his own rule as liberator of the Floridas, his own currency included; with news of a looming Spanish counter-attack, and with Dona Josefa pregnant, MacGregor abandons the island and his forces there, sailing for Nassau. The island would soon end up an American territory, but MacGregor had found a pattern he could re-create.

10. Calvin P. Jones, "The Images of Simón Bolívar as Reflected in Ten Leading British Periodicals, 1816–1830," *Americas*, vol. 40, no. 3 (January 1983): 382. Linda Colley (*Britons*, 288–289) has shown the importance of uniforms as a status symbol for volunteer regiments in the Napoleonic Wars. They were, as was true in the case of the South American wars, expensive, impractical, and attractive. They were met to establish soldiers as gentleman.

11. Frank Trentmann, *Free Trade Nation* (Oxford: Oxford University Press, 2007), 20.

12. James Hackett, *Narrative of the Expedition Which Sailed from England in 1817, to Join the South American Patriots* (London, 1819), 68, 25; W. D. Weatherhead, *An Account of the Late Expedition against the Isthmus of Darien, under the Command of Sir Gregor McGregor, London, Longman, Hurst, Reese . . .* (London, 1821), 1.

13. In 1698, thirteen hundred colonists had sailed from Firth, Scotland, bound for Darien, on the east coast of the Panama isthmus. The stretch of land, rich in disease and jungle, had been the claim of the Spanish for centuries. William Paterson, of

the Bank of England plan, pushed Darien shares in London. Subscriptions at their peak reached £400,000, claiming one-fourth to one-half of Scotland's coinage. This was confidence that gave way to exuberance and ultimately tragedy, as over 70 percent of all who sailed to Darien died. Scotland's independence would soon disappear like the colony itself, partly as a result of the Darien scheme, with the signing of the Act of Union in 1707.

14. Weatherhead, *An Account*, 37, 25; John Besant, *Narrative of the Expedition under General MacGregor against Portobello* (London and Edinburgh, 1820), 26.

15. Weatherhead, *An Account*, 43.

16. Weatherhead, *An Account*, 43, 102, 99.

17. Moises Enrique Rodriguez, *Freedom's Mercenaries: British Volunteers in the Wars of Independence of Latin America* (Lanham, MD: Hamilton Books, 2006), 9.

18. Hackett, *Narrative of the Expedition*, x; G. Hippisley, *A Narrative of the Expedition to the Rivers Orinoco and Apure, in South America* (London, 1819), vi.

19. Hackett, *Narrative of the Expedition*, 68; Weatherhead, *An Account*, 65.

20. *Proceedings of an Inquiry and Investigation, Instituted by Major General Codd, His Majesty's Superintendant and Commander-in-Chief at Belize, Honduras, Relative to Poyais* (London: Lawler and Quick, by order of the Magistrate of Honduras, 1824), 100; David Sinclair, *The Land That Never Was: Sir Gregor MacGregor and the Most Audacious Fraud in History* (Cambridge, MA: Da Capo Press, 2004), 14.

21. Thomas Strangeways [Gregor MacGregor?], *Sketch of the Mosquito Shore, Including the Territory of Poyais, Descriptive of the Country, with some information as to its Productions, the best mode of Culture, and Chiefly Intended for the Use of Settlers* (Edinburgh, 1822), 65. For those who may have wanted to consult a map on Poyais's exact location, numerous could be found in London. In 1819, W. Gentle, of Fleet Street, London, published the map, "The British Settlement in Honduras," which featured Poyais and detailed the Mosquito Coast. In 1820, R. Holmes Laurie, chart seller to the Admiralty, published a similar map with details of the Port of Truxillo, Port Royal, the Black River, and Poyais. Both can be seen at the British National Archives, Kew.

22. In a great many of these approaches, MacGregor parallels the later career and frauds of Sir Edmund Backhouse as told in Hugh Trevor Roper's *Hermit of Peking* (New York: Knopf, 1977). As Trevor Roper notes, Backhouse, a British-born scholar and swindler, succeeded in defrauding intelligent officials, academics, and other victims through a combination of force of conviction, massive scale of operation, and apparent plausibility sold through minute attention to detail.

23. Strangeways, *Sketch of the Mosquito Shore*, 329.

24. Thomas Chalmers, *The Christian and Civic Economy of Large Towns*, volume 1 (Glasgow, 1821), 169. Like particular advocates of the country ideology, Chalmers remained convinced that land was the source of all value in the economy. The influence of Malthus is obvious.

25. Boyd Hilton, *The Age of Atonement: The Influence of Evangelicalism on Social and Economic Thought, 1795–1865* (Oxford: Clarendon Press; New York: Oxford University Press, 1988), 123.

26. William Kuhn, *The Politics of Pleasure* (London: Pocket Books, 2006). Bulwer-Lytton recalls him as wearing "green velvet trousers, a canary coloured waistcoat, low shoes, silver buckles, lace at his wrists, and his hair in ringlets." Robert Blake, *Disraeli* (New York: St. Martin's Press, 1967), 59.

27. Blake, *Disraeli*, 3. William Kuhn called him "one of the greatest liars in British history." Kuhn, *Politics of Pleasure,* 18. Despite appearances, the observation is really something of a compliment, and meant as such.

28. Blake, *Disraeli*, 66.

29. Frank Griffith Dawson, *The First Latin American Debt Crisis: The City of London and the 1822–1825 Loan Bubble* (New Haven, CT: Yale University Press, 1990), 21.

30. *London New Price Current*, October 20, 1820.

31. Dawson (*First Latin American Debt Crisis*, 13–14) suggests that newspapers can be read as both participants and measures of the bubble.

32. "Report from the Select Committee on Consular Establishment; together with the minutes of evidence, and appendix" (1835) (499), appendix no. 12, p. 145. Parliamentary reports accessed at House of Commons Parliamentary Papers (http://parlipapers.chadwyck.com).

33. Irving Stone, "British Direct and Portfolio Investment in Latin America before 1914," *Journal of Economic History*, vol. 37, no. 3 (September 1977); Dawson, *First Latin American Debt Crisis*, appendix 1. Because of British restrictions on interest payments, the Colombia loan was signed in Paris so that it could offer 6 percent. The same would be done in the case of Poyais loans.

34. Niall Ferguson, *The House of Rothschild*, volume 1 (New York: Viking, 1998), 123–125; Stone, "British Direct and Portfolio Investment," 694, table 1.

35. For more on bubbles and their life span, see Hyman P. Minsky, "The Financial Instability Hypothesis," Levy Economics Institute of Bard College, working paper no. 74 (May 1992). Minsky, upon whom the great economic historian Charles Kindleberger draws, noted that capitalist economies could move without exogenous shock from stability to a bubble. In fact, it was something of a natural process: "In particular, over a protracted period of good times, capitalist economies tend to move from a financial structure dominated by hedge finance units to a structure in which there is large weight of units engaged in speculative and ponzi [borrowing to repay interest] finance" (8). Government, in Minsky's model, plays a crucial role, as does the innovating banker. To anybody familiar with the subprime crisis of 2008, Minsky's observation of bankers will certainly ring true: "Bankers whether they be brokers or dealers, are merchants of debt who strive to innovate in the assets they acquire and the liabilities they market" (4). Also see Robert Shiller's now famous *Irrational Exuberance* (Princeton, NJ: Princeton University Press, 2000).

36. British Library, record 1881.c.16.(7.).

37. Mary Anne Lloyd, "To the Gentlemen of the Stock Exchange. Lines on the Poyais Bonds, 12 August, 1823, being his majesty's natal day, etc. Lines on a neglected rose tree" (London, 1823), British Library, record 1881.a.1.(39.).

38. Sinclair, *Land That Never Was*, 77; G. A. Low, *The Belise Merchants Unmasked; Or, A Review of Their Late Proceedings against Poyais, etc.* (London, 1824).

39. *Proceedings of an Inquiry and Investigation*, 75–80, 100.

40. *Proceedings of an Inquiry and Investigation*, 100. With regard to order no. 17, while MacGregor was concerned with not making enemies of the natives to the Mosquito Coast, his principle concern was likely with controlling the supply of land.

41. T. M. Devine, *To the Ends of the Earth* (Washington, DC: Smithsonian Books, 2011), 19–30.

42. "Police," *Times*, October 21, 1823.

43. *Proceedings of an Inquiry and Investigation*, 47–49.

44. *Proceedings of an Inquiry and Investigation*, 47–149; "Police," *Times*.

45. *Times*, January 15, 1823; January 16, 1823; and March 14, 1823.

46. *Times*, August 22, 1823; and November 11, 1823.

47. "To the Editor of the *Times*," *Times*, June 14, 1823.

48. Low, *Belise Merchants Unmasked*, 34–48, 57.

49. Low, *Belise Merchants Unmasked*, iv.

50. "Poyais Settlement," *Times*, September 1, 1823. The letter was dated May 13 and was dispatched from the Belize River's mouth, Bay of Honduras.

51. *Proceedings of an Inquiry and Investigation*, 98.

52. "Remarks on the Late Accounts Received from the Poyais Settlers," *Edinburgh Magazine and Literary Miscellany*, vol. 13 (September 1823): 326.

53. George Smeeton, *Doings in London: Or, Day and Night Scenes of the Frauds, Frolics, Manners, and Depravities of the Metropolis* (London, 1828), 90.

54. This deal was better than that received in some of the later issues. It was also likely the best deal Colombia could have gotten with no credit history. See Dawson, *First Latin American Debt Crisis*, 2. It is worth remembering that defaults are something of a regular historical occurrence. Spain itself would default seven times in the nineteenth century, according to economists Carmen M. Reinhart and Kenneth S. Rogoff, while France had defaulted eight times from 1500 to 1800. Reinhart and Rogoff, *This Time Is Different: Eight Centuries of Financial Folly* (Princeton, NJ: Princeton University Press, 2009), 88.

55. See Dawson, *First Latin American Debt Crisis*, 21; Platt, *Latin America and British Trade*, 17–25.

56. The damage done to the markets in general was significant. One visitor to Montevideo in 1826 estimated the population had shrunk by two-thirds. Success was staying static as the population of Venezuela was said to have halved. See Platt, *Latin America and British Trade*, 4–6 and chapter 1.

57. Margaret E. Rankine, "The Mexican Mining Industry in the Nineteenth Century with Special Reference to Guanajuato," *Bulletin of Latin American Research*, vol. 11, no. 1 (January 1992): 31–34.

58. Walter Bagehot, *Lombard Street* (London, 1873), 200; Joel Mokyr, *The Enlightened Economy: An Economic History of Britain, 1700–1850* (New York: Yale University Press, 2010), 326.

59. George Robb, *White-Collar Crime in Modern England: Financial Fraud and Business Morality, 1845–1929* (New York: Cambridge University Press, 1992), 19; Charles Kindleberger, *A Financial History of Western Europe* (Boston: Allen & Unwin, 1984), 87. These joint-stock banks had to be sixty-five miles outside of London. The act also granted the Bank of England a monopoly on notes issued within those sixty-five miles.

60. James Taylor, "Company Fraud in Victorian Britain: The Royal British Bank Scandal of 1856," *English Historical Review*, vol. 122, no. 497 (200): 700–724.

61. For more details on Disraeli's early investment in South America, see Blake, *Disraeli*, chapter 2; Kuhn, *Politics of Pleasure*, 45–50; Dawson, *First Latin American Debt Crisis*, 214–216.

62. Benjamin Disraeli, "An Inquiry into the Plans, Progress, and Policy of the American Mining Companies," (London, 1825), 59.

63. In their sweeping study of centuries of financial history, Reinhart and Rogoff (*This Time Is Different*, xxxiv) argue that financial crises of the sort that hit Britain in 1824–1825 repeatedly occur, in part, because of the capacity of governments and regulators to convince themselves that circumstances have changed, that the present offers opportunity combined with security not known in the past.

64. Disraeli, *Inquiry*, 84.

FIVE   Principals, Agents, and Their Mutual Friends

1. Michael Slater, *Charles Dickens* (New Haven, CT: Yale University Press, 2009), 468.

2. Daniel P. Scoggin, "A Speculative Resurrection: Death, Money, and Vampiric Economy of *Our Mutual Friend*," *Victorian Literature and Culture*, vol. 30, no. 1 (2002): 99–125. On social pressures, agency, and conformity in the novel, see Molly Anne Rothenberg, "Articulating Social Agency in 'Our Mutual Friend': Problems with Performances, Practices, and Political Efficacy," *English Literary History*, vol. 71 (2004): 719–749.

3. Charles Dickens, *Our Mutual Friend* (New York: Everyman's Library, 1994; originally published 1864–1865), 123–125.

4. Daniel Friedman, *Morals and Markets* (New York: St. Martin's Press, 2008), 25–59, 96.

5. *By the King a proclamation for the better encouragement, and aduancement of the trade of the East-Indie Companie, and for preuention of excesse of priuate trade* (London, 1632).

6. "Richard Colley Wellesley to Henry Dundas," February 23, 1798, in *The Despatches, Minutes, and Correspondence of the Marquess Wellesley*, edited by Montgomery Martin (London, 1836), 6.

7. Tom Osborne, "Bureaucracy as a Vocation: Governmentality and Administration in Nineteenth-Century Britain," *Journal of Historical Sociology*, vol. 7, no. 3 (Sept. 1994): 291. Governing at a distance, writes the sociologist Osborne, required the

capacity "to preserve and utilize the 'freedom' of agents, whilst also seeking to culti-vate those agents some or other way" (291). For a general introduction to this issue, see Michael C. Jensen and William H. Meckling, "Theory of the Firm: Managerial, Be-havior, Agency Costs and Ownership Structure," *Journal of Financial Economics*, vol. 3, no. 4 (1976): 305–360.

8. For an overview of the legal precedent, see William Paley, *A Treatise on the Law of Principal and Agent*, 2nd edition (London, 1819); also see "Report from the Select Committee on the Law Relating to Merchants, Agents, or Factors; &c." (1823), 5–7. Parliamentary reports accessed at House of Commons Parliamentary Papers (http://parlipapers.chadwyck.com).

9. Hugh Fentwick Boyd and Arthur Beilby Pearson, *The Factors' Acts (1823 to 1877): With an Introduction and Explanatory Notes* (London, 1884), 9.

10. Sean Thomas, "The Origins of the Factors Acts," *Journal of Legal History*, vol. 32, no. 2 (2011): 159.

11. It is worth noting that even in a so-called free market, where the government plays a limited role either as a regulator or as a stimulator, it is still likely to play a role in shaping risk distribution. Limited liability, as David A. Moss shows, is a good ex-ample of this. It may well have further unleashed market forces, but it was the govern-ment that played the active role in structuring this redistribution risk. Moss, *When All Else Fails* (Cambridge, MA: Harvard University Press, 2002).

12. "For his great public virtue," Paley dedicated his tome to Lord Ellenborough.

13. Paley, *Treatise*, 23.

14. The Factors Act, 1823, 4 Geo. IV. C. 83; The Factors Act, 1825, 6 Geo. IV. C 94; The Factors Act Amendment, 1842, 5 and 6 Vict. C. 39; The Factors Act Amendment, 1877, 40 and 41 Vict. C. 39.

15. Paley, *A Treatise*, 170.

16. Paley, *A Treatise*, v.

17. "Committee of Merchants, Bankers and Others. Law Relating to Principal and Factor. Address delivered by Mr. James William Freshfield to the Select Commit-tee of the House of Commons, short-hand by W.B. Gurney" (London, 1823), 10. See also "Select Committee on the Law," which is the record from the proceedings. The proceedings were recorded by the same W. B. Gurney who kept the shorthand at the trial of Lord Cochrane.

18. "Select Committee on the Law," 3.

19. According to testimony, it was usual to draw anywhere between half and two-thirds of the consignment or invoice value.

20. "Select Committee on the Law," 98.

21. "Select Committee on the Law," 10.

22. The Factors Act, 1823, 4 Geo. IV. C. 83, p. 2.

23. For changes in the political landscape, see Thomas, "Origins of the Factors Acts."

24. Commercial Association of Liverpool, *Law of Principal and Factor. State-ments of Its Defects and Remedy* (Liverpool, 1842), 18–23. They reiterated the point: "In

a question between two innocent parties, the owner who has selected the agent, who has confided his goods to him, and who has thus given him an appearance of credit, ought to be the one to bear the loss occasioned by the fraud or insolvency of his own agent" (23).

25. Commercial Association of Liverpool, *Law of Principal and Factor*, 5–11.

26. James Cook, *On the Law of Principal and Factor* (London, 1840), 24. Like many before him, Cook also bemoaned what he saw as England's comparative disadvantage on the matter: "We are the only *European* nation, and we believe we may say, the *only* nation who would legalize an action of trover, for the recovery of goods on which money had been bona fide advanced" (22).

27. As quoted in Thomas, "Origins of the Factors Acts," 161.

28. The Factors Act Amendment, 1842, 5 and 6 Vict. C. 39, p. 2. The 1877 act would further clarify the burdens of risk and responsibility in three-party transactions, but the 1842 act laid the crucial groundwork.

29. Robin Pearson and David Richardson, "Business Networking in the Industrial Revolution," *Economic History Review*, vol. 61, no. 2 (2003): 672; Sunderland, *Social Capital, Trust and the Industrial Revolution* (London: Routledge, 2007); Mokyr, *The Enlightened Economy*.

30. "Report from the Select Committee on Consular Service and Appointments; together with the proceedings of the committee, minutes of evidence, appendix and index" (1857–1858), 56. Parliamentary reports accessed at House of Commons Parliamentary Papers (http://parlipapers.chadwyck.com).

31. "Select Committee on Consular Service," 203.

32. Dickens, *Our Mutual Friend*, 7.

SIX   Reputation Contagion

1. A number of Victorian authors made use of fraud as a way to examine the contemporary machinations of commercial and financial exchange, most notably D. Morier Evans in *The City; or, the Physiology of London Business; with Sketches on Change, and at the Coffee House* (1845) and *Facts, Failures, and Frauds: Revelations Financial, Mercantile, Criminal* (1859). This practice has been taken up by a number of historians. Some of the most notable works include George Robb, *White-Collar Crime in Modern England: Financial Fraud and Business Morality, 1845–1929* (New York: Cambridge University Press, 1992); James Taylor, "Company Fraud in Victorian Britain: The Royal British Bank Scandal of 1856," *English Historical Review*, vol. 122, no. 497 (2007): 700–724; and Paul Johnson, "Civilising Mammon: Fraud and Profit in Nineteenth-Century London," *Fathom* (2002): fathom.lse.ac.uk/Features/121984/, retrieved April 18, 2011.

2. "The Exchequer Bill Fraud" and "Court Circular," *Times*, October 30, 1841.

3. It was Beaumont's uncle, Sir Sidney Smith, who had achieved the greatest fame in the family, having helped hold back Napoleon's siege of Acre.

4. Phil Handler and James Taylor have both shown the great attention given to fraud throughout the nineteenth century. See Handler, "Forgery and the End of the 'Bloody Code' in Early Nineteenth Century England," *Historical Journal*, vol. 48, no. 3 (2005): 683–702; and Taylor, "Commercial Fraud and Public Men in Victorian Britain," *Historical Research*, vol. 78, no. 200 (May 2005): 230–252.

5. Randall McGowen, "The Bank of England and the Policing of Forgery," 83; Handler, "Bloody Code in Early Nineteenth Century England," 692.

6. In today's value, £1,010,000,000 (see www.measuringworth.com). Numerous options are available for converting past value to that of the present. As the amount of money involved was large and government issued, I have chosen here to use percentage of gross domestic product.

7. James Macdonald, *A Free Nation Deep in Debt* (New York: Farrar, Straus and Giroux, 2003), 176.

8. He did, as we shall see, achieve his own infamy, but officers at the Exchequer and subsequent archivists on into the twentieth century chose to preserve only the letters with links to Sir Sidney.

9. Smith to Fanny, April 4, 1829, British National Archives: TS.27.106.

10. When, in 1829, a young Beaumont Smith wrote his sister from his office at the Exchequer to inform her that he would be placing his financial affairs ahead of those of his family, he also alluded to his recent appointment at the treasury. The appointment may have been a result of the connections of his father, the colonel, or his famed uncle, Sir Sidney Smith, but the power was wielded by Lord Grenville, also known as George Nugent Grenville, the Duke of Buckingham's brother. "I have written," Smith observed as an aside atop the letter, "to thank Lord Grenville for my appointment which I saw yesterday." Smith to Fanny, April 4, 1829, British National Archives: TS.27.106.

11. Smith to Fanny, April 4, 1829, British National Archives: TS.27.106.

12. Sir Sidney to Smith, September 20, 1834, British National Archives: TS.64.398.

13. Sir Sidney to Smith, September 29, 1837, British National Archives: TS.64.398.

14. Sir Sidney to Smith, December 21, 1838, British National Archives: TS.64.398.

15. June 13, 1840, British National Archives: TS.27.106.

16. "Exchequer Bills Forgery: Report of the Commissioners" (London, 1842), 8. Parliamentary reports accessed at House of Commons Parliamentary Papers (http://parlipapers.chadwyck.com).

17. Secretary of the Parthenon Club to Smith, June 10, 1840, British National Archives: TS.64.398.

18. "Exchequer Bills Forgery. Report of the Commissioners," xv.

19. "List of Property," British National Archives: TS.64.398. The government claimed ownership of all his goods.

20. "Exchequer Bill Fraud," *Examiner*, December 4, 1841: 778.

21. "Exchequer Bill Fraud," 778–779.

22. "Exchequer Bill Fraud," 779.

23. Randall McGowen, "The Bank of England and the Punishment of Forgery," *Past and Present*, vol. 186, no. 1 (2005): 81–116; Handler, "Forgery," 689. See also Rob

Sindall, "Middle-Class Crime in Nineteenth-Century England," *Criminal Justice History*, no. 4 (1983): 23-40.

24. "Exchequer Bills, Report Made to the Lords of Her Majesty's Treasury by the commissioners appointed to inquire and ascertain in what manner exchequer bills have been made out and issued" (London, 1842), 10-12. Parliamentary reports accessed at House of Commons Parliamentary Papers (http://parlipapers.chadwyck.com).

25. "Exchequer Bills, Report Made to the Lords," 11.

26. "Exchequer Bills, Report Made to the Lords," 10-11.

27. "Exchequer Bills, Report Made to the Lords," 12.

28. "Exchequer Bills, Report Made to the Lords," 11.

29. G. B. Mainwaring quoted in McGowen, "Bank of England," 83.

30. "The Exchequer-Bill Fraud," *Times*, January 1, 1842.

31. "Exchequer Bills Forgery. Report of the Commissioners," iv.

32. Mark Casson, *The Entrepreneur: An Economic Theory*, second edition (Northhampton, MA: Edward Elgar, 2003), 169.

33. Lord Monteagle, chancellor at the Exchequer until 1839, testified to Parliament that the office was not necessarily any busier in 1840 than it had been in 1820. It was commonplace to produce bills that did not make it into circulation, making an exact figure of those that entered the market difficult to pin down. Nonetheless, the issue numbers tend to confirm this story. In 1825, for example, two warrants led to the production of a first issue of £20 million and then a second of £10.5 million. That, however, was an exceptionally busy year. In 1836, there were two issues, one for £15 million and a second for just over £14 million. In 1840, the two issues were each for around £11 million. The average annual issue of such bills does not seem to have grown much from the 1820s to the 1830s or early 1840. From 1818 to 1824, 52,700 bills were printed but not issued, there being no need presumably for further short-term debt. The ratio of extras was about one to five that were ultimately issued. By 1831, according to, who else, Beaumont Smith, £7,022,200 worth of exchequer bills were held by the office of the comptroller-general. "Exchequer Bills. Report Made to the Lords," 80-81 table.

34. "Exchequer Bills Forgery. Report of the Commissioners," xvii, case I.

35. "Exchequer Bills Forgery. Report of the Commissioners," xix, case II.

36. "Exchequer Bills Forgery. Report of the Commissioners," 134.

37. "Exchequer Bills Forgery. Report of the Commissioners," 137, 338.

38. Larry Neal and Lance Davis, "The Evolution of the Structure and Performance of the London Stock Exchange in the First Global Financial Market, 1812-1914," *European Review of Economic History*, vol. 10 (2006): 282.

39. Taylor, "Company Fraud in Great Britain"; Robb, *White-Collar Crime in Modern England*.

40. "Exchequer Bills Forgery. Report of the Commissioners," 79.

41. "Exchequer Bills Forgery. Report of the Commissioners," 236-238.

42. "Exchequer Bills Forgery. Report of the Commissioners," 75.

43. Casson, *Entrepreneur*, 176.

44. "Exchequer Bills Forgery. Report of the Commissioners," 118.

45. "Exchequer Bills Forgery. Report of the Commissioners," 17–22. The Stock Exchange, though it threatened defaulters with expulsion, was actually quite lenient on the matter. Robb shows that 265 brokers were expelled from the stock exchange for defaulting between 1867 and 1877. Of the 116 who would later apply for readmission, 105 were granted a second membership. Robb, *White-Collar Crime*, 87.

46. "Exchequer Bills Forgery. Report of the Commissioners," 22.

47. "Exchequer Bills Forgery. Report of the Commissioners," 34.

48. "Exchequer Bills Forgery. Report of the Commissioners," 29–30.

49. "Exchequer Bills Forgery. Report of the Commissioners," 36.

50. "Exchequer Bills Forgery. Report of the Commissioners," 122.

51. "Exchequer Bills Forgery. Report of the Commissioners," xv.

52. William Mariner, *Exchequer Bills Forgery: A Statement by William Mariner* (London, 1843), 72.

53. In "Exchequer-Bill Fraud" the *Times* wrote of him sarcastically: "The opportunity of clearing his character (if he can) by a trial at the Old Bailey is still open to him, should he feel disposed to return to take advantage of it."

54. Mariner, *Exchequer Bills Forgery*, 16.

55. Mariner, *Exchequer Bills Forgery*, 19.

56. Mariner, *Exchequer Bills Forgery*, 23.

57. Mariner, *Exchequer Bills Forgery*, 72.

58. *The History and Mystery of the Exchequer Bills Forgery Examined: A Letter to Rt. Hon. Henry Golbourn* (London, 1842), 16.

59. Charles Dickens, *Our Mutual Friend* (New York: Everyman's Library, 1994; originally published 1864–1865), 114.

60. "Exchequer Bills Forgery. Report of the Commissioners," xxxvii.

61. "Exchequer Bills Forgery. Report of the Commissioners," xxxix.

62. "A Bona Fide Holder of Detained Exchequer-Bills," *Times*, April 13, 1842.

63. Commercial Association of Liverpool, *Law of Principal and Factor. Statements of Its Defects and Remedy* (Liverpool, 1842), 18–23; James Cook, *On the Law of Principal and Factor* (London, 1840), 24; Factors' Act Amendment, 1842, 5 and 6 Vict. C. 39, p. 2. The 1877 act would further clarify the burdens of risk and responsibility in three-party transactions, but the 1842 act laid the crucial groundwork.

SEVEN The Detection of Lies, Lives, and Agents

1. Jonathan Levy, *Freaks of Fortune* (Cambridge, MA: Harvard University Press, 2012), 63. Though the insurance industry undoubtedly benefited from and helped fuel urbanization and industrialization, it is also important to note, as Levy points out, that maritime insurance and its development played a significant role in facilitating the risk management dimensions of the Atlantic slave trade. See Levy, *Freaks of Fortune*, chapter 2.

2. For a more extensive discussion of the intellectual foundation of insurance, see Ferguson, *The Ascent of Money*, 188–190.

3. Ian Dunlop, "Provisions for Ministers' Widows in Scotland—Eighteenth Century," in *The Scottish Ministers' Widows Fund, 1743–1993*, edited by Ian A. Dunlop (Edinburgh: Saint Andrews Press, 1992).

4. Timothy Alborn, *Regulated Lives* (Toronto: University of Toronto Press, 2009).

5. Dunlop, "Provisions for Ministers' Widows," 14.

6. Barry Supple, "Insurance in British History," in *The Historian and the Business of Insurance*, edited by Oliver M. Westall (Manchester: Manchester University Press, 1984), 2–3.

7. Supple, "Insurance in British History," 2–3.

8. An astounding expansion in insurance also took place in the United States over the course of the nineteenth century. According to Levy (*Freaks of Fortune*, 61), measuring in 1860 dollars, the value of insurance held expanded from $168,000 in 1825 to $4.5 million in 1870 and $2.3 billion in 1870.

9. J. Hooper Hartnoll and Robert Christie, *The Annual Balance Sheets of the Insurance Companies* (London, 1852), 6. The American market, Levy shows (*Freaks of Fortune*, 197), was also vulnerable to widespread collapses. In the United States, between 1988 and 1877, ninety-eight commercial life companies closed and thirty-two failed completely.

10. "Assurance companies. Return by the Registrar of Joint Stock Companies of the names, places of business, and objects of all assurance companies completely registered, from the passing of the act 7 & 8 Vict. c. 110, to the 5th day of February 1852, stating the dates of complete registration, and of every account registered by such companies, conformably with the provisions of the said act, since the return of the 20th day of April 1849" (1852). Parliamentary reports accessed at House of Commons Parliamentary Papers (http://parlipapers.chadwyck.com).

11. David A. Moss, *When All Else Fails* (Cambridge, MA: Harvard University Press, 2002), 30.

12. "Globe Insurance, Pall-Mall and Cornhill, London," *Aetheneum*, no. 579 (December 1838): 860.

13. Hartnoll and Christie, *Annual Balance Sheets*, 5. Hartnoll and Christie selected twenty-five new companies for study and found that of £460,032 paid in, only £86,704 remained. See also J. H. Treble, "The Record of the Standard Life Assurance Company in the Life Insurance Market of the United Kingdom, 1850–1864," in Westall, *Historian and the Business of Insurance*, 101.

14. *The Facts and Fictions of the Life Assurance Controversy, addressed to Plain People by one of themselves* (London, 1852), 2–6.

15. *Facts and Fictions*, 2, 9–11.

16. Treble, "Record of the Standard Life Assurance Company," 97.

17. As Gregory Anderson points out, personal contact with management of a firm was essential to acquiring clerical positions. See Anderson, *Victorian Clerks* (Bath, UK: Manchester University Press, 1976).

18. *Old Bailey Proceedings Online* (www.oldbaileyonline.org, version 6.0, April 28, 2011): April 1833, trial of Robert Byers (t18330411-199).

19. Anderson, *Victorian Clerks*, 3.

20. British Library: Playbills 378.

21. "Town and Country Talk," *Examiner* (April 6, 1850): 219

22. Godfrey Turner, *First Nights of My Young Days* (London, 1877), 124.

23. Turner, *First Nights*, 123.

24. Edmund Yates, *His Recollections and Experiences* (London, 1884), 207.

25. "News of the Week," *Leader* 17 (July 20, 1850): 385.

26. "News of the Week," 385.

27. Guildhall, City of London: Ms 11656/1071.

28. "Globe 1803, Rules and Regulations," Guildhall, City of London: Ms 11656, p. 37. Subsequent directors were expected to have twenty shares paid out.

29. Guildhall, City of London: Ms 11679, policy 84251; Ms 11679, policies 86826, 87063–87065; Ms 11679.

30. *The East-India register and directory, for 1820; corrected to the 26th September 1820* (London, 1820); John Phipps, *A Guide to the Commerce of Bengal* (Calcutta, 1823).

31. *Mercein's city directory, New-York register, and almanac, for the forty-fifth year of American independence* (New York, 1820).

32. "Minutes of the Board," February 24, 1853, in Special Committees, no. 2 reports, Guildhall, City of London: Ms 11662/1, pp. 9–12.

33. "Report of Chairs on Business of Year 1854," February 22, 1855, no. 2 reports, Guildhall, City of London: Ms 11662/1, p. 247; "Special Committee of Accounts," January 29, 1857, in Globe Insurance, Minutes of the Committees of Insurance, Accounts, and Treasury, Guildhall, City of London: Ms 11659/1, p. 146.

34. Gilbert Currie, *The Insurance Agent's Assistant: A Popular Essay on Life Assurance, Its Nature, Use and Advantages* (London, 1852), 7.

35. Currie, *Insurance Agent's Assistant*, 9.

36. Levy, *Freaks of Fortune*, 87.

37. Archibald Hewat, "Policy Values Popularly Explained and Illustrated by an Actuary," in *Papers by Archibald Hewat, Actuary, 1873 to 1886* (Glasgow, 1887). We might also assume, though Hewat did not mention it, income.

38. Hewat, "Policy Values," 4–6.

39. Hewat, "Policy Values," 4–6.

40. "Report of Chairs on Foreign Business," September 22, 1853, no. 2 reports, Guildhall, City of London: Ms 11662/1, p. 48; "Report of Chairs on Business," February 22, 1854, no. 2 reports, Guildhall, City of London: Ms 11662/1, p. 140.

41. "Report of Chairs on Foreign Business," 50.

42. "Report of Chairs on Business," February 22, 1854, p. 139.

43. "Report of Chairs on Foreign Business," 35–45.

44. D. T. Jenkins, "The Practice of Insurance against Fire, 1750–1840, and Historical Research," in Westall, *Historian and the Business of Insurance*, 18.

45. Domestic data from D. T. Jenkins, "Practice of Insurance against Fire," 18; Guildhall, City of London: Ms 11679; "Report of Chairs on Business of year 1852," February 22, 1853, no. 2 reports, Guildhall, City of London: Ms 11662/1, p. 18.

46. Globe, like most life insurers, offset potential losses from the life business by acting as a bank of sorts. In 1854, the interests list of Globe included Blackwall Railway, East Anglia Railway, South Eastern Railway, and the East and West India Docks.

47. Jenkins, "Practice of Insurance against Fire," 25.

48. Jenkins, "Practice of Insurance against Fire," 101–102.

49. "Report of Chairs on Foreign Business," 35–40.

50. "Report of Chairs on Business of Year 1854," 238–240.

51. "Report from the Committee of Insurance on the Fire and Life Businesses," March 14, 1855, no. 2 reports, Guildhall, City of London: Ms 11662/1, p. 268.

52. "Report of Chairs on Business of Year 1854," 229–230.

53. Jenkins, "Practice of Insurance against Fire," 101–102.

54. "Report of Chairs on Business," February 22, 1854, p. 137.

55. "Minutes of the Board," 11.

56. "Finance Committee," August 11, 1864, Guildhall, City of London: Ms 11670/1, p. 7; October 13, 1864, p. 20; October 20, 1864, p. 22.

57. Guildhall, City of London: Ms 11678, Loans on Life Policies, Ledger no. 1.

EIGHT   The Observance of Trifles

1. Arthur Conan Doyle, *Memories and Adventures* (London: Hodder and Stoughton, 1924), 273.

2. Marc Flandreau, Norbert Gaillard, and Frank Packer, "To Err Is Human: Rating Agencies and the Interwar Foreign Government Debt Crisis," BIS Working Papers, no. 35, Bank for International Settlements, Basel, Switzerland (December 2010): 5–7. John Moody began security rating in 1909, and as Flandreau et al. point out, though innovation in rating agencies also took place in France, it was in the United States that the innovation "took hold."

3. Richard Sennett notes that in his fiction, Balzac employed a very similar approach: "His methods of characterization, too, were based on decoding isolated details of appearance, magnifying the detail into an emblem of the whole man." Sennett, *The Fall of Public Man* (New York: Random House, 1977), 169.

4. Arthur Conan Doyle, "A Case of Identity," in *The Adventures of Sherlock Holmes* (New York: Penguin Books, 2009; originally published 1892), 40. Sennett (*Fall of Public Man*, 169) also draws attention to this quote from Doyle, noting that "the compulsive attention to detail, the anxiety for facts which has since come to obsess us in so many ways, was born out of this anxiety about what appearances symbolize."

5. Carlo Ginzburg, *Clues, Myths, and the Historical Method* (Baltimore, MD: Johns Hopkins University Press, 1989). If, as Ginzburg suggests, medical examiners practiced "medical semiotics," bankers practiced asset semiotics.

6. Arthur Conan Doyle, "Boscombe," in *Adventures of Sherlock Holmes*, 101; Conan Doyle, "A Scandal in Bohemia," in *Adventures of Sherlock Holmes*, 7.

7. Sharonna Pearl, *About Faces: Physiognomy in Nineteenth-Century Britain* (Cambridge, MA: Harvard University Press, 2010). As Pearl states in her history of physiognomy: "The most information physiognomy could provide was precisely what was lacking in the urban environment, names, a system of establishing reasons to trust, and, equally important, identifying whom not to trust. Without the lengthy timescale of rural life, and with the hustle and bustle of the streets, physiognomy emerged as a way to make sense of the city" (11).

8. Eden Warwick [George Jabet], *Nasology; or Hints Towards a Classification of the Nose* (London, 1848), 7, 8. The nose did have its limits, Jabet acknowledged. It could not reveal a man's or woman's passion or temper. It did, however, hold the secret to an individual's "Power or Energy to carry our Ideas, and the Taste or Inclination which dictates or guides them."

9. Jabet, *Nasology*, 14.

10. Jabet, *Nasology*, 11.

11. *Cornhill Magazine* (1861), quoted in Pearl, *About Faces*, 148.

12. Jans Breman, "Introduction: Race, a Class Apart," in *Imperial Monkey Business: Racial Supremacy in Social Darwinist Theory and Colonial Practice*, edited by Jans Breman (Amsterdam: VU University Press, 1990), 2.

13. Simon Cole, *Suspected Identities* (Cambridge, MA: Harvard University Press, 2001).

14. Both quoted in Cole, *Suspected Identities*, 77, 90.

15. Cole, *Suspected Identities*, 94.

16. Geoffrey Scott, *A Plan for Effecting one of the chief objects of ordinary life insurance without Medical or any other form of Examination* (London, 1884), 3–4.

17. Charles Lyman Greene, *The Medical Examination for Life Insurance* (London: Rebman, 1902), 30–69.

18. Joseph Bell, lecture February 3, 1903, reprinted in *Transactions of the Insurance Society of Edinburgh, 1901–1904* (Edinburgh: H & J Pillans & Wilson, 1904), 117–121.

19. "Finance and Accounts Committee," Guildhall, City of London: Ms 11670/1.

20. Little, apparently, was thought of voting rights—a holder without title had none.

21. "The Negotiability of American Railway Share Certificates," *Economist*, May 17, 1890: 620.

22. "The Liverpool Bank Frauds," *Economist*, November 30, 1901: 1764–1765.

23. John Hutchinson, *The Practice of banking embracing the cases at law and in equity bearing upon all branches of the subject*, 2 vols. (London: Effingham Wilson, Royal Exchange, 1881, 1883), 1:90.

24. Hutchinson, *Practice of banking*, 2:387. The science continues:

There appears to be only one kind of ink, the "combined carbonaceous ink," really indelible in its nature, and which cannot be erased from ordinary paper; but, from its composition, this species of ink cannot be well used for general purposes. A new means of fraud, it may be added, has presented itself in the anastic process of printing recently invented. By this kind of printing, bank notes, cheques, and other documents and writings can be so exactly copied or reproduced as to defy scrutiny, elaborate engraving or beauty of design affording in such case no protection, but rather facility to the fraud. A safeguard to this, however, is offered in Glynn's patent paper, which not only prevents copy of its contents being taken, but is itself destroyed when submitted to the process in question. In further reference to improvements in paper, it may be mentioned that, by the application of asbestos, a fire-proof paper has been lately produced.

Consider this in comparison with the instruction Holmes would issue: "The envelope was a very coarse one, and was stamped with the Gravesend postmark, and with the date of that very day," describes Watson, before ceding to Holmes in "The Man with the Twisted Lip": "The name, you see, is in perfectly black ink, which has dried itself. The rest is of greyish colour which shows that blotting-paper has been used. If it had been written straight off, and then blotted, none would be of a deep black shade. This man has written the name, and there has then been a pause before he wrote the address, which can only mean that he was not familiar with it. It is, of course, a trifle, but there is nothing so important as trifles." Doyle, "The Man with the Twisted Lip," in *Adventures of Sherlock Holmes*, 104.

25. Hutchinson, *Practice of banking*, 2:1.

26. "Liverpool Bank Frauds."

27. *Times*, September 8, 1908: 8; "Fraud on a London Bank," *Times*, September 28, 1908; "The Fraud on the London and South-Western Bank," *Times*, April 21, 1909; "Attempted Fraud on a Bank," *Times*, January 23, 1910.

28. *Financial News*, May 30, 1905.

29. *How to Protect Capital Invested in Stocks and Shares* (London: Investment Registry and Stock Exchange Ltd., 1905), 73.

30. *Investment Risks and How to Avoid Them*, 5th revised edition (London: Investment Registry, 1905), 33–35.

31. *How to Protect Capital*, 33.

32. *Proceedings at the Twenty-Fifth Annual Ordinary General Meeting . . . Tuesday, the 14th November, 1905. Sir John Rolleston, M.P. presiding*, Investment Registry, Ltd., 3, British Library: 8229.s.

33. Kevin H. O'Rourke and Jeffrey G. Williamson, *Globalization and History: the Evolution of a Nineteenth-Century Atlantic Economy* (Cambridge, MA: MIT Press, 1999), 14; Harold James, *The End of Globalization* (Cambridge, MA: Harvard University Press, 2001), 11, 34–35.

34. O'Rourke and Williamson, *Globalization and History*, 215; James, *End of Globalization*, 12.

35. David Rubinstein, "Cycling in the 1890s," *Victorian Studies*, vol. 21, no. 1 (Autumn 1977): 51; A. E. Harrison, "Joint Stock Company Flotation in the Cycle, Motor-Vehicle and Related Industries, 1882–1914," *Business History*, vol. 23, no. 2 (1981): 165–190.

36. David Itzkowitz, "Fair Enterprise or Extravagant Speculation: Investment, Speculation, and Gambling in Victorian England," *Victorian Studies*, vol. 45, no. 1, (Autumn 2002): 124.

37. Speculation was not gambling. This was a distinction fundamental to the late nineteenth century. As the century had worn on, chance restrictions on gambling increased while those on speculation diminished. Itzkowitz, "Fair Enterprise or Extravagant Speculation," 126.

NINE A Gorgeous Vulgarity

1. See Tim Jeal, *Stanley: The Impossible Life of Africa's Greatest Explorer* (New Haven, CT: Yale University Press, 2007).

2. See Jeal, *Stanley*, as well as Adam Hochschild, *King Leopold's Ghost* (New York: Pan Macmillan, 1998).

3. T. M. Devine, *To the Ends of the Earth* (Washington, DC: Smithsonian Books, 2011), 75.

4. As quoted in Robb, *White-Collar Crime: Financial Fraud and Business Morality, 1845–1929*, (Cambridge and New York: Cambridge University Press, 1992), 108.

5. Frank Trentmann, *Free Trade Nation* (Oxford: Oxford University Press, 2007); Thorstein Veblen, *The Theory of the Leisure Class* (New York: Modern Library, 1989; originally published 1899), 71.

6. Eustace Clare Grenville Murray, *Under the Lens: Social Photographs*, vol. 1, 2nd edition (London, 1886), 126, 157.

7. Horatio Bottomley, *Horatio Bottomley: Hys Booke* (London, 1892), 7.

8. Robb, *White-Collar Crime*, 104–108.

9. Robb, *White-Collar Crime*, 124.

10. Simon J. Potter, "The English Press," in *Newspapers and Empire in Ireland and Britain*, edited by Potter (Dublin: Four Court's Press, 2004), 47.

11. Tony Ballantyne, *Orientalism and Race: Aryanism in the British Empire* (Houndmills, UK: Palgrave, 2002), 12. See also Simon J. Potter, "Webs, Networks, and Systems: Globalization and the Mass Media in the Nineteenth- and Twentieth-Century British Empire," *Journal of British Studies*, vol. 46 (July 2007): 629.

12. Tom Standage, *The Victorian Internet* (New York: Walker, 1999).

13. For an extended discussion of the process of laying the four-part Persian Gulf submarine cable, see Christina Phelps Harris, "The Persian Gulf Submarine Telegraph of 1864," *Geographical Journal*, vol. 135, part 2 (June 1969): 169–190. The cost of the effort, according to Harris, was £411,751, the majority of which was paid by the British government, with the remainder paid by the government of India.

14. John B. Thompson, *The Media and Modernity: A Social Theory of Media* (Stanford, CA: Stanford University Press, 1995), 154–155.

15. Griset Pascal and Daniel R. Headrick, "Submarine Telegraph Cables: Business and Politics, 1838–1939," *Business History Review*, vol. 75, no. 3 (2001): 544, 559, 560–561; Daniel R. Headrick, *Tentacles of Progress* (New York: Oxford University Press, 1988), 108.

16. Potter, "Webs, Networks, and Systems," 630–633; Jeal, *Stanley*, 132; Vary T. Coates and Bernard Finn, *A Retrospective Technology Assessment: Submarine Telegraphy: The Transatlantic Cable of 1866* (San Francisco: San Francisco Press, 1979), 79–89; Daniel Headrick, *Tools of Empire* (New York: Oxford University Press, 1981). Peter H. Lindert and Jeffrey G. Williamson, "English Workers' Living Standards during the Industrial Revolution: A New Look," *Economic History Review*, vol. 36, no. 1 (February 1983): 4, table 2. Steven C. Topik and Allen Wells note that the telegraph favored not only large businesses and news services but also imperial control: "The telegraph was useful in mobilizing troops of central authorities against local or regional resistance, so in many places the wire reinforced the power of the few over the many." See Topik and Wells, "Commodity Chains in a Global Economy," in *A World Connecting*, edited by Emily S. Rosenberg (Cambridge, MA: Belknap Press, 2013), 665.

17. Topik and Wells, "Commodity Chains," 663. Topik and Wells provide some useful comparisons: in 1870, the United States sent 9 million telegrams, a number that rose to more than 160 million by 1913. In that same year, 60 million telegrams were sent from Asia, two-thirds of which were sent by Japan and its colonies.

18. Coates et al., *Retrospective Technology Assessment*, 70–76. Coates et al. also provide further background on the effect upon inventories, middle men, foreign exchange, and credit.

19. Coates et al., *Retrospective Technology Assessment*, 68; Pascal and Headrick, "Submarine Telegraph Cables," 551; Headrick, *Tools of Empire*, 101.

20. John M. MacKenzie, "Empire and the English Press," in Potter, *Newspapers and Empire*, 76.

21. "[*Financial News*] Its Birth and Progress, with Some Account of Its Management, Policy and Surroundings," *Financial News*, October 4, 1886.

22. Dilwyn Porter, "'A Trusted Guide of the Investing Public': Harry Marks and the *Financial News* 1884–1916," *Business History*, vol. 28 (1986): 2.

23. Porter, "Trusted Guide," 1.

24. "[*Financial News*] Its Birth and Progress, with Some Account of Its Management, Policy and Surroundings," *Financial News*, October 4, 1886.

25. J. A. Hobson, *Imperialism* (London: J. Nisbet, 1902), 60.

26. Trentmann, *Free Trade Nation*, 91.

27. *Financial News*, July 1, 1884: 1, 3. Where the newspaper article had no title in the case of the *Financial News*, I have included page numbers when applicable.

28. *Financial News*, July 25, 1884.

29. *Financial News*, February 5, 1886: 1.

30. "A Promoter of the Period," *Financial News,* June 11, 1886.

31. Thomas Rickard, *The Gold Fields of the Transvaal, with an Appendix on the Adjacent Coal and Iron of Natal* (London, 1884), 48–49.

32. "On the Problem of Fraud," *Economist*, December 24, 1898: 1853.

33. "Its Birth and Progress."

34. "Its Birth and Progress."

35. *Old Bailey Proceedings Online* (www.oldbaileyonline.org, version 6.0, April 17, 2011): Old Bailey, Central Criminal Court, Second Session, "George Washington Butterfield, Breaking Peace, Libel" (December 15, 1890), ref. no. t18901215-91, 285.

36. In the first decades of the nineteenth century, Philip Harling shows, seditious libel was used as a tool, but more often a threat, to intimidate radical pamphleteers and journalists. Harling, "The Law of Libel and the Limits of Repression, 1790–1832," *Historical Journal*, vol. 44, no. 1 (March 2001): 107–134. Harling estimates that Crown lawyers were involved in over two hundred cases between 1790 and 1832.

37. *Old Bailey Proceedings Online*, tabulating decade against offense category where offense category is libel, and then counting by offense. The conviction rate was relatively high, with 457 cases ending in some form of guilty verdict.

38. Quoted in "Report from the Select Committee on the Law of Libel; together with the proceedings of the committee, minutes of evidence, and appendix" (1878–1879), 68. Parliamentary reports accessed at House of Commons Parliamentary Papers (http://parlipapers.chadwyck.com).

39. Quoted in "Report from the Select Committee on the Law of Libel," 52.

40. "George Washington Butterfield," 260. No copies of the pamphlet are known to have survived, but it became the basis of the case brought by Marks, and as such, its contents and accusations can be divined from the trial that followed.

41. "Marks and Butterfield," *Saturday Review of Politics, Literature, Science and Art*, vol. 70, no. 1834 (December 20, 1890): 701.

42. "George Washington Butterfield." Most responses to questions about the relationship can be found on pp. 206–268.

43. "George Washington Butterfield," 206.

44. David R. Green and Alastair Owens, "Gentlewomanly Capitalism? Spinsters, Widows, and Wealth Holding in England and Wales, c. 1800–1860," *Economic History Review*, new series, vol. 56, no. 3 (August 2003): 524–525.

45. "George Washington Butterfield," 208.

46. British Library: BT 31/4302/27933, p. 41.

47. "The Rae (Transvaal) Gold Mining Company Limited," *Financial News*, January 17, 1887.

48. J. R. Seeley, *The Expansion of England: Two Courses of Lectures* (London, 1883), 12. Seeley instead favored a Greater Britain, composed of colonies of white settlement united with London in a sort of federal union. This union—which would theoretically prove a counterbalance to rising Russian and American power—had explicit cultural and ethnic overtones. It was also a vision forged by globalization. Whereas once Seeley thought the distance of the colonies precluded a more formal relationship of governance, now technology enabled global connections. "In the present day," he wrote, "it is quite easy to imagine such a sense of common interest existing between us and even the remotest of our colonies, because in the present day distance has been almost abolished by steam and electricity" (64).

49. Robert V. Kubicek, *Economic Imperialism in Theory and Practice* (Durham, NC: Duke University Press, 1979), 22.

50. Hobson, *Imperialism*, 60.

51. "The South African Goldfields," *Financial News*, August 14, 1886.

52. "The South African Gold Fever," *Grahamstown Journal*, reprinted in the *Financial News*, September 9, 1886.

53. "Its Birth and Progress."

54. *Financial News*, January 15, 1887, 2.

55. "George Washington Butterfield," 239, 228.

56. "George Washington Butterfield," 222–234.

57. "George Washington Butterfield," 279.

58. "George Washington Butterfield," 257.

59. "George Washington Butterfield," 279.

60. J. H. Curle, *The Gold Mines of the World, containing concise and practical advice for investors* (London, 1899), 10.

61. Curle, *Gold Mines of the World*, 9.

62. "Marks and Butterfield," 702.

63. See Bernard Wasserstein's marvelous history, *The Secret Lives of Trebitsch Lincoln* (New Haven, CT: Yale University Press, 1998).

64. J. C. Haig, *Electioneering Up-to-Date . . . with Three additional Chapters on the Case of Thanet* (London, 1906).

65. G. K. Chesterton, "Times Abstract and Brief Chronicle," *Fortnight Review*, vol. 77 (February 1905): 345.

66. Bottomley, *Hys Booke*, 54.

67. As quoted in David Kynaston, *The Financial Times: A Centenary History* (New York: Viking, 1998), 26.

68. Kynaston, *Financial Times*, 35–43.

69. "A Retrospect by Harry Marks," *Financial News*, 20th anniversary issue, January 23, 1904.

70. "Twentieth Anniversary Number," *Financial News*, January 23, 1904. The poem "Gaudeamus" was by Lewis Morris.

71. Kynaston is especially good on this edition; see his *Financial News*, 56–57.

72. *Financial Review of Reviews*, no. 1 (November 1905), no. 2 (December 1905).

73. *Financial Review of Reviews*, no. 4 (February 1906), 84.

74. *Financial Review of Reviews*, no. 4, 110, 111.

TEN   The Verification Bureau

1. www.measuringworth.org. Numerous options are available for measuring past value to that of the present. As the amount of money involved was large and was used in financing of commodities and not the mere purchase of them for consumption, I have chosen here to use relative share of GDP. "Cotton Failure Hits 26 Firms," *New York Times*, April 23, 1910; "Expect No Big Losses Here," *New York Times*, April

23, 1910; "German Banks Loss Involved in Insolvency in Alabama Cotton Firm," *Philadelphia Inquirer*, May 1, 1910.

2. Niall Ferguson, *Empire* (New York: Basic Books, 2003), 202.

3. Herman Melville, *The Confidence-Man* (New York: Library of America; originally published 1857), 853.

4. This is opposed to relationships of coercion, which also proliferated in the empire. The capitalism that emerged from the anxiety, uncertainty, energy, and insights of the late eighteenth century took numerous forms, all of which interacted with an expanded empire and arena of global commerce. Many historians have pointed to the coercive component of nineteenth-century capitalism. Slavery in the New World, indentured servitude in Asia, and repressive labor regimes during the Industrial Revolution are seen as the oppressive building blocks of nineteenth-century capitalism and the wealth of the West. It is not only labor but also the use of credit and capital that has been represented as coercive, particularly in the way that lenders used credit and interest rates to tie labor to the land. On the importance of imperial expansion for such wealth, see Kenneth Pomeranz, *The Great Divergence* (Princeton, NJ: Princeton University Press, 2000); for two works on the role of slavery in Western capital formation, see Stanley Mintz, *Sweetness and Power: The Place of Sugar in Modern History* (New York: Viking, 1985); and Robin Blackburn, *The Making of New World Slavery* (London: Verso, 1997). Also see Sven Beckert, "Emancipation and Empire: Reconstructing the Worldwide Web of Cotton Production in the Age of the American Civil War," *American Historical Review*, vol. 109, no. 5 (December 2004): 1405–1438.

5. Thomas Ellison, *The Cotton Trade of Great Britain* (London: E. Wilson, 1886), 274.

6. Beckert, "Emancipation and Empire," 1421–1429.

7. Beckert, "Emancipation and Empire," 1421, table 2.

8. Beckert, "Emancipation and Empire," 1421–1429.

9. Louis Bader, "British Colonial Competition for the American Cotton Belt," *Economic Geography*, vol. 3, no. 2: 212, Table 1.

10. *Cotton Trade of Great Britain*, 275. A 1908 report to the U.S. Congress commissioned by the Department of Commerce and Labor similarly observed of the market before the telegraph: "At this time an extensive system of forward or future contracts was almost impossible, owing to the lack of adequate means of communication. The first successful Atlantic cable had not been laid and the telegraph was still in its infancy, while the telephone had not been invented." *Report of the Commissioners of Corporations on Cotton Exchanges, 1908* (Washington, DC: Government Printing Office, 1908), 39.

11. Auguste Bruckert, *Cotton Pamphlet Relating to the Liverpool Cotton Market* (Liverpool, 1908–1909), 5–6. This was all, as Bruckert saw it, a praiseworthy financial innovation that owed much to technology: "The facilities of communication by cable and telegraph became greater day by day, which lessened the risk to a great extent, by eliminating delay. . . . The new use of the 'Futures Contract' became rapidly a simple method to distribute risk amongst the various interested parties, from the planter to

the seller of manufactured goods, from one part of the world to the other." The 1908 Department of Commerce and Labor report to the U.S. Congress similarly observed of the market before the telegraph: "At this time an extensive system of forward or future contracts was almost impossible, owing to the lack of adequate means of communication. The first successful Atlantic cable had not been laid and the telegraph was still in its infancy, while the telephone had not been invented." *Report of the Commissioners*, 39.

12. Jonathan Levy, *Freaks of Fortune* (Cambridge, MA: Harvard University Press, 2012), 251–263.

13. Levy, *Freaks of Fortune*, 232, 239.

14. "To the Board of Managers and Members of the New York Cotton Exchange," October 15, 1908, New York Cotton Exchange Archives: Box 3999.

15. Lance Davis and Larry Neal, "Micro Rules and Macro Outcomes: The Impact of Micro-structure on the Efficiency of Security Exchanges, London, New York, and Paris, 1800–1914," *American Economic Review*, vol. 88, no. 2 (1998): 40–45.

16. "To the Board"; see also Kenneth J. Lipartito, "The New York Cotton Exchange and the Development of the Cotton Futures Market," *The Business History Review*, vol. 57, no. 1 (Spring 1983): 50–72.

17. "To the Board."

18. To give a wider description of the trade, I draw here on "To the Board" and C. S. Duncan, "The Uniform Bill of Lading," *The Journal of Political Economy*, vol. 25, no. 7 (July 1917): 679–703.

19. Duncan, "Uniform Bill of Lading," 679; *Hannay v. Guaranty Trust Co. of New York*, 187 F. 686 (S.D.N.Y. 1911), 1.

20. December 7, 1908, London Metropolitan Archives: Ms 3220.

21. Michael D. Bordo and Hugh Rockoff, "The Gold Standard as a 'Good Housekeeping Seal of Approval,'" *Journal of Economic History*, vol. 56, no. 2 (June 1996): 389–482; Niall Ferguson and Moritz Schularick, "The Empire Effect: The Determinants of Country Risk in the First Age of Globalization, 1880–1913," *Journal of Economic History*, vol. 66, no. 2 (2004): 283–312.

22. "Edward Grey to Baron Grenicke," July 5, 1909, enclosure no. 4 in *Correspondence Relating to the Conference on Bills of Exchange at the Hague,* Commercial no. 4 (June 1910), 10.

23. "Instructions to the British Delegates," enclosure no. 11 in *Correspondence.*

24. "British Delegates to Sir Edward Grey," August 8, 1910, enclosure no. 14 in *Correspondence*, 28.

25. Frank Trentmann, *Free Trade Nation* (Oxford: Oxford University Press, 2007), 158.

26. Kern to the Liverpool Cotton Brokers' Association, January 14, 1908, and November 18, 1908, London Metropolitan Archives: Ms 32206.

27. H. Kern, "Circular," January 15, 1908, London Metropolitan Archives: Ms 32206.

28. On reputational mechanisms in the nineteenth century, see David Sunderland, *Social Capital, Trust and the Industrial Revolution: 1780–1880* (London: Rout-

ledge, 2007); Joel Mokyr, *The Enlightened Economy: An Economic History of Britain, 1700–1850* (New York: Yale University Press, 2010); see also, more generally, Asa Briggs, *The Age of Improvement, 1783–1867* (New York: Longman, 1979, original edition 1959).

29. Kern to the Liverpool Cotton Brokers' Association, January 14, 1908, London Metropolitan Archives: Ms 32206.

30. Kern to Liverpool Cotton Brokers' Association, November 18, 1908, London Metropolitan Archives: Ms 32206. Numerous lists are provided from 1908 through at least 1911.

31. Kern to Liverpool Cotton Brokers' Association, January 31, 1908, London Metropolitan Archives: Ms 32206; bold and italics in original.

32. Kern to Liverpool Cotton Brokers' Association, November 18, 1908, London Metropolitan Archives: Ms 32206.

33. Kern to Liverpool Cotton Brokers' Association, October 31, 1908, London Metropolitan Archives: Ms 32206.

34. New York Cotton Exchange, *Charter, By-laws and Rules of the New York Cotton Exchange*, 15th edition (New York, 1900).

35. "Seize Failed Firm's Cotton," *New York Times*, April 25, 1910.

36. *Montgomery Advertiser*, April 21, 1910: 1.

37. "Was Bankrupt Five Years," *New York Times*, June 3, 1910.

38. "Cotton Failure Hits 26 Firms."

39. "Cotton Circles Agog," *Charlotte Observer*, April 23, 1910; "German Banks Lose."

40. "Expect No Big Losses Here."

41. "Cotton Failure Hits 26 Firms."

42. "Three Million Lost. Books of Knight, Yancey and Co. Showed Big Speculative Account, Expert Says," *Times-Picayune*, December 12, 1911. In May 1911, according to the *New York Times*, the trustee estimated the assets at $700,000 with liabilities still over $5 million.

43. "Cotton Circles Agog."

44. "German Banks Lose."

45. "Cotton Circles Agog."

46. *Lovell v. H. Hentz and Co.*, 181 F. 555 (N.D. Ala. 1910).

47. *Hannay v. Guaranty Trust.*

48. *Guaranty Trust Co. of New York v. Hannay*, 210 F. 810 (2d Cir. 1913).

49. "Banks Held Liable for Bad Lading Bill," *New York Times*, May 24, 1911.

50. *Guaranty v. Hannay.*

51. It is a commonplace that courts, be they in the United States, England, or British India, liked to extend their realm of jurisdiction. Numerous legal historians, including Lauren Benton and most recently and notably Paul Halliday, have shown how aggressive courts and governments have been, particularly in imperial settings, in attempting to do so. Benton, "Colonial Law and Cultural Difference: Jurisdictional Politics and the Formation of the Colonial State," *Comparative Studies in Society and History*, vol. 41, no. 3 (July 1999): 563–588; Halliday, *Habeas Corpus* (Cambridge, MA: Belknap Press, 2010).

52. *Guaranty v. Hannay.*

53. "Foreigners Sue Railroads," *Charlotte Observer*, January 15, 1911.

54. "Cotton Bills of Lading," *Economist*, September 23, 1911: 604.

55. Akira Iriye, *Global Community: The Role of International Organizations in the Making of the Contemporary World* (Berkeley: University of California Press, 2002), 11; Harold Jacobson, *Networks of Interdependence: International Organizations and the Global Political System*, second edition (New York: Knopf, 1984).

56. Iriye, *Global Community*, 12.

57. "Cotton Bills of Lading," *New York Times*, August 12, 1910.

58. "Cotton Bills of Lading," *New York Times*, September 16, 1910. See also "Banker's Guarantee Required for Cotton Bills of Lading," *Wall Street Journal*, September 15, 1910.

59. "Settles Lading Bill Dispute," *New York Times*, April 13, 1911; Kern to members, August 4, 1911, London Metropolitan Archives: Ms 32206.

60. Kern to members, August 4, 1911.

61. "Southern Cotton Men Thoroughly Angered: Bills of Lading Validation Clearing House in New York Is Reflection Upon and Insult to the South," *Biloxi Daily Herald*, August 17, 1911.

62. Kern to members, September 21, 1911, London Metropolitan Archives: Ms 32206. It is worth noting the degree to which international coordination after the war, as Trentmann points out in *Free Trade Nation*, was approached with a concern for just the sort of overcentralization of which the Southerners were complaining.

63. "Cotton Bills of Lading Scheme," *New York Times*, August 29, 1911; "Cotton Bills of Lading," *New York Times*, September 4, 1911: 15, and September 22, 1911.

64. "The Central Bureau's System of Checking Bills of Lading," Liverpool Cotton Bills of Lading Committee, London Metropolitan Archives: Ms 32206; bold in original.

65. Kern to members, September 21, 1911; "Cotton Bills of Lading," *New York Times*, September 22, 1911.

66. Kern to members, 21 September 1911.

67. "Bankers Indorse the Aldrich Plan," *New York Times*, November 25, 1911; American Bankers Association, *Proceedings of the Thirty-Seven Annual Convention of the American Bankers' Association* (New York, 1913), 402.

68. "Withdraw Objection to Cotton Bills," *Dallas Morning News*, November 17, 1911.

69. "Declaration by European Importers," July 16, 1912, London Metropolitan Archives: Ms 32206.

70. Kern to members, October 31, 1912, London Metropolitan Archives: Ms 32206.

71. Kern to members, July 31, 1913, London Metropolitan Archives: Ms 32206.

72. Kern to members, July 31, 1913.

73. "Knight on Witness Stand," *Dallas Morning News*, December 13, 1911.

74. The internationalism—private and public—of which Kern was a part returned after 1918, as would the backdrop of financial capitalism and empire. The Bank for International Settlements was meant to organize central banks, while trade negotiations increasingly took on the appearance of the Conference on Bills of Exchange, with numerous parties at the table rather than just two. Efforts at the unification of bills of lading continued to move forward. In 1924, representatives from dozens of governments again met in an attempt to agree upon uniform rules for bills of lading, this time regarding bills carried at sea. Similar such commercial and economic efforts were largely undone by war reparation debates, beggar-thy-neighbor currency manipulations, and trade tariffs. And though the uniform rules were adopted wholesale by many countries, the United States and Britain both chose to incorporate elements of the rules into their own national legislation rather than ratify and codify the convention itself. Britain crafted its law in conjunction with the lessons of empire and the input of the commonwealth. But this of course was nothing new: the United States and Britain had both stood on their own during the prewar Conference on Bills of Exchange. See Harold James, *The End of Globalization* (Cambridge, MA: Harvard University Press, 2001), 25–30; Barry Eichengreen, *Golden Fetters: The Gold Standard and the Great Depression, 1919–1939* (New York: Oxford University Press, 1992); Athanassios Yiannopoulos, "Uniform Rules Governing Bills of Lading: The Brussels Convention of 1924 in Light of National Legislation," *American Journal of Comparative Law*, vol. 10, no. 4 (Autumn 1961): 374–392; Imperial Shipping Committee, "Report of the Imperial Shipping Committee on the limitation of shipowners' liability by clauses in bills of lading and on certain other matters relating to bills of lading" (1921) [Cmd. 1205].

75. Halliday, *Habeas Corpus*, 312; see also James Garner, "Treatment of Enemy Aliens," *American Journal of International Law*, vol. 12, no. 1 (January 1918): 27–55; and A. W. Brian Simpson, *In the Highest Degree Odious* (New York: Oxford University Press, 1992), chapters 1 and 2.

76. Even as late as June 21, the *Times* had yet to mention the potential war as a long-term threat to financial stability. When the fallout happened, it proceeded with amazing pace. In two days, beginning on July 27, the markets of Vienna and Budapest were closed, followed shortly by the bourses in Paris and Berlin. Meanwhile, the continental markets raided deposits in Britain and sold their foreign-held securities. Paris withdrew £4 million in gold from London. By the end of the month, the London Exchange had also shut. The access to credit from British institutions upon which a great deal of the world relied, including at moments the bankers of New York and the cotton merchants of the American South, had effectively ground to a halt. Niall Ferguson, "Political Risk and the International Bond Market between the 1848 Revolution and the Outbreak of the First World War," *Economic History Review*, vol. 59, no. 1 (February 2006): 70–112; Kindleberger, *A Financial History of Western Europe*, 282. The classic example, of course, is Norman Angell's *The Great Illusion: A Study of the Relation of Military Power in Nations to Their Economic and Social Advantage* (London: W. Heinemann, 1911).

CONCLUSION "Money, Money, Money, and What Money Can Make of Life!"

1. Joseph A. Schumpeter, *Capitalism, Socialism and Democracy* (New York: Harper Perennial, 2008; originally published 1942), 73.

2. Schumpeter, *Capitalism, Socialism and Democracy*, 127–137.

3. Charles Dickens, *Our Mutual Friend* (New York: Everyman's Library, 1994; originally published 1864–1865), 460.

4. "Company Promoting Frauds," *Economist*, January 25, 1890: 105; "On the Problem of Fraud," *Economist*, December 24, 1898: 1853.

5. Ken Alder, "A Social History of Untruth: Lie Detection and Trust in Twentieth-Century America," *Representations*, vol. 80, no. 1 (Fall 2002): 1–33.

6. Frederick Winslow Taylor, *The Principles of Scientific Management* (New York: W. W. Norton, 1967; originally published 1911).

7. Francis Fukuyama, *Trust* (New York: Free Press, 1995); Peter Drucker, *Management*, rev. ed. (New York: Collins Business, 2008; originally published 1973). See also Edward C. Banfield, *The Moral Basis of a Backward Society* (New York: Free Press, 1958); and Robert Putnam, *Making Democracy Work: Civic Traditions in Modern Italy* (Princeton, NJ: Princeton University Press, 1993).

8. John C. Torpey, *The Invention of the Passport: Surveillance, Citizenship and the State* (Cambridge: Cambridge University Press, 2000). See also Charles Maier, "Leviathan 2.0," in *A World Connecting*, edited by Emily S. Rosenberg (Cambridge, MA: Belknap Press, 2013): 29–281.

9. Adam Smith, *The Wealth of Nations* (New York: Modern Library, 1994; originally published 1776), book 1, chapter 2, part 1, 16.

10. Friedrich A. Hayek, *The Road to Serfdom* (Chicago: University of Chicago Press, 2007; originally published 1944), 70.

11. Friedrich A. Hayek, *The Constitution of Liberty* (Chicago: University of Chicago Press, 2011; originally published 1960), 139.

Selected Primary Sources

Archives

British Library, London
Guildhall, City of London

London Metropolitan Archives
British National Archives, Kew
New York Cotton Exchange Archives, University of Texas at Austin

Government Reports (Chronological Listing)

"Report from the Select Committee on the Law Relating to Merchants, Agents, or Factors; &c." (1823) (453). All parliamentary reports accessed at House of Commons Parliamentary Papers (http://parlipapers.chadwyck.com).

"Report from the Select Committee on Consular Establishment; together with the minutes of evidence, and appendix" (1835) (499).

"Exchequer Bills, Report Made to the Lords of Her Majesty's Treasury by the commissioners appointed to inquire and ascertain in what manner exchequer bills have been made out and issued" (London, 1842).

"Exchequer Bills Forgery: Report of the Commissioners' (London, 1842).

"Assurance Companies. Return by the Registrar of Joint Stock Companies of the names, places of business, and objects of all assurance companies completely registered, from the passing of the act 7 & 8 Vict. c. 110, to the 5th day of February 1852, stating the dates of complete registration, and of every account registered by such companies, conformably with the provisions of the said act, since the return of the 20th day of April 1849" (1852) (171-I).

"Report from the Select Committee on the Law of Libel; together with the proceedings of the committee, minutes of evidence, and appendix" (1878–1879) (343).

Old Bailey, Central Criminal Court, Second Session, "George Washington Butterfield, Breaking Peace, libel" (December 15, 1890), ref. no. t18901215-91.

"Correspondence Relating to the Conference on Bills of Exchange at the Hague," Commercial. no. 4 (June 1910).

Acknowledgments

I would like to thank friends who either commented on chapters or provided intellectual accompaniment during the writing: Ken Weisbrode, Stefan Link, James Esdaile, Jason Rockett, Amanda Fazzone, Dylan Yaeger, Martin Oehmke, and Frode Saugerstaad—all bona fide experts. In Washington, DC, Cambridge, and London I owe particularly large debts of gratitude. Liz Hylton welcomed me to Washington. Brynn and Jed Wartman graciously provided me a room, a home, in Cambridge as I commuted from Washington and New York. In London, I owe my greatest debt to Elizabeth and Ashley Mitchell, who housed me on every round of research in London. Scaffolding on the Georgian homes of Frognal Street and Church Row came and went, as did Hampstead's seasonal visitors of foreign wealth, and I kept returning to find a warm welcome and Indian food.

I had numerous homes within the Harvard University community, all of which provided remarkable support. At the history department, I would like to thank Eddie Lee, Jesse Halvorsen, and Janet Hatch. A special debt of gratitude is reserved for Gail Rock and Matthew Corcoran. The Weatherhead Center for International Affairs provided a wonderful interdisciplinary working environment, owing in no small part to the guidance and work of Steven Bloomfield and the help of Clare Putnam. Finally, during the writing up of this, I was honored to be an Ernest May Fellow at Harvard's Belfer Center for Science and International Affairs, where Graham Allison and Susan Lynch did their best to make historians feel at home. Without the generous support of Clive and Whiting Fellowships, I could not have conducted my research or found the time necessary to write. Additionally, I am grateful for the generous help of the staff at Harvard's Widener Library; the U.K. National Archives at Kew; the British Library at Euston and Colindale; the London Metropolitan Archives, Guildhall; the Northamptonshire Records Office; the New York Public Library; and the Dolph Briscoe Center for American History at the University of Texas. I'm also grateful to the images department at the British Museum, as well as that at the U.K. National Maritime Museum in Greenwich. I'm appreciative of the long-distance help from the Liverpool Record Office, Liverpool Libraries, and Roger Hull in particular.

Bill Frucht made this book incalculably better and was a pleasure to work with, as were the entire team at Yale University Press, including Jaya Chatterjee and Mary Pasti, and Angela DeFini and the production team at Westchester Publishing Services. I am particularly grateful to Andrew Wylie and Kristina Moore for fantastic representation and guidance. I have also received great support in professional endeavors from Leon Wieseltier, Lucas Wittman, and George Andreou. Finally, I'm grateful to the blind readers who offered helpful commentary on the manuscripts, as well as on early discrete chapters and parts in other forms. I owe intellectual debts to a number of historians, including Peter Stansky, Iver Bernstein, Gerald Izenberg, and Henry Berger; Felicity Heal at Jesus College, Oxford; and David Blackbourn and Roger Owen at Harvard. I was also helped along the way by Peter Gordon and Emma Rothschild. Tracking down fraudsters is not easy, and often you need a starting point. I am particularly grateful to the work of David Cordingly, David Sinclair, and David Kynaston on Lord Thomas Cochrane, Gregor MacGregor, and Harry Marks for laying some groundwork, as I am to Paul Johnson and George Robb for braving the dangerous and ignored territory of white-collar crime. Most important, I'd like to thank Niall Ferguson, Charles Maier, and Maya Jasanoff. They are all three remarkable historians, but perhaps even better teachers.

While the views represented herein are entirely my own, I finished this book while working as a member of the Policy Planning Staff at the U.S. Department of State. For that remarkable opportunity, I'd like to thank Secretaries of State Hillary Rodham Clinton and John Kerry, as well as Cheryl Mills and Jake Sullivan. Jake, along with his successor, David McKean, more than capably filled the large shoes of George Kennan. I'd also like to thank Sheba Crocker, Ed Lacey, Dan Baer, Marisa McAuliffe, and Drew McCracken, as well as my wonderful colleagues on the staff and in the wider policy community. Finally, thank you Patricia, Robin, and Evan, as well as Tom and Mary Anne. Thank you Spottiswoode.

Laurie, somehow this work has followed us from Alphabet City to the West Village to 20th street, to Washington, DC, to France, Sonoma, Bavaria, and Croatia, and that is to leave 88 Hancock Street unmentioned. At moments it and much else felt like a Poyais to me, but you have never wavered.

Index